DOES HAPPINESS WRITE BLANK PAGES?
ON STOICISM AND ARTISTIC CREATIVITY

Piotr Stankiewicz
University of Warsaw, Poland

Series in Philosophy
VERNON PRESS

Copyright © 2019 Vernon Press, an imprint of Vernon Art and Science Inc, on behalf of the author.

All rights reserved. No part of this publication may be reproduced, stored in a retrieval system, or transmitted in any form or by any means, electronic, mechanical, photocopying, recording, or otherwise, without the prior permission of Vernon Art and Science Inc.

www.vernonpress.com

In the Americas:	*In the rest of the world:*
Vernon Press	Vernon Press
1000 N West Street,	C/Sancti Espiritu 17,
Suite 1200, Wilmington,	Malaga, 29006
Delaware 19801	Spain
United States	

Series in Philosophy

Library of Congress Control Number: 2018959960

ISBN: 978-1-62273-675-1

Also available:

Hardback: 978-1-62273-446-7

E-book: 978-1-62273-568-6

Product and company names mentioned in this work are the trademarks of their respective owners. While every care has been taken in preparing this work, neither the authors nor Vernon Art and Science Inc. may be held responsible for any loss or damage caused or alleged to be caused directly or indirectly by the information contained in it.

Every effort has been made to trace all copyright holders, but if any have been inadvertently overlooked the publisher will be pleased to include any necessary credits in any subsequent reprint or edition.

Cover design by Vernon Press.

to Olga

The root of all human creativity lies in pursuit of unhappiness[1].

Slavoj Žižek

[For those] whose work is of the spirit [...] it would be the loss of losses to be deprived of their subtle irritability and be awarded in its place a hard Stoic hedgehog skin[2].

Friedrich Nietzsche

[...] the structure of Stoicism: intimate and full of sophisticate contradictions[3].

Henryk Elzenberg

Table of Contents

Foreword	vii
Introduction	ix
Stoicism, happiness, and tormented artists	ix
Stoic happiness and happiness in general	x
Why Stoicism?	x
Challenges facing Stoicism	xiii
Why artistic creativity?	xvii
Remarks on methodology	xix
The argument	1
1. Stating the problem	1
2. Defining creativity	1
3. Why is artistic creativity a challenge to Stoicism?	11
4. Methodology	21
5. The theme of fame	26
6. The profit theme and the ascetic misinterpretation of Stoicism	30
7. The preservation theme	42
8. The expressive theme	50
The first variant: artist's self is created through the creative act	51
The second variant: artist's self exists prior to the creative act	55
9. The cognitive theme	62
10. The revolutionary theme and the conservative misinterpretation of Stoicism	70
11. The axiological theme	84

12. The autotherapeutic theme	89
The possibility of cooperation	91
The possibility of contradiction	94
13. The didactic theme	97
Conclusions	**107**
Acknowledgements	**115**
Endnotes	**117**
Bibliography	**145**
Index	**155**

Foreword

The arrival of this book is good news. It tackles an annoying but persistent criticism of the Stoic account of emotion, tranquility, and happiness – namely that there is a conflict between stoic ideals and necessary ingredients of high-level artistic creativity. There is no such conflict, as the author carefully shows. Moreover, in the process of making that case, a similar concern emerges with the human desire for happiness itself – namely that there is a conflict between aiming for it and one's chances of getting it. There again, the Stoic conception of those things is illuminating.

The author is well-placed to open up both of these discussions in a challenging and productive way. He is a poet as well as a philosopher; a public intellectual as well as a private one; and a practical Stoic as well as a theoretical one. Moreover, it is refreshing to have these discussions pursued by a genuinely cosmopolitan author whose concerns are shaped not only by his European roots, deep appreciation of the ancient Stoic texts, and contemporary philosophical discussion of them, but by his wide reading on the subjects involved.

One further comment in advance may be useful. It seems to me that in its most general sense, the problem addressed in this book is about whether or not there is some kind of damaging, dangerous, or even tragic relationship between the quest for happiness and the quest to make great art. But worries about this have a long, troubling history. The root idea seems to be that there might be some sort of self-defeating internal relation between happiness and great art, such that each sort of quest is not only self-defeating (in the way that seeking happiness – or seeking to write the Great American Novel – seems to be self-defeating) but also defeats the other one of the pair. After all, seeking to write the Great American novel usually leads to despair, not happiness. And seeking happiness, often as not, leads to artistic failure as well. Is this a genuine problem or just a confused pseudo-problem raised by people who should know better? How do we get clear about that?

Addressing the problem when it is raised against the Stoic conception of happiness is particularly promising. For Stoics, there is only one good, and that is neither happiness nor great art. It is rather Virtue, which is the rarely achieved perfection of practical wisdom in pursuit of active and effective rational agency in its attempt to integrate and coordinate the whole range of human virtues while subordinating the vices. Achieving Stoic Virtue is a necessary and sufficient condition, the Stoics maintained, for the achievement of happiness. Of course one rarely achieves it. But as long as one is making progress toward it, one can remain intensely motivated to continue making progress. There need not be anything tragic or self-defeating about that whether it involves the attempt to make great art or not. Instead, we go on – perhaps after having some effective Stoic therapy. But never mind. The philosophical problem seems to have been effectively dealt with – and not only for Stoicism.

Lawrence C. Becker

Fellow of Hollins University; Prof. of Philosophy Emeritus, William & Mary

October 20, 2018

Introduction

Stoicism, happiness, and tormented artists

The aim of this book is to examine whether Stoicism and artistic creativity contradict or conflate. I will juxtapose the Stoic and artistic ideals of life and I will try to verify whether they can be pursued simultaneously or not. In simpler terms, I will ask if it is possible for a follower of Stoic ethics to also be an artist.

The title of the book is based on a passage from Henry de Montherlant's *Don Juan*. Don Juan declares there that "happiness writes in white ink on white pages."[4] I adopt this phrase as a tagline for the commonplace intuition that a content life cannot produce meaningful work of art. This very notion is reflected in the figure of a "tormented artist," or "cursed poet," which is a cultural motif that shackles the highest creative capacities to suffering. According to this view, the unavoidable trade-off for the creative gift is the incapability of coming to peaceful terms with oneself and with the world. Thus, if one prefers pursuit of happiness over creative pursuits, then one's creativity will wither away. This is what Montherlant's Don Juan says: if someone is happy, she cannot be a creative artist. And the other way around: whoever wishes to create true art must be inherently unable to be happy.

But the inability to be happy sounds preposterous to a Stoic ear. The goal of Stoic philosophy is to teach its adherents how to be happy under any conditions, including dire misfortunes and extremes of physical adversity[5]. Is then creativity a greater challenge to Stoicism than being on the rack?

This book sets out to examine this paradox. Stoicism and artistic creativity represent pinnacles of human spirit, and it's amazing that their position in respect to one another has hitherto received stunningly scarce attention. The ambition of this book is to fill the gap. Yet, before we get to it, there are certain issues which require clarification.

Stoic happiness and happiness in general

One of the basic facts about Stoicism is that it was never meant to be a purely theoretical school. It has always been a therapeutic endeavor too. "The philosopher's school [...] is a surgery,"[6] as Epictetus put it. "Everyone must discover," Foucault remarks in *The Care of the Self*, "that he needs to receive medication and assistance."[7] This "medication and assistance" is – in this case – nothing else than Stoic philosophy itself. In this vein, we may say that the goal of the Stoic philosophy is to attain happiness. Indeed, to their adherents, the Stoic philosophers promise nothing short of a divine bliss. They promise the Marcus Aurelius' "waveless bay"[8] and Epictetus' "time without perturbations and free from every thing."[9] "A wise man," as Seneca puts it, "is one who full of joy, lives as happy in his condition, as the gods can do in theirs, ever cheerful, placid and unshaken."[10]

We need to remember though, that there are other, non-stoical types of happiness. Happiness is a broad notion and the Stoic account of it – is just one of many. Yet, this book is a book on Stoicism, and it focuses on whether the *Stoic* way of happiness can be agreed with artistic creativity. I make no claim to an overall treatise on creativity and happiness in general. It would be just too broad a topic, requiring not just another book but a shelf full of books.

Why Stoicism?

> [Marcus Aurelius' work is] a veritable eternal gospel, which will never grow old, for it affirms no dogma [...] The book of the *Thoughts* [i.e., *Meditations*] remains young yet in life and truth. [...]
> No revolution, no advance, no discovery can change it[11].
>
> Ernest Renan

There is, I assume, no need to explain at length why Stoicism is worth discussion and critical evaluation. "Stoicism," as William Davidson wrote, "may be confidently affirmed to have perennial value."[12] It has been widely recognized and respected, and its ideal of ethical life has been a hub of Western morality for the past 23 centuries. Importantly, the Stoic influence is not confined to the realm of philosophy. As Jacqueline Lagreé said, "Stoicism ceases to be a true philosophy and becomes instead an ethical and then legal *attitude*."[13] In the words of Bernard Russell: "[The Stoic ideal of egalitarianism] could not be consistently realized in [antiquity], but it influenced legislation, particularly in improving the status of women and slaves. [...] And when at last, in the seventeenth century, the opportunity came to combat despotism effectually, the Stoic doctrines of natural law and natural equality [...] acquired a practical force."[14] Today ideas akin to Stoicism can be found in psychoanalysis and psychotherapy[15], not to mention other popular methods of soul-healing, such as, e.g., coaching. Even the most elusive and most enduring human device, the language itself, testifies to the persistent presence of Stoicism. While no one ever speaks of being "Fichtean" about something and no one talks of living a "Leibnizian" life, the words "stoic" and "stoical" are indelible parts of common parlance. As Robert Arrington put it, "when people today speak of 'being philosophical' about some issue or series of events, the attitude or frame of mind they refer to is precisely the one recommended by the Stoics."[16]

Eminence of Stoicism has been acknowledged by many authors and philosophers. Schopenhauer claimed that "the highest point to which man can attain by the mere use of his faculty of reason [...] is the ideal represented in the Stoic sage."[17] Wilhelm Windelband proclaimed that Stoicism is "one of the most powerful and pregnant creations in the history of the conceptions of human life."[18] MacIntyre declared that "Stoicism remains one of the permanent moral possibilities within the cultures of the West."[19] Hume asserted that "the ancient schools, particularly that of Zeno, produced examples of virtue and constancy which seem astonishing to present times."[20] Montesquieu affirmed that "there has never been one [sect of philosophy] whose principles were more worthy of men."[21] In Dilthey's judgment, Stoicism has had "the strongest and most lasting influence that any philosophical ethic had been able to achieve."[22] Even Emmanuel Levinas, whose own philosophy is quite antipodal to Stoicism, paid his respect and named Stoicism among the "highest, exceptional hours"[23] of Western philosophy. The list goes on and on.

The late 20th and early 21st century have witnessed an upsurge of interest and publications on Stoicism – something that might be called "a Stoic boom." This includes theoretical and interpretative works[24], new translations of the classical Stoic works[25] and new biographies of the ancient Stoics[26]. This boom, however, transcends the boundary of scholar study. The goal is greater: it's an attempt to reestablish Stoicism as a viable philosophy of life. Among authors germane in this regard we should count, first and foremost, Lawrence Becker[27], then William B. Irvine[28], Massimo Pigliucci[29], Donald Robertson[30], William Stephens[31] and many others (and, last and least, myself[32]). Many of them share Becker's manifesto of reinterpretation, i.e. the idea that "it is interesting to try to imagine what might have happened if stoicism had had a continuous twenty-three-hundred-year history; if stoics had had to confront Bacon and Descartes, Newton and Locke, Hobbes and Bentham, Hume and Kant, Darwin and Marx."[33] As mentioned, this approach has overflowed the usual brim of scholarship, and it picks up momentum as a popular movement. There is, for example, the Modern Stoicism endeavor[34], there are events like the annual "Stoicon," there are various online Stoic communities[35] and blogs[36], and there is an increasing presence of Stoicism in the social media[37]. This revival of interest in modern, applied Stoicism adds of course to the relevance of the subject matter of this book.

This book doesn't lay out any definition of what Stoicism is. I outline specific concepts whenever necessary, but this work is by no means an introductory volume. It is justified by the practical reasons since it would be difficult to fit both the exposition of the doctrine and the critical discussion into just one book of reasonable length. More importantly, we need to keep in mind that Stoicism has never been a closed, perfectly defined and immutable system of definite propositions. Seneca loyally reminded his reader not to "think [of him as] a deserter," who "speaks without book and authority"[38], for he wasn't the first representative of Stoicism to has his own opinion. As A. A. Long said: "Stoicism, unlike Epicureanism, was never a monolithic church."[39]

Stoicism has never been a fixed codex, and the Stoic tradition has always been to evolve. Even in the ancient school, there was no uniformity of thought. The lack of consensus between the founding fathers was almost proverbial. There was even "a dispute between Cleanthes and Chrysippus upon this very point of walking: they could by no means agree."[40] In this light, it seems acceptable to continue with a detailed discussion of Stoicism without droning too much over the basics. The discussion set forth below is legitimate even without a precise specification of what particular flavor of Stoicism I embrace. And if this is not enough, then let it be said that I would go with the interpretation of Stoicism as cheerful exercise and contemplation of one's agency. This is along Becker's understanding of Stoic virtue as perfect agency, in his own words, "we hold that, considered as an end, virtue consists in perfected agency."[41] To borrow from his idiom some more, this interpretation can be expressed as: Stoicism is about constructing and employing all-things-considered normative propositions of practical reason[42]. This reading is also akin to what MacIntyre says in *After Virtue*, that the core of Stoicism is the "right action by an agent with a rightly formed will."[43]

Another preliminary issue that requires a brief discussion is the question of "a Stoic sage vs. a Stoic in training." The question is, to speak loosely, whether this inquiry pertains to sages only, i.e., to the alleged individuals who live perfect and pristine Stoic lives, or if it also applies to the "Stoic progressors," (to use Holowchak's term[44]) who are just on their way to become Stoics and who merely aim at the elevated goal of Stoic sagacity.

The imbalance between "sages" and "progressors" has always been a factor in Stoicism. The ancient Stoics were well aware that their philosophy set a very high standard for moral behavior and that an actual Stoic sage was very hard to come by. In other words, Stoicism is self-aware that it's difficult to embrace. What follows from this is not only that the vast majority of self-proclaimed Stoics are actually merely Stoic progressors, but also that the argument presented in this book is valid throughout. It applies both to the ideal Stoic lives and to those who barely started their adventure with Stoicism.

Challenges facing Stoicism

There is a number of problems that Stoicism faces, and there is a string of charges that the Stoics may be – and have been – taxed with. Among the challenges that are most important from the today's (and mine) point of view, I should name at least the following.

[1] Stoicism has been accused of being inhumane[45]. It has been accused of demanding too much, of placing the bar too high, in a word, of calling for unmeetable standards. According to this charge, Stoicism is too difficult, or even impossible, to uphold.

This criticism has taken a plethora of specific forms. Denis Diderot reflected upon his reading of Seneca, that "demanding too much from a man, isn't it a way to achieve nothing?"[46] David Hume pointed out that "the fabric and constitution of our mind no more depend on our choice, than that of our body,"[47] and thus "nature has, in large measure, deprived us"[48] of the "resource"[49] of intellectual malleability the Stoics want to build on. Also, many contemporary psychological and psychotherapeutic currents oppose the Stoic idea that it's easier to reshape one's mental framework than the external circumstances.

The ancient Stoics themselves were well aware of this problem. Seneca refers the "common outcry against the Stoics,"[50] that they "command impossibilities."[51] He declares that he knows "that the doctrine of the Stoics is unpopular among the ignorant as being excessively severe."[52] In the ancient Stoic writings, this problem is often expressed in a discussion of how rare a real Stoic sage is. In *On Firmness*, Serenus, the addressee of the treatise and Seneca's imaginary interlocutor, is, reportedly, in the habit of saying that the "wise man of ours [i.e., the Stoic sage] is nowhere to be found."[53] Seneca partially agrees and declares that "what is great [...] is not often produced."[54] He also admits that "only one [sage] appears at long intervals"[55] and even gives an approximate time frame: "[a good man of the first class] you will scarce find such a phoenix in a thousand years."[56] In a similar vein, Epictetus defies his audience to show him at least one genuine Stoic sage:

> You will find that most of you are Epicureans, a few Peripatetics [...] But show me a Stoic, if you can. Where or how? [...] Show me a man who is sick and happy, in danger and happy, dying and happy, in exile and happy, in disgrace and happy. Show him: I desire, by the gods, to see a Stoic.[57]

[2] The general charge of "inhumanity" can take the specific form of "excessive harshness toward fellow humans." According to this line of criticism, Stoicism compels us to be somewhat cruel, cold-hearted or at least less than compassionate towards others. This, as Davidson calls it, "over-emphasis on the stern, austere, unsympathetic side of morality"[58] is in part rooted in the fact that other people are unavoidably counted in the category of "things not in our power" (more on this in chapter 13). There is powerful evidence to substantiate this charge.

Some ancient Stoic formulas make our sensitivity flinch. Just consider this: " – Suppose that my friends have died [...]. – What else have they suffered than that which is the condition of mortals?"[59] Or: "My family [...] will starve. – What then? Their starvation does not lead to some other end than yours, does it?"[60] Some Stoic advice is quite brutal, to say the least: "If you are kissing your child or wife, say that it is a human being whom you are kissing, for when the wife or child dies, you will not be disturbed."[61] Some precepts are just shy of inducing trauma: "while you are kissing your child say with a lisping voice, 'Tomorrow you will die.'"[62]

The ancient Stoics didn't shrink from the rhetoric of dehumanization, which is particularly unsettling to a contemporary ear:

> Why [...] did you call him a human being? [...] Neither are the nose and the eyes sufficient to prove that one is a human being, but you must see whether one has the judgments that belong to a human being. Here is a man who does not listen to reason [...] he is an ass. Here is one whose sense of self-respect has grown numb; he is useless, a sheep, anything but a human being[63].

Finally, some of the Stoic attitudes toward other humans are downright unacceptable in the world after Auschwitz, Kolyma, and Rwanda:

> Wars and factions and deaths of many men and destructions of cities? And what is there great in all this? – What, nothing great in this? – Why, what is there great in the death of many oxen and many

sheep and the burning and destruction of many nests of swallows or storks? – Is there any similarity between this and that? – A great similarity. Men's bodies perished in the one case, and bodies of oxen and sheep in the other. Petty dwellings of men were burned, and so were nests of storks. What is there great or dreadful about that?[64]

This problem has been widely commented on by philosophers and scholars. In *On Firmness*[65] Seneca recounts the story of Stilbo, who stated that he had lost nothing although "his inheritance had been given up to pillage, his daughters had been outraged by the enemy, his country had fallen under a foreign dominion."[66] Denis Diderot remarked that he was "revolted"[67] by these words and by Seneca's praise of Stilbo conduct. Diderot calls Stilbo "a man of bronze,"[68] and says that he "must be peculiarly isolated from all that is dear to us, from all things sacred to other people."[69] Diderot also declares that if Stoicism advises to follow Stilbo's steps, then Diderot himself "is not at all Stoic and he takes pride in it."[70] "If a sage [...] cannot be found more than once, all the better. If one should resemble him, I swear never to be a sage."[71]

Bertrand Russell also wrote about a "certain coldness in the Stoic conception of virtue,"[72] which he understood as follows. "The sage does not feel sympathy; when his wife or children die, he reflects that this event is no obstacle to his own virtue, and therefore he does not suffer deeply. Friendship [...] must not be carried to the point where your friend's misfortunes can destroy your holy calm."[73] The conclusion is simple: "Love, except in a superficial sense, is absent from [the Stoic] conception of virtue."[74] John Rist, put it this way: "Each man has one and only one object of value to be cherished, namely his own higher self. By a law of nature, he is not able to love others as he loves himself."[75] Nancy Sherman formulates her doubts starkly: "If we are to prepare ourselves to see the loss of children and friends as little different from bidding adieu to a favorite crystal goblet that breaks, then what is the point of building a life around family and friends? [...] This is the unacceptable face of orthodox Stoicism."[76] In the "Defects of Stoicism" section of his 1917 book William de Witt Hyde says this:

> It may be well enough to treat things as indifferent, and work them over into such mental combinations as best serve our rational interests. To treat persons in that way, however, to make them mere pawns in the game which reason plays, is heartless, monstrous [77].

Finally, Edwyn Bevan articulates it this way: "The Wise Man was not to concern himself with his brethren [...] Benevolence he was to have [...] but there was one thing he must not have, and that was love. [...] Pity, in the sense of painful emotion caused by the sight of other men's suffering, is actually a vice."[78]

[3] Today's meaning, status, and validity of the flagship Stoic principle of "following nature" is far from clarity. This issue deserves a book-length study of its own, but the gist of the problem is this. **First**, the onset of the scientific discourse in recent centuries has pushed the teleological view of nature into a much more irrational (or even mystical) sphere than the ancient Stoics originally conceived. **Second**, the Darwinian revolution undermined our reliance on teleology even further. **Third**, "conformity with nature" was quite a self-evident concept for the ancient Stoics. Today it's quite the contrary. We have a gamut of possible interpretations of it. Some of them are highly tautological[79], some are ethically empty[80], some make the very term "nature" redundant[81], and none of them is superior or more convincing than others. **Fourth**, the social, political, scientific and technological progress has made "nature" incomparably more malleable than the Stoics had held. **Fifth**, the rhetorical power of the "appeal to nature" can be used for unethical purposes, for example when it is applied to support the alleged superiority of genders, races, nations or sexual orientations. **Sixth**, "following nature" may dangerously devolve into a form of Nuremberg defense, i.e., it may relinquish responsibility for our actions and transfer it upon abstract and inhuman "nature" whose "higher orders" cannot be disobeyed.

[4] Finally, Stoicism has also been criticized for making its adepts miss certain elusive but essential elements of human experience. This point was particularly inspiring to me, and this book originated as an assessment of such a "price tag" on Stoicism. My intention was to study whether pursuing a good Stoic life forces us to renounce some vital aspects of our humanity.

What are these aspects? For instance, the Stoics made their followers avoid something so intrinsically human as laughter. Their stance was quite unequivocal in this respect. "Let not your laughter be much, nor on many occasions"[82] and "take care also not to provoke laughter"[83] as Epictetus advised. Another example is the argument that Stoicism demands us to "petrify" ourselves. Alexander Pope put it this way: "In lazy apathy let Stoics boast / Their virtue fix'd; 'tis fix'd as in a frost."[84] Common criticism (particularly in recent times) that the Stoics require their adherents to suppress their emotions is yet another facet of this problem. In John Rist's words: "The picture-book Stoic wise man is devoid of passions, emotionless and unfeeling. In some respects this picture is accurate, but in a number of others it is an influential caricature."[85] In Dorothea Frede's phrasing: "Stoicism is a philosophy of moral rigor. This rigor has given rise to [...] [a stereotype that] a Stoic either has no feelings or successfully suppresses them."[86] Last and foremost, we have Nietzsche who explicitly claims that for some people assuming the Stoic position might be a loss (or even a loss of losses): "[For those] whose work is of the spirit [...] it would be the loss of losses to be deprived of their subtle irritability and be awarded in its place a hard Stoic hedgehog skin."[87]

Why artistic creativity?

The last passage from Nietzsche serves as one of the mottos of this book, and it does so for a reason. I won't dwell much on the thickness of the Stoic skin, but we may safely assume that "those whose work is of the spirit" are artists, writers and creative persons of all sorts[88]. And this is the central idea of this book: to analyze whether it would be a "loss of losses" for artists to adopt the Stoic philosophy of life. In other words, the big question is about whether Stoicism dams artistic creativity, or, in yet another formula, whether the essential tenets of our contemporary understanding of artistic creativity are translatable into the Stoic idiom or not.

Why does artistic creativity deserve interest at all? Why is it so important? There are a few specific reasons for this.

[1] There is a cluster of premises which make us suspect that there is a fundamental divergence between the Stoic and artistic models of life (I will analyze them in detail in chapter 3). Given that our culture holds both Stoicism and artistic creativity in exceptionally high regard (details will follow), we face a landscape in which two apexes of the human spirit possibly negate each other. It seems promising and inspiring to pursue an analysis of this alleged conflict.

[2] Artistic creativity is an idea that our contemporary Western world attaches great importance to. As George Steiner puts it, it "is considered the highest capacity that human beings possess."[89] Henryk Elzenberg calls artistry "the highest, the most perfect embodiment of the sense of life"[90] (and assesses that Marcus Aurelius "lacked it completely"[91]). In Alexander Pope's words, "invention" is "the highest capacity of man, a near-divine attribute."[92] It's clear that the zeitgeist of our era hinges more directly on artistic creativity than that of antiquity did. It would undoubtedly raise eyebrows if we heard someone applying the words of Epictetus to *Hamlet*, condescendingly asserting that Shakespeare's work is nothing more than "perturbations of men who value externals."[93]

[3] Artistic creativity today has also a broader sense and even wider impact. It's linked to the capability of reinventing oneself and reinventing the discourse as such. In other words, artistic creativity connects with the ability, audacity, and will to advance new ways of life, new outlooks on the world and new vocabularies (in the Rortian sense of the word[94]). As Isaiah Berlin and Richard Rorty have argued, and as I will discuss in detail in chapter 2, this implies that our present understanding and experience of "the human" can be – to a certain extent – explained in terms of creative capacities. This way, the discussion of Stoicism and artistic creativity contributes to the discussion of the relevance of Stoicism as such.

[4] Focus on the possible contradiction between Stoicism and artistic creativity provides an organized and useful platform to study several other problems yielded by either Stoicism itself or by its juxtaposition to modern sensibility. This will happen in chapter 6 with the "ascetic misinterpretation" of Stoicism and in chapter 10 with the "conservative misinterpretation." In other words, salient parts of the discussion of the current validity of Stoicism can be neatly arranged around artistic creativity.

[5] The problem of Stoicism and artistic creativity is greatly underrepresented in the existing literature of the subject. As far as I'm aware, there exists neither a comprehensive work to discuss the issue, nor even one to provide a clear and explicit exposition of it. Scholars and researchers have done extraordinary work reconstructing the Stoic doctrine and accounting for its intricacies. Yet, gaps between Stoicism and other realms of human experience have received less attention. The Stoic scholars haven't been drawn to the problems of artistic creativity and, on the other hand, authors writing on artistic creativity haven't exhibited great interest in Stoicism. This book fills this gap. It's needed particularly given the last upsurge of popular interest in Stoic philosophy and its insistence on the practical approach. The Stoic boom of recent years only adds weight to the question of compatibility between Stoic and other ideals of human life.

* * *

All that said, we can now address one final issue, namely, artistic creativity as contrasted with creativity in general. Just like the Stoic understanding of happiness is one among many, artistic creativity is a specific instance of creativity in general. How does it play out here?

Chapter 2 contains a detailed presentation of the understanding of artistic creativity assumed in this book. It's the *artistic* creativity, not creativity in general, that I juxtapose with Stoicism. I believe that there are substantial reasons to do so.

First of all, an examination of artistic creativity and Stoicism is, so to speak, more philosophically weighty than a discussion of Stoicism and creativity in general. This so happens because artistic creativity is a much more specific and particular subject than creativity in general. If I had focused on the latter, the conclusions would have been vaguer. **Second**, an attempt to discuss the whole spectrum of creativity, not just its artistic subdomain, would be infeasible in a single book. From the practical point of view, it would just be too complex and too multifarious a subject. **Third**, this is all uncharted territory. Stoicism has never been positioned against neither creativity as such, nor artistic creativity specifically. Thus, it's prudent to deal with a narrowed-down and well-defined subject before the immense and blurred complexity of the greater problem is taken on. Particularly given that, **fourth**, this limited subject is of extraordinary significance. Artistic creativity enjoys its very special status in our culture; it has its own gravity and weight. Artistic creativity holds – culturally – a very special, elated, or even somehow "magical" or "sacred" position. All of this makes the Stoic assessment of it an inspiring and pressing issue.

Remarks on methodology

The methodology I employ in this book can be best described on two levels. On the tactical level, the argument will be organized around a string of dialectical exchanges. I anticipate counter-arguments, and I reply to them. This approach is rooted in my core belief that the convincing power of any philosophical position doesn't come from blind devotion which ignores the darker side of the coin. The value of things and value of arguments comes not from hiding the existing cracks but rather from the courage to bring them to the spotlight. Ideas get their strength and vigor not from careless ignorance but from tackling the problems head-on.

On the strategic level, I use presentism, i.e. "an attitude toward the past dominated by present-day attitudes and experiences."[95] In saying this, I intend both to make a methodological declaration and to answer a possible objection. This objection is that my approach to Stoicism and the demands I make from it are heavily influenced by today's conceptual grid and by the modern understanding of certain concepts, particularly the concept of artistic creativity. This is unacceptable – the objection goes – because an ancient philosophy cannot be confronted with expectations which are only expressible in the contemporary terms. The idiom of ancient Stoicism and the current idiom of artistic creativity are incompatible, hence it's fundamentally illegitimate to juxtapose the two.

I acknowledge this objection, and my answer is this. The power of reinterpretation of Stoicism throughout history and its ability to retain validity across historical eras comes precisely from that it takes questions about any given present. There is a continuous reception of Stoicism since antiquity, and it has its impact throughout the centuries – it is so because every new interpretation of Stoicism is presentist. If Marcus Aurelius was possible if Justus Lipsius was possible and if Lawrence Becker is possible, they are possible because they ask Stoic questions from within their very own time. Thus, it seems only right to juxtapose the contemporary understanding of artistic creativity with a contemporary reading of Stoicism.

One more methodological remark is that in this book I frequently assume the position of an inquisitor who examines whether or not a given notion is agreeable with Stoicism. This is of course merely a convention, a rhetorical device. I don't aspire to be an *arbiter Stoicorum* or any other embodiment of an omniscient spectator. As mentioned before, Stoicism is a pluralistic school of philosophy, and I'm – as Seneca would put it – not the first one to speak from his own opinion.[96]

Also, I'm far from suggesting that what is at odds with Stoicism is inferior. Quite the opposite, this book is inspired by a great reverence for *both* Stoicism and artistic creativity. A conclusion that a given outlook on artistic creativity cannot be reconciled with the Stoic way of thinking is not a reason to condemn it. If a personal viewpoint be admitted, I would say that whenever some Stoic and creative concepts contradict each other, it rather saddens me. I would imagine that in some utopian world they would always concur.

When it comes to the sources, I rely in great measure – possibly exceedingly – on the three Roman Stoics: Seneca, Epictetus, and Marcus Aurelius. The reasons for this are as follows. [1] Obviously, in Long's words: "We have only scraps of the pre-Roman Stoics."[97]. Only the mentioned trio can offer us a bigger picture, coherent, however warped, instead of snippets, dispersed fragments or second-hand reports. [2] To quote Long again, "it is the Stoicism of Seneca, Epictetus, and Marcus which has had greatest influence on later authors."[98] [3] There is the position held by Troels Engberg-Pedersen, that the views of the late Roman Stoics could actually be much closer to the original Old Stoa than the scholars originally assumed. As he puts it: "it is gradually becoming clear that late Stoicism [...] represents something of a return to early Stoicism across the developments that took place in the middle Stoicism of philosophers like Panaetius [...] and his pupil Posidonius [...]."[99]

Introduction

What I want to pursue in this book is philosophy which is English in language, analytical in clarity and continental in scope. The frame of this book, alas, is predominantly Western and my loyalty to the good old hopes of traditionally understood liberalism can clearly be seen in some portions of the book. On the larger view, this book is undoubtedly a part of the "West," where the term stands for the amalgam of Greek philosophy, Roman law and Jewish religion transmitted by the Western Roman Empire and Latin Christianity, and further shaped by the Renaissance, Protestant Reformation, Enlightenment, Colonialism, Industrial Revolution and the heavy legacy of the 20th century. Obviously, this is not because of lack of deference to non-Western cultures, but because it's the Western history of ideas that Stoicism is a part of and because non-Western cultures are, sadly, beyond my area of expertise. This book quotes authors who wrote in Danish, English, French, German, Greek, Latin and Polish. Some Russian poets are mentioned, but Russian philosophers aren't. Not a single example is summoned from the great realms of the Arab, Persian, Indian, Chinese, Korean, Japanese, African, Latin American, and other traditions.

The book is a result of my ongoing interest and research in Stoicism. The motivation which has drawn me to it is twofold: personal and professional. On the personal level, I have been captivated – as so many others have – by the grandiose ambitions of the Stoic ethics which promise freedom from fear and doubt. This personal matter swiftly yielded professional interest. As a philosopher, I became curious what the limits and restrictions of the Stoic commitment are and whether Stoicism can be a viable solution in the 21st century. This book is one of the products of my inquiry thus fueled.

Unless otherwise specified, all translations from French were done by Olga Kaczmarek, all translations from German were consulted with Michał Dobrzański, and all translations from Polish are my own. Obviously, all the slips of thought and shortcomings of argument are also my own.

The argument

> ...he became a poet and thus he belonged to the race forever cursed by the powerful of the earth [100].
> Alfred de Vigny

1. Stating the problem

As the commonly acknowledged and greatly simplified picture goes, Plato banned poets from his ideal state. He thereby established an enduring tradition which assumes that creative, open-minded individuals, the "free artists of themselves"[101] cannot be consistently incorporated into the tissue of a reasoned and prospering state. The problem I tackle in this book follows an analogous vein. I ask whether the Stoics mimic Plato in ordering their followers to ban creative elements from their mind and spirit.

Dropping the metaphor and applying plain terms: I intend to investigate the question of whether living in accordance with the Stoic principles can be agreed with being a creative artist in the contemporary sense of the term. In other words, the question is this: can artistic creativity be coherently translated into the Stoic idiom and expressed in it? Yet another way to phrase the problem is as follows: is forgoing our human capacity of artistic creativity a necessary price for using Stoicism to secure a good life and happiness?

An analysis of this must begin with a discussion of terminology, which I will now turn to.

2. Defining creativity

There is a law in chemistry which states that under given conditions only a limited amount of a solute can dissolve in a given amount of solvent. For example, with temperature and pressure fixed, only a limited mass of salt can dissolve in a given volume of water. Accordingly, in philosophy (or at least in the sort of philosophy this book affiliates with), every body of writing can only contain a limited number of question marks and limited degree of methodic doubt. While every concept and every term can be undermined and deconstructed, it's impossible to undermine and deconstruct all of them simultaneously. Some concepts and some terms must serve as axiomatic bricks on which we rely while questioning others. Obviously, it's not unalterable which of them we rely on and which we undermine (the catty would add that authors sometimes swap what they undermine and what they rely on within a single sentence and without telling the reader). Yet, in every single moment, our exploring attention is always focused somewhere, and the other "somewheres" are left out of focus. And what's left out of focus is taken as – at least temporarily – established.

These remarks don't, however, allow me to give up definitions and abandon the effort of explanation. They aren't an excuse for opaqueness, and I won't avoid clarifications. Yet, I want to make it plain that the primary aim of this book isn't an inquiry about creativity itself. Obviously, one can try to topple the entire reasoning by claiming that I assume oversimplified, outdated or otherwise inadequate understandings of "creativity" and "artist." Yet, as I've just declared, some terms and concepts must serve as working tools and must be temporarily agreed upon as fixed. In this book "creativity," "artistic creativity" and "artist" will be such terms. This, however, doesn't mean I wouldn't clarify them – I will now turn to this.

A preliminary, a bit sketchy but still revealing way of framing my approach to artistic creativity is this. "*To create*" means "to try to create new meanings," particularly having taken into account the reasonable doubt whether any genuinely new meaning is even possible. Respectively, "artistic creativity" signifies the capability and willingness to produce new meanings, or at least capability and willingness to try to do so[102]. This preliminary definition (or maybe just a preconception) can be called a "hermeneutic" one. It's not meant to satisfy the desire for precision and accuracy, but it can provide an organizing guideline.

A more detailed definition of the term is as follows.

"Creativity" is a good contender in the well-cast competition for the most confusing notion ever. As the literature of the subject reassures us, there is neither consensus on the exact meaning of it, nor even a consensus on its most legitimate context. "The conceptual status of creativity is largely unsettled,"[103] as Albert Rothenberg wrote. Keith Negus and Michael Pickering comment that "[creativity] is one of the most used and abused of terms. [...] [It] is deployed in so many different contexts, and with reference to so many different activities, that we may well ask if it has not been drained of any valid meaning or any useful critical application."[104]

Furthermore, we mustn't forget the diachronic lens. The meaning of creativity has greatly evolved over the centuries. To say the very least, it has shifted from an exclusively divine activity to a human one, and then, in the 20th century, "creativity" has turned from a philosophical term into one entangled primarily in psychological and cognitivist discourses[105].

The very verb "to create" is rooted in Latin "*creo, creare.*" The Oxford Latin Dictionary presents its meaning in the following way. First, if it refers to human beings, it can mean one of the following: "to procreate," "to beget," "to give birth to," "to be born," "to institute (an office)," "to conceive (an idea)," "to bring about, occasion, cause" "to appoint."[106] Second, if it refers to nature and life forces in general, it can mean "to cause or allow to grow," "to bear fruit."[107] Finally, if it refers to "God, Nature [...] as the source of all life," it can mean "to bring into being," "to create."[108]

There is a telling disparity among mentioned meanings, and it's symptomatic of the early idea of "*creatio.*" The original, strongest sense of it, the act of calling something into existence, is associated solely with superhuman powers: with God, Nature and other forces inchoate but grand. Humans are also able to "*creare,*" but only in a more particular, more down to earth sense of the word, as when we talk about "creating someone a baron," or, in a modern context, "creating jobs." Importantly, in this sense, we can say that one human "*creavit*" another, but it would only mean "one human begot another human" or "one human gave birth to another human." In particular, a statement that a human "*creavit*" herself would make no sense. The idea of one's self-creation as an individual is inexpressible in these terms[109].

It wasn't until the 16th and 17th century that the strong, metaphysical sense of "creation" became associated with humans[110]. In his 1626 work *De Perfecta Poesii*, the Polish author Maciej Kazimierz Sarbiewski wrote that "It is only the poet who – in a way like God – by narrating in his words something as existing makes it present [...] and as if he creates it anew."[111] Both "creates anew" ("*de novo creari*") and "like God" ("*instar Dei*") have been reported to be the first use of the terms in reference to a poet[112]. Yet, the deep connection between "*creatio*" and the divine domain was lasting, and it took time for the new meaning to take hold. In Shakespeare's 1594 play *The Comedy of Errors* we find Antipholus' of Syracuse words, in which he asks Luciana "Are you a god? would you create me new?"[113] It's worth noticing because the line plays directly on the association between the ability to create something new and God's discretion. Similarly, in the sermon delivered by John Donne on Easter, April 21, 1622, we find the famous phrase that "Poetry is a counterfeit Creation, and makes things that are not, as though they were."¹¹⁴ This again reverberates with the tension between the old meaning of the creative act, God's sole authority, and poetry, its new, controversial rival¹¹⁵.

These birth pangs now gone, we find it natural today to speak about humans and artists "creating" things, including creating art and creating themselves as individuals. The sense employed by the authors of the Vulgate in the opening line of Genesis, "In the beginning God created the heavens and the earth,"¹¹⁶ is now perfectly applicable to our human endeavors and foremost to art. Some put it even stronger. For instance, Alexandre Ganoczy in his 1976 book claimed that the anthropocentric meaning of creativity is the only one currently valid:

> Today, when we speak in anthropology about creation, in psychology about creativity, and in the ordinary language about a creator of a work of art, we undoubtedly do not mean anything theological. The religious tinge of these concepts is not any more comprehensible *per se*¹¹⁷.

And consequently:

> Such thinkers as Descartes, Kant, Hegel, Marx, Nietzsche, Sartre and some neomarxists and positivists [...] are advocates of *homo creator* in his pursuit of liberating himself from *deus creator*. They represent the great adventure that the men of the West have undertaken by their attempt to autonomously reinvent the world and themselves¹¹⁸.

In the words of Tatarkiewicz: "In the 19th century [...] [art] not only was [...] regarded as creativity, but it alone was so regarded. 'Creator' became a synonym for artist and for poet."¹¹⁹

I have thus clarified the first important issue: who (or what) is the subject proper of creativity as considered in this book. In the context of what was said above, I will hereafter set aside all non-human creative agents. Creation as it refers to God, gods or any other more or less specific natural power, including personified or deified Nature herself – none of these will be the subject matter here. "Creativity" will be from now on understood solely as a human activity.

I will focus on creativity of humans, but not on every instance of it. The next step is to fix my attention on artistic creativity of humans (in the light of what was discussed in the Introduction). In saying this, I'm well aware that specifying what "artistic" means is in a way more demanding than defining creativity itself. There is neither any universally recognized definition of the term, nor any commonly accepted consensus on its usage, nor any clear criteria for distinguishing artists from non-artists and

The argument

artistic work from non-artistic work. "There exists no clear-cut definition of the term 'artist',"[120] as Catherine Soussloff wrote.

Due to these difficulties, I will again take advantage of what I said about terms temporarily taken as established, and I will keep to the meaning that is attributed to the word "artistic" in the ordinary language. The Oxford English Dictionary defines "artistic" as "relating to, befitting, or characteristic of an artist" or "relating to art or a work of art."[121] Thus, "artistic creativity" in turn means "creativity of an artist" or "creativity within a field of some art." This outlines the paradigm I intend to work in. I follow Soussloff's line in it: "In contemporary discourse, the artist is separated from other categories of human beings by virtue of what [she] does: [she] makes art."[122] In other words, in my discussion of "creativity" I will refer to creativity of poets, writers, playwrights, painters, sculptors, photographers, filmmakers, actors, theater directors, performers, stand-up comedians, composers, musicians, dancers, singers, songwriters, designers and all others who we usually regard as "artists," rather than creativity of scientists, politicians, prophets, social utopists and activists, inventors, engineers, entrepreneurs, military planners, project managers or businessmen. I take the word "artist" in its broad meaning, that is, including representatives of ancient disciplines, like sculpture or literature, as well as the recent ones, such as computer graphics or social media stunts. I also don't bring up the distinction between "visual arts such as painting, design, and sculpture, as distinguished from literature, music, etc."[123] "Artist" as referred to in this book comprises a poet and a novelist as well as a painter and a designer.

Thus, when speaking of creativity, I will have in mind Shakespeare's creativity in playwriting rather than George Washington's in establishing sovereign countries, Walt Whitman's creativity in poetry rather than Steve Jobs' in creating new companies, Isadora Duncan's creativity in dancing rather than Trotsky's in creating armies, Picasso's in painting rather than Chairman Mao's in envisioning new social deals, Mozart's in composing operas rather than Fosbury's in inventing new techniques in high jump, Proust's in writing novels rather than Einstein's in propounding theories of relativity and Rodin's in sculpting rather than Oppenheimer's in inventing nuclear weapons. All mentioned individuals did create something specific and new. But, clearly, our ordinary use of language attaches the word "artists" only to half of them, and this common intuition marks the track I would like to follow.

An inquiry into the phenomenon of artistic creativity won't be comprehensive unless it's pursued from the social perspective, or at least with the social perspective recognized. By this I mean, at the very least, the issues of how and to what extent the social context makes artistic creativity possible, how and to what extent the social context conditions the dynamics, patterns and outcomes of creativity, and finally, how and to what extent the social context determines the evaluation of the product of the creative process[124]. Most of this, however, I will have to pass over. I will leave aside most of the social intricacy of artistic creativity, and I will consider it rather as an activity of a given individual. I will study it as a phenomenon which occurs within the event horizon of a single human monad, rather than within the web of interactions.

This approach, as simplified as it may seem, offers an undeniable advantage as it reduces the complexity of the task to a manageable level and allows for a single method. But above of all, it seems justified and promising because of the specificity of the Stoic philosophy. Stoicism, at least according to the traditional views, is fundamentally focused on the individual[125] and it might be troublesome to apply the social perspective to examine the Stoic outlook on artistic creativity. For these reasons, I have decided to scale down my task to artistic creativity explainable within the scope of a single subject.

Human artistic creativity can vary greatly in its characteristics, qualities, methods, means, and outcomes. Similarly, approaches to it vary in method, scope, and interpretative tools, making navigation through the maze of theories and aesthetical doctrines a demanding business. Thus, I won't attempt to construct a comprehensive account of these theories – this isn't necessary for my line of argument. What is necessary is to single out a model of artistic creativity (more precisely: a model of artistic creativity and a model for contextualizing it), which organizes the analysis. The model I chose might be roughly called the "Romantic" one. I will now try to spell out its content.

There are several notions that are usually associated with the Romantic model of artistic creativity. In the first approximation, it might be outlined as a model in which: **(a)** originality is valorized more than conventionality, **(b)** invention more than imitation, **(c)** imagination and inspiration more than logic and closed "systematicity," **(d)** activity more than passivity, **(e)** responsibility for one's individual voice more than adaptability to the chorus, **(f)** relying on personal idiosyncrasies more than trusting common clichés, **(g)** exploring the inchoate and unobvious (or even the concealed and dark) more than repeating trivial truths already present in plain sight, **(h)** creation of the new more than rediscovering and reaffirming the old, **(i)** transformation and reshaping the world more than submissive acceptation of it. Furthermore, **(j)** the Romantic model of creativity assumes that there no longer exists a given universal and common symbolic code and it attempts to provide a code of its own[126]. Consequently, **(k)** the Romantic model is not satisfied with using the old alphabet to create a new work of art but rather dares to create both a new alphabet and a new work of art. Finally, **(l)** it aims at creating its own new truth rather than defending old and debunked ones.

Let me now turn to the work of Isaiah Berlin to substantiate this. Berlin provides one of the most convincing and enduring accounts of Romanticism[127]. In his account, Romanticism was a wide and thoroughgoing transformation of the Western culture, pursued simultaneously on many fronts, by artists of various genres, by art theoreticians and philosophers. The importance and influence of this transformation are hard to overestimate. For Berlin, Romanticism is far more than an artistic, philosophical or political movement of the 19th century. It's rather a pivotal point in the course of Western civilization, a turning point that defines all of its subsequent history, in a word, nothing short of a keystone of the contemporary Western mind[128].

Berlin claims that it was Romanticism that begot the following cluster of ideas: **first**, there is not one universal Truth but many truths. **Second**, these truths are untranslatable into one another, and they usually do not overlap[129]. **Third**, different people espouse different truths, and they have an undeniable right to do so. **Fourth**, there is no method of determining which truth is "the truest one" and to ask which of any two given truths is "the truer one" is to ask the wrong question. **Fifth**, these truths not only tend to contradict one another but they also might be self-contradictory. **Sixth**, these truths don't have to be rational, transparent, easily comprehensible, consistent and logically coherent. Quite the contrary, the irrational, the hardly-embraceable and the perennially self-conflicted truths can prove far more insightful. **Seventh**, none of these truths is or is supposed to be universal, ultimate, final and exhaustive. Rather, whatever and whenever a truth is advanced, it's by necessity only a stage in an unfinished, perpetually unfolding process[130]. **Eighth**, espousing any given truth is much more than just passive reception: it's active adoption of certain framework which makes this particular truth possible[131]. **Ninth**, sincere devotion to one's truths can be valued independently of the content of these truths[132]. **Tenth**, things that are subconscious, peripheral or associated with a minority, bear truths of their own. These truths are not only legitimate but often more interesting and revealing than the official mainstream truths[133]. **Eleventh**, humans don't have to be subjected to the rules of this world as they are. Humans can and should transform these rules (and transform themselves) according to their own values[134]. **Twelfth**, these values are not preordained and immutable but they could and should be created by human agents themselves[135]. **Thirteenth,** "creating" in this context is taken in the strong sense, that is, it doesn't stand for transforming, realigning or reshaping something that had already been there, but rather creating *ex nihilo*, establishing something which hadn't existed before[136].

In Berlin's account, all of these ideas were major novelties advanced by Romanticism, and they have become vital elements of the Western mind ever since. They have caused a permanent transformation of the Western culture, and they still define the way we think[137]. In other words, Berlin claims (somewhat akin to the saying popular in antiquity that had there been no Chrysippus, there would have been no Stoa[138]) that had there been no Romanticism, there would be no contemporary era as we know it. There would be no liberalism, no pluralism, no insistence on tolerance[139], no individualism in our modern sense, and we would have neither the will nor the ability to determine ourselves.

Applying the Romantic lens doesn't distort the outlook on artistic creativity as a whole. Quite the opposite, I use the Romantic account in order to frame artistic creativity in a way that sounds most natural to our contemporary ears. Berlin argues that Romanticism had a tremendous impact on Western sensibility and that it was one of the key factors shaping it. Romanticism is inseparably associated with a specific understanding of creativity – to the extent that the latter might be used to define the former. Hence, if we agree that we are heavily indebted to the Romantics, we immediately have a specific understanding of creativity to work with.

In choosing this approach, I neither defy common sense nor do I depart from the ordinary meaning of the terms. Berlin is right that many ideas drawn from the Romantic model are present in various contemporary intellectual currents. Values such as originality, independence, devotion to one's individual voice, willingness to give the floor to the previously unheard, willingness to create a code which enables expression of truths previously unspeakable – all of these reverberate in the today's understanding of artistic creativity.

Moreover, focusing on the Romantic paradigm allows me to address an important doubt that may be raised here. This doubt is particularly justified in our time, when we have largely lost faith in universal standards and objective criteria for telling "good art" from "poor art." The problem at hand is the distinction between (i) just "creating art" and (ii) "creating *true* art," i.e., valuable, inspired and innovative art. For instance, let us consider someone who plays the guitar (badly) and sings in the streets of a

The argument

vacation town in summer time to entertain the tourists and earn some money. Or someone who, like Raymond Dufayel in Jean-Pierre Jeunet's *Amélie*, repaints one and the same Renoir's work every year just for his own pleasure. Quantitatively, they produce (or perform) lots of art. But qualitatively? Would we call them "true artists"? Clearly not in the Romantic sense. Focusing on the Romantic approach allows me to distinguish these two cases, i.e., an actual, innovative and inspired artist and a mere "manufacturer" or recreational "performer" of art. As I will show later on, this distinction is important since both cases look different from the Stoic point of view.

To sum it all up. "Artistic creativity" will hereafter mean, **first**, creativity *of human beings*, not that of God, gods, nature or any other super- or nonhuman forces. **Second**, it will mean the *artistic* creativity of human beings: not political creativity, entrepreneurial, scientific or religious. **Third**, it will mean chiefly the *Romantic* (in the sense described) type of artistic creativity of human beings: not the mimetic, classical or postmodern one.

* * *

Certainly, this approach is still open to objections. The weightiest of them is the problem of bias: one might say that focusing on the Romantic paradigm is too lopsided and that it rules out too many of the other accounts of artistic creativity. This objection is sound in the sense that the Romantic account – however influential – is obviously not the only one but one of many. Yet, I never declare that this book pretends to consider all the existing theories. This would be plainly impossible, given their abundance. What is more, striving to take too much into account often leads to obscurity. Being aware of this, and being aware that this book is a pioneering enterprise in the field, I have decided against venturing into a territory of which I have no chart and no entitlement to wander around. I rather chose to follow the early Wittgenstein's vein of "whereof one cannot speak, thereof one must be silent."[140] This secure pathway is also somehow pragmatically justifiable. As the following chapters will unfold, I do arrive at some results, however preliminary they may be.

For the sake of a bigger picture, I will now outline two examples of approaches to artistic creativity which are *not* covered in this book. The first of them comes from Jean Baudrillard. To quote from his famous *The Precession of Simulacra*: "The medium/message confusion is certainly a corollary of that between the sender and the receiver, thus sealing the disappearance of all dual, polar structures that formed the discursive organization of language."[141] It will be clear from the next chapters that the methodology I adopt rests heavily on those "polar structures" and particularly on the distinction between the sender and receiver. Thus, it would be challenging to apply it to the theories of creativity which follow Baudrillard's line. Certainly, this might be called a theoretical weak spot of my argument, but, as I stressed earlier, *some* specific methodology must be adopted and no one can be reasonably expected to construct an exhaustive account of all existing theories at once.

The second example is supplied by an influential book by Boris Groys, titled *Gesamtkunstwerk Stalin* in original German. It has been translated as *The Total Art of Stalinism*[142], yet the title could also be rendered in English as "Stalin as the Total Work of Art" or "Stalin as the Ideal Work of Art." As Piotr Kozak put it, this book presents Stalin as "the most eminent artist of the avant-garde, or even as the most eminent work of art of the avant-garde."[143] Sure enough, the actual Joseph Stalin is well known for his political accomplishments and mass atrocities. By no account, however, is he known for his artistic creativity[144] and a paradigm which interprets him as an artist or even as a work of art himself – is a paradigm clearly distinct from the one employed in this book. All these caveats aren't supposed to undermine the legitimacy and fruitfulness of these other approaches to creativity. I just want to be clear what's within the scope of this book and what's beyond it.

All this sheds more light on the problem presented in the Introduction, i.e. "artistic creativity" as contrasted with "creativity in general." I focus on the former, and I don't propose a discussion of non-artistic strands of creativity. The rationale for this should be clear at this point. One underlying tenet of this book is to evaluate how different pinnacles of human spirit relate to each other. Stoicism is one such pinnacle, artistic creativity is one, while non-artistic creativity doesn't have the same level of eminence. It's the *artistic* creativity that enjoys a very special place in our post-Romantic culture (to use Berlin's view again). It's the artistic creativity that we are used to perceive as somehow elated, or even sacred. The non-artistic human creativity, as necessary as it is for technology and society, doesn't enjoy this special status. It's valued but in more practical and instrumental terms.

There are also more "tactical" reasons here. Since I focus on the "culturally superior" (in the discussed sense) understanding of creativity, I may expect that the subsequent findings will – in some measure – trickle down, from the more subtle discourse to the less subtle. This wouldn't happen the other way around. If I started off with the "lower" aspects of creativity, like creativity understood as the ability to envision new policies, innovativeness in business or technology, I wouldn't obtain conclusions

The argument

relevant *also* to writing poems or music. It is so because the "higher" (artistic) domain is something "more," something irrational, sometimes transcendental or even magical, something which goes beyond the established frame of logic and reason.

3. Why is artistic creativity a challenge to Stoicism?

> Happiness is a reactionary idea for stupid people. The root of all human creativity lies in pursuit of unhappiness [145].
>
> Slavoj Žižek

Having outlined the meaning of the essential terms, I can now turn to the critical question: why is there a suspicion that artistic creativity poses a challenge to Stoicism? Or, in other words, why think that the model of ethical life proposed by the Stoics is incompatible with the demands of artistic creativity? Grounds for that can be rounded up under seven headings which I will now inspect one by one.

[1] First and foremost: we have direct, explicit and abundant textual evidence that the ancient Stoics expressed reluctance, aversion and even open hostility to art.

Marcus Aurelius pithily sums up performances "in the amphitheater and such places" as "wearisome"[146] and includes them in a lowly company of "the idle business of show, plays on the stage, flocks of sheep [...] a bone cast to little dogs, a bit of bread into fish-ponds, laborings of ants and burden-carrying."[147] Another juxtaposition is even more straightforward: "Neither tragic actor nor whore."[148] Marcus' disdain of theater closely parallels Epictetus' advice that "it is not necessary to go to the theatres often."[149] Epictetus contemptuously summarizes them as something unfit and unproductive: "For what else is tragedy than the perturbations of men who value externals exhibited in this kind of poetry?"[150]

Equal scorn is cast on literature, which is presented as the interplay of false impressions and wrong judgments. "The *Iliad* is nothing else than appearance and the use of appearances"[151], Epictetus says. And later on: "what tragedy has any other beginning? The *Atreus* of Euripides, what is it? An appearance. The *Oedipus* of Sophocles, what is it? An appearance. The *Phoenix*? An appearance. The *Hippolytus*? An appearance."[152] Reading poetry is a waste of time, which should be avoided: "Cicero affirms, that were his days to be doubled, he should not find time enough to read the Lyric Poets."[153] To the Stoics, the works of poets seemed too loose with the facts. "The poets think that it is of no importance to speak the truth, but are either forced by the exigencies of metre, or attracted by sweetness of sound, into calling every one by whatever name runs neatly into verse."[154] Poetry was clearly considered something inferior. "As for those other follies, let them be left to the poets, whose purpose is merely to charm the ear and to weave a pleasing story."[155] Poetry was scornfully counted in the ranks of "flippant and mythical talk, and such old wives' reasoning."[156] Symptomatically, in the first book of *Meditations* Marcus Aurelius thanks gods for having not "wasted [his] time on writers."[157]

In general, the arts are despised on the grounds that they provide no contribution to ethical progress. Literary arts do not provide any:

> The Grammarian's principal study is to speak accurately; and if he [goes] out any further, it is to have some knowledge in history; and his largest stretch is but a taste in poetry. Now what is there in all these that leads to virtue? The weighing of syllables, and the propriety of words, the remembrance of stories, the scanning of verses, and the laws of poetry? Which of these can take away fear, can root out a fond desire, or bridle headstrong lust?[158]

Neither does study of intricacies of literature:

> Are you curious to know whether Ulysses so long wandered in his travels, rather than to take care that we wander not ourselves daily in the road of life? It is all one to me, whether he was tossed about in the straights between Sicily and Italy, or in some unknown seas [...] It is certainly of more consequence to reflect upon the tempests of the mind that daily toss us[159].

Nor is music in any way contributive to virtue:

> Here you teach me how the treble and bass agree together; and how from strings of a different tone arises harmony. Teach me rather how my mind may agree with itself, and my thoughts be free from jarring discord. You show me what notes or key are proper to express sorrow; show me rather how in adversity I may abstain from sighs and groans, and such lamentable sounds[160].

The Stoics associated art with vanity, futility, and fruitlessness, they claimed that it didn't serve the purpose of living an ethical, judicious and flourishing life. But their reluctance was not exhausted by this. They went further, claiming that art not only offers no help for a good life but actively deters from it. As Chrysippus put it, "Do not painters and sculptors divert men's minds from industry to pleasure?"[161] Creativity and works of art draw human attention away from what should be the principal human enterprise. Seneca explores this vein saying that "we are not to catch at old or new-coined words, or extravagant metaphors and rhetorical flourishes of speech, but [we need] to observe such precepts as may prove of use."[162]

The argument

Art, generally, promotes coarseness and indecency: "The manners of men are such, that poverty is a cursed disgrace, and consequently despised by the rich, and hateful to the poor. To this besides are added the ingenious labors of the poets, who are forever inflaming this affection in us."[163] Seneca goes even further and explicitly compares charming melodies to tempting evil:

> As when we have heard a concert of music, we carry away the modulation and sweetness of the air, that engages our thoughts, nor will suffer us to give attention to any thing more serious; so the voice of flatterers, and of such as commend vice, stays longer with us than the time we give it hearing; nor is it an easy matter to shake off from the fond mind the pleasing sound[164].

The praised Stoic life was clearly distinct from a life in which beauty of art and ornaments were praised. Musonius Rufus asked: "Why are there courtyards surrounded by colonnades? Why are there paints of different colors? Why are there gilded ceilings?"[165] According to the Stoics, admiration of art is just foolish admiration of fleeting, vain and skin-deep things:

> Children [...] think [that] glaring trifles [are] of great value, and prefer their penny bracelets and toys to the love of either fathers or brothers. What difference is there [...] between them and us, unless that we are more expensively silly, in being mad after pictures and statues? They are pleased with the shells and little stones of various colors [...] and we with the variegated marble pillars, [...] brought from sandy Egypt or the deserts from Africa [...] We so greatly admire the walls inlaid with plates of marble, [even though] we know what is behind them, and what they serve to hide [...] we know that beneath this show of gold is concealed vile and worm-eaten wood[166].

In a word, according to the Stoics attention to artistic merit is a litmus test of the condition of one's soul. If the attention is excessive, it's a clear sign of trouble. "Know that when you see or hear a labored and over-nice discourse, that the mind of the author is taken up with trifles and vanity."[167]

[2] There is a certain cluster of associations which often accompanies artistic creativity and its Romantic model in particular. Those associations share a common trait: they are all somehow alien to the model of life advanced by the Stoics.

The first of them is the inclination to trust and exploit the emotional, subconscious and irrational realms. Their link to artistic creativity is even older than the Romantic model of art. The archetypical example of this is

Plato's *Ion*, in which Socrates asserts that "Lyric poets [...] are not in their right minds when they make those beautiful lyrics,"[168] and, a moment later, "For a poet is an airy thing [...], and he is not able to make poetry until he becomes inspired and goes out of his mind and his intellect is no longer in him."[169] This was also acknowledged by the Stoics themselves. For example, Seneca in his *On Tranquility of Mind* investigates the necessity of rest and leisure, which leads him to address the issue of drinking wine which in turns makes him notice that

> [we need to] cast off dull sobriety for a while. If we believe the Greek poet, 'it is sometimes pleasant to be mad,' again; Plato always knocked in vain at the door of poetry when he was sober; or, if we trust Aristotle, no great genius has never been without a touch of insanity. The mind cannot use lofty language, above that of the common herd, unless it be excited[170].

This problem has been explored by many later authors. Goethe, for instance, stated that

> No productiveness of the highest kind [...] is in the power of any one; but such things are elevated above all earthly control. [...] They are akin to the demon [...] In such cases, man may often be considered as an instrument in a higher government of the world[171].

The common denominator of the mentioned positions is clear. They all assume that "creative persons [...] are dependent on a source beyond their [...] powers"[172]. And it's clear that such a dependence is at odds with the Stoic teaching on autonomy and on the things in and not in our power.

The second presumably nonstoic association is a cluster of networked concepts varying from "spontaneity" through "disobedience towards given laws" to "rebellion." Artistic creativity, especially in its Romantic incarnation, is usually tied to the ideas of spontaneous development, unrestrained manifestation, and resistance to the rules imposed from the outside.

Spontaneity is claimed to be both a right and an obligation of an artist: she wouldn't be able to create if she was stripped of her spontaneous freedom. In fulfilling the artistic vocation spontaneity must be exploited to the highest pitch. As Theodor Adorno puts it, there is an "instinctive spontaneity" on which "the emancipated capacity for expression depends."[173] The issue of spontaneity is bordered by the broader problem of the artist's attitude to laws, regulations, rules and pre-existing vocabularies. It's clear that subordination to the discourses of others isn't her primary concern. An artist is seldom actuated by an urge to obey and follow.

The argument

She isn't inclined to accept, reproduce and replicate the order of discourse, but rather to re-read, redefine and recreate it. The merit of artistic creativity consists in breaking free from what is fixed, not in subjecting to it. This happens both on the symbolic level, where artists strive to advance their own symbolic codes to describe the world, and in the more mundane sense. It's not a coincidence after all that artists are a social group which is statistically prone to run afoul of the world and of themselves (more on this soon).

In a word, artists are more likely to rebel. This rebellion can turn against the external world and society, with its norms and niceties, as in Berlin's account of "the worlds of Byron's gloomy heroes – satanic outcasts, proud, indomitable, sinister – Manfred, Beppo, Conrad, Lara, Cain – who defy society and suffer and destroy. They may, by the standards of the world, be accounted criminal, enemies of mankind, damned souls."[174] But the rebellion may well take the form of a self-destructive struggle against the artist herself, which brings attention to the figure of a tormented, auto-tormented or otherwise cursed artist. I will expound this thread in detail in points [6] and [7].

[3] One important way of understanding Stoicism, associated primarily with Michel Foucault, is to interpret it as a system of "cultivation of the self," or "care for the self." "Taking care of one's soul," in Foucault's own words, "was a precept that Zeno had given his disciples from the beginning, and one Musonius was to repeat."[175] Furthermore, Foucault says that

> Man is defined in the *Discourses* as the being who was destined to care for himself. This is where the basic difference between him and other creatures resides. The animals find "ready prepared" that which they need in order to live [...] [while] man, [...] must attend to himself[176].

In other words, the task of taking care of oneself is a "privilege-duty, a gift-obligation,"[177] the highest responsibility of a human being.

But, if it is so, what about artistic creativity? Artistic creativity has been described by others in the exact same way (remember the Introduction): as the highest human capacity and the finest human obligation. It's not unreasonable to say that it is indeed the capability of art-making (and not of "caring for oneself") that differs us from animals.

Let's now turn to the following remarks by Foucault:

> [Taking care of oneself] [...] demands that one [...] spares no effort in order to "develop oneself," "transform oneself," "return to oneself." [...] Marcus Aurelius [confesses that] neither reading nor

writing must keep him [...] from the direct attention he must give to his own being[178].

In this view, the care of oneself is not only the single most important duty of a human being. It's also a very demanding project. It's a practice which requires us to withdraw from tending to other things, including, not coincidentally, reading *and writing*. Doesn't it then require us to withdraw from creating art? Doesn't the exhaustive task of caring for oneself disable us from just as exhaustive task of creation? Can these two great projects be pursued simultaneously? If one devotes their time, energy and spiritual capacity for one of them, is there anything left to be devoted to the other?

Creating true art is never easy, and we know that the psychological cost of it ranges anywhere from draining to devastating (see later in this chapter). Is a balance between the care-for-self vs. creativity even possible? It's definitely a question worth an inquiry. To use a loose metaphor, we may say that Foucaultian "care for oneself" and artistic creativity are two vocations which are highly and destructively jealous, like God of the Old Testament. Can they tolerate each other? Can they be tempered and synced into one tune? This is the question this book deals with.

[4] Another reason which makes artistic creativity a challenge to Stoicism follows from the materialism of the Stoics. "No idea is more deeply ingrained in Stoic philosophy," as Hahm puts it, "than the conviction that everything real is corporeal."[179] How does it relate to my subject matter?

The proposition "the Stoics are materialists" can also be expressed as "the Stoics deny transcendence." The Stoics hold that the present, material universe of our worldly experience is the only true universe and that all beyond it – is a mere illusion. This material world is the one in which we must flourish and excel, one in which must live and thrive, one in which we must exercise our virtue. This doesn't necessarily contradict all of artistic creativity. But it is clearly with odds with these accounts of it in which the purpose of an artist is to express the humanity's transcendent yearnings and experiences. The Romantic model is – surely – one of them.

[5] "Happy families are all alike; every unhappy family is unhappy in its own way."[180] The famous opening of Leo Tolstoy's *Anna Karenina* captures the gist of another argument that can be made from the "artistic" position against Stoicism. The Stoic ideal – the argument goes – venerable as it is, is a very single-tracked one. All the Stoics achieve their fulfillment in the same way. This is repetitive, boring, impoverishing. Artistic fulfillment is quite the contrary. It can be found in a plethora of ways and particularly

The argument

the Romantic approach is that every artist should try to explore her very own, unique way. Thus, the potential for artist's experience is broader; her account is more diverse, more multidimensional, more open to the variety of the world we live in. The opulence of life and openness to its various phenomena is a value in itself, and it shouldn't be easily rejected – as it happens in Stoicism.

[6] It's not a coincidence that the passage from *Anna Karenina* refers to happiness and unhappiness. The ambition of this book is – in some measure – to tackle the vague notion that the state of ultimate and permanent happiness (as the Stoics promise us) is a violation of a profound tenet of the human condition. On this notion, humans are shackled to some extent of discontentment, disappointment, and suffering. These shackles *can* be broken (e.g., by applying Stoic ethics) yet it is not clear whether they *should* be broken. Eradicating suffering – the thinking goes – impoverishes us because it reduces the complexity of human experience. This is precisely what makes the artist's way more exhaustive and comprehensive. An artist accounts for the spheres of the human condition that the Stoics make us immune to. Moreover, since unhappiness and suffering can be seen as sources of creative powers, it follows that an artist is obliged not only not to soothe and heal her soul but to cultivate, prolong and reproduce her misery. In this view, suffering is part of the artist's vocation and to try to negate it would be an act of treason.

In other words, a critic of Stoicism may say roughly the following. "A Stoic is akin to a happy Mill's pig: she is withdrawn, she doesn't account fully for the complexity of human experience, in a word, her humanity is painfully limited. It's nobler in the mind and more desirable to be a full-fledged yet unhappy human than a happy yet limited one." This view translates directly into the dispute between artists and Stoics. After all, the embodiment of a fully developed human spirit is often to be found in an artist, and the account of the whole of human experience – in artistic creativity.

The permanent presence of suffering in the artistic experience can be illustrated by the recurring discontent in *The Gypsy Song* by iconic Soviet bard Vladimir Vysotsky. Youtube might be of use here – I particularly recommend the clip where the song is set to a selection of scenes from the *Yesenin* TV miniseries. The lyrics display a succession of places and walks of life which are one by one rejected. Neither a drunk night, nor the morning after, neither tavern, nor church, neither up the hill, nor down the slope, contentment is nowhere to be found and the gut sense that things are not right echoes again and again.

Another example comes from another Russian poet, Sergei Yesenin (the one from the mentioned TV show) who confessed in 1925 (the last year of his short and troubled life) that for him being a poet means nothing short from self-flailing one's own skin so that the blood can appease souls of others[181]. Interestingly, the opening of Søren Kierkegaard's *Either/or* bears a striking resemblance to this diagnosis:

> What is a poet? A wretch who conceals deep torments in his heart, but whose lips are formed in such a way that as the sighs and shrieks stream out over them they sound like beautiful music[182].

[7] Finally, there is a wealth of biographical material about artists whose lives were at odds – to put it mildly – with what we usually conceive of as the ideal of a Stoic sage. There is a long tradition of "cursed poets," to borrow a phrase from Alfred de Vigny and Paul Verlaine[183], or of wedding "creativity and madness," to use the title of Albert Rothenberg's work[184]. This can be traced back through the Western history at least to François Villon in the 15th century. It's a continuous tradition of troubled lives, full of self-harm and social sins. I will spell out a few examples in detail. I draw them from recent memory since temporal proximity secures most credible and precise accounts.

To begin with, there have been artists who weren't able to handle their fondness for liquor. Ernest Hemingway was reported by Buck Lanham to be "drinking gallons [of booze]"[185], or, in a more precise report by Leicester Hemingway, "about seventeen Scotch and sodas a single day."[186] He "tried to restrict himself to only three or four drinks before dinner but could never manage to do so."[187] Janis Joplin happened to "pause between songs to swig from a bottle of [...] Southern Comfort"[188] and lived it up to her own standard of what controlled drinking means. "She'd start in the morning; she'd pass out in the afternoon. She'd recover by the time of her concerts; she'd get drunk later. [...] On the days of no performance, she'd break the routine and drink straight through."[189] William Faulkner used to "drink himself into a violent state"[190] which shocked Saxe Commins, his friend and editor, who was called for help in October 1952:

> Faulkner lay on a couch in stupor, his face covered with bruises and contusions, his body battered and bloated. [...] [He] pleaded for a drink, tossed and mumbled deliriously [...] Commins had virtually to carry him to the bathroom. [...] [He] wrote his wife [...] "It is the complete disintegration of a man."[191]

There have been artists deeply and often gravely troubled with other chemicals. The most dramatic case is surely the plethora of rock stars of the second half of the 20th century. It can be best seen through the lens of

The argument

Annie Leibovitz's adventure, who was reported to have needed months to regain sobriety and altogether recover after accompanying The Rolling Stones on their North American tour in 1975. There have been artists who suffered from severe and recurrent breakdowns, like Truman Capote, who described his experience as follows. "Every morning I wake up and [...] I'm weeping [...] I just cry and cry. [...] Every night the same thing happens. I take a pill, go to bed [...] and suddenly I start to cry. There's just so much pain somebody can endure. [...] I'm *so* unhappy. [...] There is something wrong."[192] Others were almost incapacitated by their pathological fixations, like the actress Joan Crawford, who

> was extreme in her phobias. [...] [She] washed her hands dozens of times each day and changed her clothes almost hourly [...] When her meal arrived, she ordered the maid to rewash the glasses, plates and silverware[193].

Alike Enrico Caruso who "had a chronic dread of infection. He would change shirts every two or three hours, have his room sprayed constantly with perfumed atomizers, and carry an assortment of syringes, medicines, and gargles with him on his travels."[194] There have been artists who were not able to manage their desires for underage women, like Roman Polanski who, as a legal consequence of his infamous 1978 actions, couldn't set foot on American soil for most of his filmmaking career. Finally, there have been these, who yielded to quasi-religious fervors and fevers, like quoted Sergei Yesenin, who once

> was trying to jump out of the stairwell window. Isadora [Duncan – his wife at the time] [...] advised [...] to soak his head in cold water. Since it did not help, Yesenin was then tied up with a washing line [...] He resisted [...] he screamed he would report to Trotsky, he cried "Crucify me!"[195]

Admittedly, these accounts are piecemeal and informal. Due to the nature of this problem, it would be hard to provide hard statistical data[196]. And yet, there is no denying that there is merit to the words of John Dryden that

> Great Wits are sure to Madness near ally'd;
> And thin Partitions do their Bounds divide[197]

There undeniably exists the stereotype of a troubled, self-tormented and insanity-inclined artist. If it was merely a stereotype, we could easily glide over it. But this stereotype can be substantiated with meaningful arguments ([1] – [6], as discussed before). All of this in sum brings us to the conclusion that there are major reasons to believe that artistic creativity and Stoic ethics may be mutually incompatible.

An objection can be raised at this point. "What about," one may well ask, "the numerous artists who have lived tranquilly and venerably, respectfully of law and social niceties? What about their sober and successful lives? Aren't they a counterexample?" It is surely a fine point and it needs to be addressed.

My answer is as follows. First of all, I never make a claim that *all* artists are tormented artists. I don't advance a thesis that *every* artist must *always* and *necessarily* suffer because he or she creates art, or that she must suffer *in order* to create valuable art. Apparently, a certain number of great artists were able to do their work without paying the price of suffering, struggle and looming madness (or at least this is the story they managed to convince us to). But does this nullify the problem? Does it invalidate the project I take up in this book? It doesn't. The fact that certain patients managed to not come down with the illness doesn't undermine my ability and right to analyze the situation of the "cursed," Romantic poet.

Nor does it make her case any less interesting. The Romantic figures – the "gloomy heroes, satanic outcasts, proud, indomitable, sinister" [198] – are simply much more interesting than the artists who lived peacefully. The former pose an actual, fascinating problem. In them, we face a radical confusion, an essential disharmony with the world which is very curious from the Stoic viewpoint. To put it differently: we will learn nothing from a quiet genius examined from a Stoic position. But we will learn a lot if we critically examine the curse, Romantic artist.

Another important issue that deserves mention is the particular case of Seneca. An argument can be raised that Seneca is a great case study for this inquiry because he was both a Stoic philosopher and a playwright. Shouldn't he get special attention then?

In this book, I extensively quote Seneca, but only his philosophical works. I refrain from analyzing the "case of Seneca," that is, from studying the twists and turns of his life and how his philosophical projects interacted with his playwriting. This is not a coincidence, but a thought-out methodological decision. Why is that so? I'm interested in an intellectual inquiry into a well-defined problem and not in a psychological, or biographical study of any individual. It's the possibility of a great clash between Stoicism and Romantic art that captivates me, not the fate or mindset of any specific human. "The case of Seneca" may indeed seem tempting, but I figure that, for the sake of honesty and intellectual scrutiny, it's methodologically important to be restrained about it.

Seneca is a difficult specimen and taking him as a representative of a larger problem would mislead us. The relationship between what he preached in his philosophical works and the facts of his biography is complex (to say the least). Adding his non-philosophical works to the mix would obscure the picture even more. Moreover, it's a broader methodological problem. Relying on the biography of any single person in arguing for a larger case is always doubtful. Particularly if this person lived 2000 years ago and the sources are limited. Let's remember what Pierre Hadot says in the concluding passage of his *Philosophy as a Way of Life*'s chapter on Marcus Aurelius. "We [can't] deduce Marcus' psychological states from any of the preceding. Was he an optimist or a pessimist? Did he suffer from a stomach ulcer? The *Meditations* do not allow us to respond to these questions. All we can learn from them is about [Stoic] spiritual exercises."[199] Similarly in Seneca's case. To draw conclusions directly from his life would be too close to anecdotal evidence, which is the type of argument I prefer to avoid.

4. Methodology

In order to deal with a complex issue, one has to arm oneself with a trustworthy method. The tougher the subject, the more reliable the method needs to be, so that we don't get lost in the maze. In dealing with artistic creativity, a careful and well-reasoned procedure is a must.

The methodology I chose can be best described as a step-by-step one. Instead of confronting the intricacy of the problem all at once, I approach it piece by piece. It's essential because, as discussed, the realm of artistic creativity is far too broad, multi-layered and polyphonic to be encompassed with just one outlook. With the systematic and analytical approach I will – hopefully – avoid one-sidedness and I will aim at a specific, yet manifold, outcome. In other words, I will examine the nodal points of the problem and sketch a roadmap of it.

The core methodological concept is this. I will discuss nine distinct paradigms for framing artistic creativity, and I will examine them one by one. Each time I will ask whether or not they are compatible with Stoicism. For brevity, I will call these paradigms "themes." In saying this, a few things require emphasis.

First of all, this methodology is a methodology and a methodology only. It's not an ideology and it's not a grand theory. It's neither an account of any pre-existing structure nor an assumption that such a structure exists. It's s just a tool which seemed most convincing and most promising to me.

The utility of this tool is proven by the outcome it provides and only by it. I don't claim that it reveals the utter mystery of artistic creativity.

The methodology is based on a classification, but it's not sociological. It's neither statistics nor typology. I neither offer a self-proclaimed taxonomy of artists nor do I need one. The outline I present isn't meant to match any particular empirical study, and I don't rely on quantitative data. Also, this classification isn't a psychological one. I don't dare, and I don't intend to analyze any particular artist's mind and soul. In a similar vein, I don't differentiate between how self-aware artists are. It doesn't matter here whether a given artist proudly boasts about her inspirations in press interviews or, as it often happens, if she would be genuinely surprised and deeply opposed to what is revealed on the therapist's couch.

Furthermore, I don't claim that any particular artist's work can be explained in terms of a single theme. Similarly, I don't believe that any work of art can be explained in terms of one theme only. The truth is quite the opposite: most creative acts cover a combination of several themes. This combination is usually a snarl, often impossible to disentangle. Moreover, some themes in a given situation tend to be hidden from sight. They may be opaque to the audience or even denied by the artists themselves. Yet, nothing of this disproves the legitimacy of my approach. Even if the themes are routinely knit together, we are still entitled to discuss them separately. It holds true as long as this systematicity provides clarity and analytical transparency of the argument.

The very concept of "theme" requires attention too. I intended to pick a term that adds as little misleading associations as possible. I strive for both clarity and impartiality. My aim is to stay out of the fray and to not side *a priori* with any specific theory. This is due to my respect and reverence for artistic creativity and due to its key role – as argued – in constituting us as humans. Artistic creativity deserves no coarse reductions. Thus, I'm careful of great discourses which aspire to totality and force pseudo-ultimate explanations. I'm aware that what I offer is close to some form of teleological approach, but I don't want to concede to it fully. Neither I prefer to cave in to genetic approach ("the source of artistic creativity is…"), nor to causal approach ("the cause of artistic creativity is…"). Above all, I strive to avoid psychological approach ("the artist is motivated by…") which poses a clear and great danger of reductionism and one-sidedness. The last point leaves the word "motive" out of question, since Oxford English Dictionary defines it as "an inward prompting or impulse," "a circumstance or external factor inducing a person to act in a certain way," […] or as "a purpose, end, or interest which motivates someone to commit an illegal, esp. criminal, act."[200] This is not satisfying, due to the

The argument

manifest psychologization of meaning and – in the last point – its excessive legal sense. Moreover, the term "motive" has the added liability of a direct connection to Latin *motus* (motion). As I will explore in detail in chapter 8, associations with dynamics, transformation and flux are present in some understandings of artistic creativity. Yet not in all of them. Therefore, for the sake of mentioned impartiality, I won't bind this analysis to a term which is too close to the idea of motion.

Following this line of reasoning, and having rejected using "motif" as too eccentric, I chose the word "theme." It provides the desired measure of both neutrality and generality. According to the Oxford English Dictionary "theme" is "[a] subject of discourse, discussion, conversation, meditation, or composition; a topic."[201] Yet, it also includes the meanings of "an exercise written on a given subject, esp. a school essay; an exercise in translation"[202] and, in music, "the principal melody, plainsong, or canto fermo in a contrapuntal piece; hence, any one of the principal melodies or motives in a sonata, symphony, etc.; a subject; also, a simple tune on which variations are constructed."[203] This net of meanings is quite suitable for me, and thus, for mentioned reasons, I will settle for the term "theme."

We can now turn to the themes themselves and eventually unpack the meat of the method. The procedure will be simple. I will examine the following themes of artistic creativity one by one, and I will assess their compatibility with Stoicism.

Chapter 5 – the theme of fame.

Chapter 6 – the profit theme.

Chapter 7 – the preservation theme.

Chapter 8 – the expressive theme.

Chapter 9 – the cognitive theme.

Chapter 10 – the revolutionary theme.

Chapter 11 – the axiological theme.

Chapter 12 – the autotherapeutic theme.

Chapter 13 – the didactic theme.

The plan is clear, but it raises a few questions and doubts. First of all, what is the rationale for such a limited set? The basic reply is: the minimalistic, safe approach mentioned earlier. This study is a pioneering endeavor and investigates a matter which hasn't been touched so far. This reason alone merits a secure pathway. The cart shouldn't come before the horse, and this book will only pave the way for more advanced studies.

I take care to eschew the worryingly popular custom of advancing a thesis based on a single passage cherry-picked from a million others. Yet, if we suspend that restriction for just a minute, we will see that, presumably, my methodology would have seemed suitable for the ancient Stoics themselves. Let's turn to Seneca's epistle 65 in which he outlines Plato's and Aristotle's views on causality. Presenting the latter's concept of the final cause, Seneca says:

> The fourth cause is the design [i.e., purpose] in making it [e.g., a statue], for without this it had not been made what it is. What then is design [purpose]? It is that which invites the artist, and which he constantly has in view in the prosecution of his work, whether it be money, if the artists intends what he makes for sale, or glory, if he works for reputation, or devotion and piety, if he designed it for a gift to some temple[204].

Seneca explicitly refers to two themes analyzed in this book: the profit theme and the theme of fame. Roughly speaking, the methodology of this book might be seen as an attempt to follow this intuition and to extrapolate this view.

As mentioned, an instance of creative effort is rarely explicable in terms of just one theme. In real life, there is usually a plurality of themes. Furthermore, the setup of themes often alters between one creative activity and another, not to mention that it varies greatly from one artist to another. I'm aware of all this. Thus, what I try to scrutinize in this book is a set of – to use mathematical imagery – basis vectors. Any particular instance of artistic creativity might be expressed as a finite linear combination of them. In another picture, the nine examined themes will serve as notes of which a melody is composed. Whichever phrasing we use, the bottom line is the same: plenty of complicated patterns might be rendered as combinations of the basis vectors or of notes. Instead of tackling the infinity of possible patterns, I decompose them into a small set of basic examples and only then launch the investigative effort.

One may also point out that there are other themes, not included in the list. A careful reader might have noticed that the analogy with a vector space fails in one respect: in mathematics the basis of a vector space spans it, i.e., every element of the vector space can be expressed as a combination of the basis vectors. In our case things are different. There are creative phenomena that cannot be expressed in terms of the mentioned themes. Indeed, many interesting cases are left out.

This incompleteness is a sound line of criticism. Yet, I hold that it doesn't undermine my argument. I want to emphasize again that I don't claim that this methodology is the ultimate one or that it covers all possible

The argument

scenarios. I'm determined to focus only on the themes I can discuss with competence and in which I can arrive at specific results. Thus, some common intuitions are split into a few distinct themes while many others are left aside completely. In the spirit of mentioned Wittgenstein thesis no. 7, I prefer to draw a workable map a limited area rather than get lost in an uncharterable territory. What's to be found in that territory? Here are a few possible examples of themes of artistic creativity that I don't discuss. **(a)** Creating for pleasure ("to satisfy the desire to create"[205]); **(b)** creating to praise somebody or something; **(c)** creating to maintain the world in its existence; **(d)** creating to play with conventions; **(e)** artistic creativity understood as "rallying everything that remains, and not to sanctify nor propound."[206]

One may also say that this approach is wrong through and through because it's an error to even try to analyze artistic creativity by translating it into distinct paradigms. In other words: this methodology oversimplifies the problem by enforcing a blatant superficiality on a complex phenomenon. My response to this is as follows. I accept that my methodology doesn't provide complete and universal answers. True, it's just one of possible methodologies. It's just a tool, and it has its flaws and limits, as all tools do. I think, however, that it's better to pick one methodology and to follow it consistently, rather than switch haphazardly from one to another. As Seneca says, "a plant thrives not, nor can well take root, if it is moved from place to place"[207] It's also better to be aware of the limitations of one's method than to imagine that one has the ultimate key to the theory of everything. As the Marxists would put it, the truth is always biased – the idea of all-encompassing impartiality is a bourgeois one. The proof of the pudding is in the eating, and as long as my approach provides an interesting outcome, I hold that my choice is justified.

The final problem I want to discuss is the problem of subjectivity. It's actually twofold. There is, first, the question if and to what extent I assume the presence of the subject in the creative process. Second, one may also ask whether I assume a subject present in Stoicism itself. The former issue is quite clear. Yes, I tacitly assume the existence of "the subject" in the creative process. "Structuralist and poststructuralist positions calling for the 'death' of the author in literary studies"[208] are beyond the scope of this book. The chosen methodology will neither cover nor fit them. As to the other issue, there is, of course, the big question about the position of the subject in Stoic philosophy. Alas, I can't address it here. I again put in action my minimalistic explanation. I don't problematize "the subject," because it would be way too much for a single project to undertake. As already said, every argument requires some cornerstones that are not undermined. Thus, in this book the existence of a somehow coherent and clearly outlined subject is neither a metaphysical assumption nor a strong thesis. It's just a mild assumption I use to explore some ramifications of the Stoic doctrine.

Having gone through this lengthy formal discussion, we can now turn to the thrust of the argument, that is to the one-by-one analysis of creative themes as juxtaposed with Stoic ethics.

5. The theme of fame

The first theme I want to consider is perhaps the clearest and most trouble-free of all. It's the theme of fame, i.e., the framework in which creative pursuits are understood as something which is employed to gain acknowledgment and praise of fellow human beings. This theme covers a wide range of particular cases.

I use "fame" as an umbrella term for all instances of other people's recognition of the work of an artist, and all cases in which her social standing is improved as a consequence of this recognition. It includes "being famous" in the strict sense, that is, being acclaimed and admired by people whom the artist doesn't know personally. It also includes what happens on a smaller scale, when a minute circle of close friends praises her work. On the other hand, it includes the posthumous fame, when strangers in the unforeseeable future valorize a work of art from bygone past. It includes being bestowed with prestigious accolades and being rewarded with the less fungible currency of silent admiration. To create in order to be rewarded with an appreciating nod – whoever the audience consists of and whatever form this nod takes – this is what "the theme of fame" means.

The significance of this theme varies from artist to artist, and I'm skeptical if any true artist can be perfectly and sincerely indifferent to the social recognition of her work. There is something to the very idea of artistic creativity that makes it difficult for the author to be truly uncaring for the fate of the created work. It's somehow akin to the parental relationship, where the parents are genetically hard-wired to care for the prosperity of their children. Thus, surely, there are artists who have long ago unilaterally retreated to the role of a lone genius, working in seclusion, unacknowledged and forgotten, counting only on the future to appreciate the value of their work. And yet, longing for recognition can still be present in them, however, concealed (or if conscious, then denied). There are also artists who are well aware that what they do is so ahead of their era – or that it's so different from the cultural mainstream – that it's certain they won't be acknowledged in their lifetime. And yet, deep in their bones they still yearn for immediate appreciation, and they feel the absence of it as painful injustice. There are also other artists – those very rare and fortunate – who are able to create masterpieces of illustrious value and do so without compromise, no concession to plaudits, and who are still recognized by their contemporaries. There are also those who – like receptive plants – are sensitized to the subtle signals from the external world, who sweat to keep a finger on the pulse of fads and who always strive to make sure that their work is in perfect harmony with what is currently in vogue. And finally, there are those who don't mince matters and openly admit that they treat artistic creativity mainly as a means of winning praises and prizes.

Furthermore, the meaning of "fame" varies in scale. In our context "fame" includes admiration of a sole addressee for whom a work of art was created, like when a poem is composed for the sole purpose of winning the heart of a fair man or a fair lady. "Fame" also includes acknowledgement of the immediate family, a group of friends, or flocks of fans. It includes exhibitions, concerts, and performances in fourth-rated venues in the middle of a God-forgotten country, just as it includes the spotlight and red carpets in Paris and New York.

Let's now turn to the question whether the theme of fame agrees with Stoicism. Can someone try to live a Stoic life and simultaneously pursue artistic creativity in order to be acknowledged by fellow humans? Of all the themes I examine in this book, the answer is the simplest here. It's clearly a negative answer. The theme of fame cannot be consistently expressed in Stoic terms. In most of the subsequent themes, a detailed discussion will be necessary, and the outcome will be equivocal at times. But here the answer is clear: the theme of fame is at odds with Stoicism.

One of the key elements of Stoic ethics is the dichotomy of control, i.e., the fundamental division between things that are in our power and things that are not in our power. As the famous opening of Epictetus' *Encheiridion* goes: "In our power are opinion, movement towards a thing, desire, aversion; and in a word, whatever are our own acts. Not in our power are the body, property, reputation, offices, and in a word, whatever are not our own acts."[209] Note, that Epictetus explicitly counts "reputation" among the things not in our power. The word is interchangeable with "fame" as interpreted in this chapter. There should be little doubt about why Epictetus does this. Indeed, among all conceivable things, the opinions of others are most certainly beyond our control. What – in a word – could be less up to us than what other people think?

Once fame is categorized as "not in our power," inevitable consequences follow. The basic principle of the Stoic ethics implies that we are obliged to define our goals, values, and endeavors only in terms of the things within our power. Things not in our power shouldn't be employed in our discourse about ourselves and our doings. We should hold them as perfectly neutral, neither good nor bad. It follows that fame doesn't qualify as a licit goal for a Stoic to pursue and Stoic ethics cannot approve of an undertaking aimed at obtaining it. Thus, artistic creativity propelled by the lust for fame cannot be agreed with the Stoic frame of mind.

That's not all here. Even stronger statement is justified. For the ancient Stoics fame wasn't just one random instance in the string of things not in our power. Quite the opposite, it was the most eminent and the least controversial case. It was a flagship example, the embodiment of all the haplessness wrought on us by an ill-guided mental framework.

Seneca puts it flat out. "Praise or renown is not a good,"[210] and he further asks rhetorically "what can be more scandalous than a philosopher affecting popularity and applause?"[211] In the same vein, we read in the epistle 52 that it is "folly" of a philosopher if he, "when dismisses his audience, is highly pleased with the acclamations of the unskillful. What cause has a man to rejoice at being praised by those, whom he cannot praise himself?"[212] Epictetus asks: "who are they by whom you wish to be admired? Are they not those of whom you are used to say, that they are mad? Well then do you wish to be admired by madmen?"[213] Interestingly, Marcus Aurelius' writings reflect a particularly intense struggle with the temptation of fame. To some extent, it's a paradox, and to some extent, it's not. In Henryk Elzenberg's reading[214], the rhetoric of *Meditations* is calibrated against the "fame of a philosopher" rather than against the "fame of an emperor." This, of course, doesn't mean that *Meditations* approve of the latter. They indeed scorn all forms of fame equally. And yet, the imperial fame, which the author had for free, seems to be a less vivid impulse for him than the fame of a philosopher, that he was possibly secretly looking for[215].

Whichever interpretation we assume, the *Meditations* are teeming with beautiful monologues against the lust for fame. We may begin with the crucial objective claim: "Everything which is in any way beautiful is beautiful in itself, and terminates in itself, not having praise as part of itself. [...] Is such a thing as an emerald made worse than it was, if it is not praised?"[216] Then comes the general vanity argument: "the things which are much valued in life are empty and rotten and trifling and like little dogs biting one another, and little children quarrelling, laughing, and then straightway weeping."[217] Next, the illusionary character of fame: "But perhaps the desire of the things called fame will torment you. See how soon everything is forgotten, and look at the chaos of infinite time on each side of the present, and the emptiness of applause, and the changeableness and want of judgment in those who pretend to give praise, and the narrowness of the space within which it is circumscribed."[218] Finally, the perishability of fame: "He who has a vehement desire for posthumous fame does not consider that every one of those who remember him will himself also die very soon; then again also they who have succeeded them, until the whole remembrance shall have been extinguished as it is transmitted through men who foolishly admire and perish."[219]

This is supported by the views of Stoic scholars, of which I will quote just two, one from the early 20th century and one from the early 21st. "The true Stoic [...] carries the only standard of social measurement under his own hat," argues William de Witt Hyde in his essay published in 1917, "and needs not the adoration of his wife, the cheers of his constituents, the cards and invitations, the nodes and smiles [...] to assure him of his dignity and worth. If he is an author, it does not trouble him that his books are unsold, unread, uncut."[220] Hyde openly admits that if a Stoic is an artist ("if he is an author"), then it shall be of no importance to her whether her work is a success or failure.

In order to be precise, however, we must acknowledge that the described position isn't equal to "artistic creativity of a Stoic mustn't be actuated by her lust of fame." It's logically possible that one desires something and acts to gain it, but is still perfectly indifferent about the outcome of that action. This caveat, though, doesn't change the picture because such instances are very rare. They happen mostly on paper, not in real life. Thus, I agree with William de Witt Hyde's judgment. Artistic creativity propelled by a desire to be praised by others is indeed at loggerheads with the Stoic way of life.

The other example comes from a 2009 book by William B. Irvine, *A Guide to The Good Life: The Ancient Art of Stoic Joy*[221], in which he presents a very sincere account of his personal experience with practicing Stoicism. Irvine emphasizes the "withdrawal from the social hierarchy game" (as he finely calls it), and describes it as cutting the loop between our motivation to act and other people's responses. He writes: "As we make progress in our practice of Stoicism, we will become increasingly indifferent to other people's opinion of us."[222] For Irvine being independent and – above all – being free from the desire to please others is the fulcrum of Stoic ethics. Needless to say, this supports my line of thought. Creative pursuits of a Stoic mustn't be aimed at gaining fame and praise. The theme of fame cannot be reconciled with Stoicism.

There is one possible argument which might counter this reasoning. Artistic creativity might be understood as a focal point for certain social sentiments and the artist herself can be seen as a transmitter of these sentiments. On this take an artist detects, amplifies and expresses the sentiments that others are insensible to. The work of art is something that the public can identify with. They can and they want to identify with it because they see in the work of art something they vaguely feel themselves, but not clearly enough and not consciously enough to express it on their own. On this reading, the social dimension of artistic creativity is not just "fame" that an artist craves (while a Stoic is indifferent to) but the very mechanism of her work. Consequently, if her work is for some reason socially unrecognized, the whole point of thus understood artistic creativity is defeated.

There is merit in this insight. But does it undermine the hitherto reasoning? It doesn't because this insight is drifting away – slowly but perceptibly – into a different story. It doesn't actually depict a creative process pursued to gain fame, but it speaks of the social role of an artist. The difference is subtle but clear. The social status and societal functions of an artist aren't the subject matter of this inquiry, and they don't affect the conclusion of this chapter. Which is, again, that creative pursuits aimed at getting praise conflict with Stoicism in spades.

6. The profit theme and the ascetic misinterpretation of Stoicism

In the profit theme, creative pursuits are employed to gain financial reward. I will understand "financial reward" broadly, to include not only money but all sorts of material goods and earthly profits an artist might receive. It involves both a physical paycheck when an artist is paid for her concert, exhibition or performance, and a situation when she is paid with any sorts of exchangeable material goods. Generally speaking, the profit theme represents artistic creativity pursued for economic reasons. Or, in others words, it is the understanding of artistic creativity primarily as artist's *modus operandi* in the economical world.

The profit theme sparks complex problems. Can artistic creativity, understood in terms of economy, be expressed in Stoic terms? This question can't be discussed in isolation from a far greater problem of the overall attitude of a Stoic to the economic side of life. I will examine the profit theme in this broad context.

What I actually need to do is to address a wrong but irritatingly commonplace view on Stoicism. This view, which is a cluster of partially interdependent ill-judgments, I will hereafter abbreviate as "the ascetic misinterpretation of Stoicism." Discussing it in detail is essential to my argument here, but it also has a huge impact on the understanding of Stoicism as such.

The argument

The ascetic misinterpretation of Stoicism might be roughly formulated like this. "The way of life the Stoics promote is an ascetic one. It's a life of renunciation, abstemiousness, and austerity. It's a life in which one refrains from indulgence. If someone wants to be a Stoic, then she is obliged to quash her desires, limit herself to little and be satisfied with little. She is obliged to live simply and frugally, to restrict herself to plain and modest food and drink, to abstain from alcohol and drugs of any sort, to moderate her sexual life or abandon it altogether. In a word, in all kinds of carnal delectations, she is obliged to limit her pleasures to the simplest ones (or even to learn how to find pleasure in renouncing pleasure). Furthermore, she is obliged to prefer a life of austerity over a life of affluence, and voluntary poverty over riches. She is obliged to disdain worldly wealth, splendors, accolades and luxuries, she is bound to a never-ending, relentless battle to overcome her desires and wants. She is obliged to withdraw in order to secure herself against possible defeat, rather than stand up to the external battle and thus make herself vulnerable to unfulfillment. She is obliged to opt for the fail-safe path and desist from the struggle for earthly goods." Abandoning financial ambitions is a part of this, so it follows that the profit theme is incompatible with Stoicism unless the ascetic misinterpretation is rejected.

In Michel Foucault's language, the ascetic misinterpretation can be expressed in terms of "training through deprivation." Foucault points out that

> for the Stoics [the exercises in abstinence were] primarily a matter of preparing oneself for possible privations by discovering how easy it was, finally, to dispense with everything to which habit, opinion, education, attention to reputation, and the taste for ostentation have attached us[223].

My point is that while it is perfectly fine and necessary for a Stoic to train herself in privation, it just happens way too often that these "exercises in abstinence"[224] and in "making oneself familiar with the minimum"[225] are taken as tantamount to Stoicism *as a whole*. It's true that the Stoics compel us to exercise. But it's not true that this exercise is all they can offer.

Let me be clear here: those who fall for the ascetic misinterpretation should be easily forgiven. They are forgiven because Stoicism relatively easily lends itself to the ascetic misreading. The ancient Stoics themselves contributed to this situation. They didn't prevent it, quite the contrary, they did a lot to seduce us into the ascetic misinterpretation. There are many cues in their writings that encourage it.

First of all, Seneca provides, in a brilliant nutshell, an argument for frugality as a specific form of the "cradle argument." "No man is born rich in himself. As soon as he enters upon life, he is obliged to be content with milk and swaddling clothes."[226] This is the beginning, but once we grow up, it suddenly turns out that even kingdoms are too small for us. Accordingly: "[If you want] to improve, and attend the duties of the mind, you must either be poor, or act as such. Study will turn to little account, where there is no respect to frugality, and frugality is a form of voluntary poverty."[227] Further on, he comments on the necessity of the austere lifestyle. "Whole armies have [...] been forced to eat the roots of herbs, and such offals as are not fit to be named. And for what did they suffer all this? For a kingdom, and, what is still more surprising, for a kingdom not their own. And will anyone scruple to endure poverty, that he may free his mind from all hurtful passions, and be king of himself?"[228] Epictetus says on our attitude towards the carnal needs generally that "it is a mark of a mean capacity to spend much time on the things which concern the body, such as much exercise, much eating, much drinking, much easing of the body, much copulation."[229] And also: "take the things which relate to the body as far as the bare use, as food, drink, clothing, house, and slaves; but exclude every thing which is for show or luxury."[230] Finally, Marcus Aurelius expresses gratitude for having been taught to "to want little"[231].

Seneca openly admits that there is a clear Epicurean echo in his epistles. "Today I have been reading Epicurus, for you must know I sometimes make an excursion into the enemy's camp, not by way of a deserter, but as a spy."[232] This particular echo is about limiting oneself to little. "'Cheerful poverty,' says he [Epicurus], 'is an excellent thing.' [...] The man, whose poverty sits easily upon him, is rich. Not he that has little, but he that desires more, is the poor man."[233] Similarly: "It is not the hunger of the belly, that puts us to this expense, but ambition, pride and luxury. These belly-mongers therefore, as Sallust says, let us rank among the number of beasts not of men, and some of them not even among animals, but among the dead."[234] On the accessibility of what we truly need we read in Seneca that "We shall be rich enough. All that [...] we want is gratuitous, or of little consequence. Nature asks for bread and water. No one is so poor, but he can answer this demand, and whoever confines his desires to these, may contend with Jove himself in happiness."[235] Similarly, in epistle 110 we read "give me water, give me a barley cake, and I will not envy Jupiter his happiness."[236]

We shouldn't overlook that the attitude towards external, earthly things has been used as a litmus test for discriminating between the Stoic and the

The argument

Aristotelian ethical systems. This is traceable at least back to Cicero, who says in *On Moral Ends* that

> It is hardly consistent for us Stoics to agree that possession of what is greatly valued with regard to the body makes one happier. The Peripatetics think that no life is completely happy without bodily well-being. We Stoics could not agree less[237].

The Aristotelian idea is often understood as an assumption that a certain non-zero amount of earthly goods – wealth, health, social standing, etc. – is a requisite condition for a good life. As for the Stoics, their view is that there is no such condition. A true Stoic is able to flourish in every conceivable circumstance, including abject poverty, impaired health or public disgrace. But while it's true that a Stoic should be content even in dire straits, it's false that she would opt for them ("preferred indifferents" versus "unpreferred indifferents"). Confusion about this matter adds to the persistence of the ascetic misinterpretation[238].

The stereotypical image of a Stoic also plays part. A Stoic is often imagined as a tough and serious figure, who laughs rarely and disregards the joys of life. This stereotype has been a commonplace since antiquity, for already Diogenes Laertius reported about Zeno that "he had almost become a proverb. At all events, 'More temperate than Zeno the philosopher' was a current saying about him."[239] It's not surprising, given the following advice by Epictetus: "let not your laughter be much, nor on many occasions."[240]

It can be seen from this that the ancient Stoics are themselves responsible for the popularity of the ascetic misinterpretation. The confusion is further compounded by the imprecision of some contemporary promoters of Stoicism. It's common in their works that ascetic motifs are shoved wherever possible with neither rhyme nor reason. It seems almost like the ascetic advice is used as a handy ornament fitting everywhere and adorning everything. Asceticism, as it happens, is a noble thing, so it certainly benefits the readers, but its overrepresentation is still a distortion of Stoic ethical teaching. Examples of this tendency include *Don't Worry, Be Stoic* by Peter J. Vernezze[241] or *The Art of Living* by Sharon Lebell[242]. On the other hand, Irvine's book, *A Guide to The Good Life*[243], only partially displays it, while Becker's *A New Stoicism*[244] avoids it completely.

On a different note, one of the purposes of philosophy generally is to redress balance, i.e., to bolster these spheres of human experience which are underrepresented and underrated in a given place and time. (In Elzenberg's words: "The goal of philosophy [...] is to keep all the sound ways of understanding the world open, despite the one-sided pressures specific to every epoch. A human, in order not to suffocate, needs all those unhindered vistas"[245]). For example, the Socratean-Platonian shift towards transcendent and universal ideas can be seen as a reaction to the predominantly "materialistic" and sophistic landscape of their era. On the other hand, the Nietzsche's shift to corporality can be interpreted as a response to the spirituality of his own time.

What does it mean in our case? If philosophy is about supporting that which is neglected and if Stoicism is a philosophy of strengthening, exercising and enjoying one's agency, then it's reasonable to expect that the Stoics encourage their followers to extend their agency into areas previously untouched and unexploited. Hence, if we assume that most people don't live ascetically and that they aren't "content with little" (which seems a reasonable assumption in every era), it follows that Stoicism will support the underrepresented view, i.e., a frugal life as a way to sustain one's agency. In an imaginary world where everybody lives ascetic lives, the Stoics might well encourage exploiting agency by a more avid, carnal and multidimensional interaction with earthly life. In this perspective, asceticism is not an intrinsic principle of Stoicism but rather a "local" and contingent example of its application.

Yet another insight into the origins of the ascetic misinterpretation comes from the contrast between the Stoics and the Epicureans. One viewpoint on the difference between the two schools is that the Epicurean path is about limiting ourselves to simple needs and simple pleasures, while the Stoic path is about cheerful exercise and contemplation of one's agency. In Lawrence Becker's interpretation and idiom, this last part can be rendered as: Stoicism is about happiness and fulfillment found in applying practical reason, all-things-considered, to whatever circumstances life brings upon us[246]. In everyday language, this translates into roughly the following: the Stoics teach us how to flourish given the resources available, how to deal smartly with whatever happens to us, how to best actualize our personal values, and how to strive for our goals unimpeded. Stoic happiness is to be found in exercising our capacity for decision-making (prioritizing, designing our own hierarchy of goals and values, etc.) at any time and under any circumstance.

These principles hold in fortunate and unfortunate conditions alike. Coherence is an important tenet of the Stoic ethics, and the same approach needs to be applied when the world is our oyster and when we are miserable (in the everyday, nonstoic meaning of the term). And yet, it so happens that the extreme cases shed most light on the specificity of the Stoic framework. Under ordinary, pleasant and non-pressing circumstances of everyday life, a

The argument

Stoic, an Epicurean, and an Aristotelian might look and behave alike. It's the extraordinary situations and harsh conditions that bring the differences to full light. Thus, it's not surprising that this was the type of examples that the Stoics eagerly used in their teaching and that their discussion of these examples was most likely to survive to our times[247].

This is one of the reasons why the dramatic stories – beheadings and brazen bulls – are overrepresented in the Stoic writings. The ascetic themes are in the same boat: they are common because they provide background which exposes the specificity of Stoic ethics. Thus, through the spotlight fallacy, the ascetic misinterpretation gains its convincing and deceptive power. But we mustn't give in to it. We mustn't be misled into thinking that what the Stoics hold about certain extreme cases exhausts all they have to say. Stoicism is a comprehensive system of living which covers the whole spectrum of circumstances. From whatever it asserts about one end of this spectrum, we shouldn't infer that applicability of Stoicism is limited to that end only. The Stoics don't require us to retire to an austere but easily-comprehensible ascetic abode. They don't demand that we reject all the amazing and overwhelming lushness of the world in order to live a rigorous life, just because the rules would be simpler. The ascetic misinterpretation not only distorts Stoicism but also simplifies it, makes it lopsided and narrow. And far less interesting than it really is.

In this context, we can easily name the differences between Stoicism, Epicureanism and the pleasantly commonsensical ethics of Aristotle. In this regard, it's all about scale. The Epicurean answer is valid only within the limited circumstances of a simple and frugal life. Hence, Epicureanism requires its adherents to restrain themselves, to ensure that they remain within the theory's limits of applicability. As for Aristotle, it's the other way about. The Aristotelian ethics openly admits that it won't work unless a certain amount of earthly goods is secured. Having put it in this perspective, we can clearly see where the superiority of the Stoic ethics stems from. Stoicism is neither as narrow as Epicureanism, nor it is based on such preconditions as Aristotleanism is.

Rejecting the ascetic misinterpretation immunizes Stoicism to one of the most serious objections that can be raised against it. It's the negativity objection: that Stoicism is not autonomous and independent, but it makes sense only against some pre-existing adversity. In this view, Stoicism is nothing more than a cure or remedy, relevant only when there is some ailment to be treated. It might be felicitously summed as "Stoic ethics is like medicine: it tries to eliminate the very thing that makes it necessary."[248] Or, in another picture, that it is like a wildfire, which lasts only as long as there is something more to devour, and then extinguishes. Yet, the validity of this objection rests on the ascetic misinterpretation. It's the ascetic reading of Stoicism that reduces it to an obligation to renounce, reject and abstain from earthly goods. Once we accept that Stoicism is about handling worldly affairs rather than dismissing them – the negativity objection loses much of its relevance.

An interesting loop emerges when a commonsensical argument against asceticism as such is applied to the ascetic misinterpretation of Stoicism. This argument can be tagged as "all ascetics are the same" and the gist of it is this. "The ascetic life is more single-tracked and more monotonous than a non-ascetic life is. All ascetics conform to the same boring and overarching principles. They follow the same path and achieve their fulfillment in the exact same way, while the non-ascetics have a wide range of possibilities to choose from. This is the price the ascetics pay: they renounce the diversity and blooming teemingness of the world."

Does this argument disprove the ascetic misinterpretation of Stoicism? Not on the spot, since it invites an immediate reply: "This argument is *a priori* reductionist. There is a tacit – and highly doubtful – premise in it, namely, that the spectrum of earthly life is the only right measure to assess human fulfillment." In other words, the presented argument is akin to criticizing monks for living dull lives. It rests on the assumption that the only "true" and interesting life takes place outside the walls of the monastery. At the same time, it completely ignores the possible diversity and exuberance of the monks' spiritual lives.

This argument isn't particularly sound if aimed against asceticism as such. It gains power, however, once we apply it specifically to Stoicism. Why? Because the Stoic model of life was (and is) about thriving and excelling at worldly life, not finding an escape route from it. The Stoics promote Pantheism and materialism, while they reject transcendence. They don't accept transcendent currency, so they can't be paid with it for turning back on the material world.

There is another argument against the ascetic misinterpretation. It goes along the following line: a mass-scale conversion to ascetically-understood Stoicism would bring negative consequences on society and civilization in general. Let's imagine, if everyone suddenly became literally content with little, it would make the economy collapse, because the demand for most products would plunge dramatically. Of course, if this were the whole story, this argument would be valid only from the pro-capitalism point of view (capitalistic economy is good, hence what threatens it – is evil). The reasoning goes further though. Such a mass-scale adoption of ascetic Stoicism would undercut all progress and development of civilization.

The argument

After all, why toil to invent technologies that could make human life less painful and easier, if widely-accepted asceticism prompts everyone to forgo all amenities in favor of frugal lives? This point is valid regardless of our position on capitalism.

Finally, one more argument against the ascetic misinterpretation may be advanced along the following line. We, humans of the 21st century, have "more to lose" than the ancients had. Our modern life is more complex than the life of people in bygone centuries was, and we live in a much more interconnected universe than they did. Thus, if someone adopts the ascetic understanding of Stoicism today, one has to disentangle oneself from many more strings than one would have to in antiquity. Such disentanglement is both harder and more costly.

Let's illustrate this on the practical level. Let's say that an ancient Stoic chose to withdraw from social commitments and political engagement. Back in her time, it could simply be achieved by avoiding the forum and focusing on private life. In the 21st century though, far more than that is required to achieve the very same goal. Even in the tranquil abodes of our own homes, we are still haunted by the shadow of information society, and we still remain the citizens of the global village. In order to fully disconnect ourselves, we would have to withdraw from using our smartphones and the Internet. That, in turn, would seriously impair our ability to have any job. The Stoic dogma states, of course, that "where a man can live, there he can also live well"[249] so it's perfectly possible to live well offline. And yet, this is a challenge that our predecessors didn't face. There is a difference: to espouse the ascetic way is heavier with consequence today than it used to be. Our social life is more complex and more exuberant, hence the higher price for withdrawing from it.

This last argument might be criticized as follows. "It's just an illusion that the ascetic way is any more difficult in the contemporary world than it was in the past. Opting for asceticism is an autonomous choice of the moral agent, and it's independent of external circumstances. Realities do change over the course of history, but the core metaphysical condition of a human being is fixed and immutable. Thus, the choice of asceticism isn't any tougher or easier in any historical circumstance." This is a fair point to make. Yet, validity of this criticism hinges on the conservative assumption that the world and human condition don't change. We thus arrive at an interesting point: the ascetic and conservative misinterpretations of Stoicism are, to a degree, interdependent. As long as this line of reasoning is concerned, one has to assume the latter to argue against the former. The conservative misinterpretation will be discussed in detail in chapter 10.

Let's get back to the main storyline. I will now substantiate the crucial anti-ascetic claim, i.e., that the essence of Stoicism is to seek happiness in the exercise and contemplation of one's agency (or, in other words, in applying practical reason, all-things-considered, to whatever the circumstances are[250]). If this holds, it follows that Stoicism is fit to work in all cases, i.e., it's not limited to asceticism. Accepting this claim translates into falsifying the ascetic misinterpretation.

The best argument can be expressed in terms of Stoic axiology, which, let's recall, asserts that only things in our power may be either good or bad, while all the things not in our power are neutral. These neutrals (or externals) can be seen as raw material from which valuable things are formed. They are like bricks or like letters that can be turned – by a human agent only – into buildings or words. All bricks and letters are perfectly neutral, it's only the building itself that can be well or poorly built and it's only the words that can be either beautifully crafted or coarse. The result depends on the human actor only, not on the materials involved.

The core Stoic formula is that being either healthy or sick, famous or forgotten, influential or powerless is neither good nor bad. It's only what we do with our health, fame, power, or lack thereof, that can be either good or bad. In particular, it's neutral whether we are rich or poor, prosperous or struggling – the only thing that counts is how we handle whatever we possess. Money itself is neither good or bad, it's only our use of it that can be either. Hence, nothing in Stoicism requires us to eschew money or refrain from earning it. Hence the ascetic interpretation is wrong, hence a Stoic, if she happens to be an artist, may well create in order to live off her art.

This axiological framework is supported by an apt picture provided by Epictetus. "This is the rod of Hermes: touch with it what you please, as the saying is, and it will be of gold. I say not so: but bring what you please, and I will make it good. Bring disease, bring death, bring poverty, bring abuse, bring trial on capital charges: all these things through the rod of Hermes shall be made profitable."[251] Almost entire chapter 5 in the second book of *Discourses* is devoted to this topic. "Things themselves are indifferent; but the use of them is not indifferent. [...] He imitates those who play at dice. The counters are indifferent; the dice are indifferent. [...] To use carefully and dexterously the cast of the dice, this is my business."[252] And then: "should we use such [indifferent] things carelessly? In no way. [...] We should act carefully because the use is not indifferent."[253] Consequently:

The argument

> So we should do: we must employ all the care of the players, but show the same indifference about the ball. For we ought by all means to apply our art to some external material, not as valuing the material, but, whatever it may be, showing our art in it. Thus too the weaver does not make wool, but exercises his art upon such as he receives. [...] When then you have received the material, work on it [254].

The same concept expressed in Seneca's words:

> By things indifferent, I mean such, that are neither good nor bad, considered in themselves, as sickness, pain, poverty, punishment, death. [...] Poverty is not commendable, but it is commendable not to be dejected and bowed down by it. So neither is banishment, but he that is not grieved at suffering it, is praise-worthy[255].

Marcus Aurelius expressed this idea in his snappy parlance: "to me that which presents itself is always a material for virtue, both rational and political."[256] Finally, John Rist summed it up as follows. "The standard position in Stoicism before Panaetius [...] is that the wise man makes use of externals, employs them as the material on which he builds his virtue."[257] The conclusion is clear. A Stoic doesn't reject externals, but she makes use of them – a wise use[258].

There are also passages in the ancient Stoics which directly oppose the pro-ascetic fragments quoted earlier in this chapter. In this vein, there is Seneca who states: "I prefer [...] to show myself in public dressed in woolen and in robes of office, rather than with naked or half-covered shoulders."[259] Epictetus in his inimitable style ridicules those who follow the ascetic interpretation: "if you are told that you ought not to wear garments dyed with purple, go and daub your cloak with muck or tear it!"[260] Next, if extra-textual evidence be admissible, there is the meaningful episode of young Marcus Aurelius, who initially had followed the ascetic misinterpretation ("a plank bed and skin, and whatever else of the kind belongs to the Grecian discipline"[261] in his own words) only to realize in his later years, that it's a distortion of Stoicism. Marcus Cornelius Fronto helped him learn the error of his ways, by appealing to a founding father: "your own Chrysippus, [...] used to get mellow, so they say, every day in the year."[262] Seneca is even a better example in this regard. He lived in great affluence while his wealth, according to some accounts, hadn't been accumulated entirely legally. We can suppose that the controversy around the ascetic misinterpretation was quite a personal issue to him. After all, he had a direct interest in proving that a Stoic isn't required to renounce his fortune. Finally, we need to remember Lawrence Becker who explicitly rejects the ascetic misinterpretation saying that it is not true that the ideal life of a Stoic is "devoid of the ordinary pleasures of sex, food, drink, music, wealth, fame, friends, and so on."[263]

Let's recap. I've argued that the ascetic misinterpretation is a false reading of Stoicism. Stoic philosophy doesn't require its followers to reject the earthly goods on principle. Stoicism isn't about limiting oneself – it's about smart management of what is at hand. In particular, it doesn't require rejecting the money. It gives its adherents the green light to live inside modern economy without desperate attempts to find a refuge on Robinson Crusoe's deserted island, on Mount Athos, in a hippie commune, or in a noble but still unreachable future of a just society where all money is abandoned. Thus, the conclusion is that the profit theme is agreeable with Stoicism. Indeed, there is nothing incoherent in a Stoic receiving money for her creative work, and there is nothing nonstoic in her doing that work with the profit in mind.

This isn't, however, the last word in the matter. We've discussed the problem from the Stoic side, but we need to shift the perspective now, so an important point isn't missed. How does it all look from the artist's point of view? She can make a bitter remark of course, that the above reasoning is irrelevant because true art all too often doesn't find a customer to pay for it. It is, sadly, quite true (as Paul Auster points out : "Unless you turn out to be a favorite of the gods [...], your work will never bring in enough to support you, and if you mean to have a roof over your head and not starve to death, you must resign yourself to doing other work to pay the bill"[264]), but it's not what I mean here.

The point is that the financial reward isn't the most inspiring part of artistic creativity. In particular, the Romantic artist doesn't create *because* she wants to pay the bill. In the discussion of the Romantic model back in chapter 2, we didn't talk about annual income. We rather talked about "imagination," "exploring the dark and the concealed," "a new alphabet," "rebellion," "vocation," "unrest." These are two distinct discourses, even though they can describe one and the same artist at a given moment of time.

But why are they distinct? Why assert that analyzing the figure of a Romantic poet through the lens of the profit theme is inadequate or unsatisfactory? Let's summon two examples. The first one is an excerpt from Salvador Dalí's memoir, which he titled, quite straightforwardly, *A Diary of a Genius*. In the entry from May 1, 1952, we read:

> I have always been greatly impressed by gold [...] Ever since [...] I learned that Miguel de Cervantes [...] died in blackest penury [...] my prudence has strongly advised me [...] to become [...] a

multimillionaire. And this [...] has been done. The simplest way to refuse all concessions to gold is to have it oneself[265].

The same idea is expressed – even more flat-out – in an entry from May 13, 1953, where we read simply: "Painters, be rich rather than poor. And to this end, follow my advice."[266]

My point is this. These two passages wouldn't make sense they make if we hadn't certain preconceptions about Dalí. These preconceptions are of a clear Romantic affiliation: we expect an artist like him to rise over the mundane monetary issues. We expect him to occupy a sphere inaccessible to mere mortals and detached from ordinary worries (Epicureans might well call that place intermundia). Moreover, we are – on the rational level – fully aware that it's just a fantasy, but we still somehow cling to it. In his diary, Dalí plays on the tension between reality and the archetype ingrained in us. If the notion of the Romantic artist wasn't present in us, the quoted passages wouldn't sound provocative. They would just seem awkward.

The second example plays even more directly on the image of an "elevated" artist, untainted by anything as earthly as money. Consider *Shakespeare in Love*, a 1998 movie by John Madden. Financial matters provide half of its humor: Hermes, not Aphrodite, brings the baseline tension to the plot. For us, the jaded 21st century readers, *The Most Excellent and Lamentable Tragedie of Romeo and Juliet* is also the most classical tragedy of all. We have a clear preconception of William Shakespeare as an almost incorporeal author of the plays that form the backbone of the Western canon (or even, as Harold Bloom asserts, are the canon itself[267]). The movie, however, presents his work as a web of financial dependencies, debts, greed, and fraud. Just as with Dalí, we theoretically know well that Shakespeare was a man of flesh, blood, and pouch, but we agree to temporarily forget it and yield to the charm of the movie. Laughter while watching *Shakespeare in Love* comes from the defiance of our "elevated" concept of the artist – and is thus another proof that it deeply influences our thought.

The conclusion is this. Despite the common and ill-conceived misinterpretation, Stoicism is not necessarily an ascetic philosophy[268]. Hence, there is nothing nonstoic in artistic creativity taken as a means to make money. Yet, such understanding of it is neither the primary focus of this book nor the most interesting case.

7. The preservation theme

The preservation theme is a framework of understanding artistic creativity as a means to capture some specific fragment of the universe and preserve it. Importantly, this "fragment" can be understood widely, encompassing all levels and categories of being. It stands for almost anything conceivable, including individual humans, their personal stories, grand histories, objects and events of every kind, deeds, nations, religions, churches, cities, all natural phenomena, all instances of magnanimity and meanness, of virtue and vice, of certitude and doubt, of will to power and faltering, of victory and defeat, love and hatred, life and death, flourishing and perishing.

The long and abstract list doesn't exhaust all possible instances, but it provides – I hope – a certain intuition. Generally speaking, the willingness to preserve maybe based on the artist's conviction that the object in question is simply worth it. Anything of positive value can stand as an example: a brave deed, a beautiful view, a brilliant game of chess. Importantly, objectivity and rational justification aren't crucial here. A creative act usually relies on the artist's own perspective, and so does my argument. The positive value of the object to-be-preserved may be actual or just apparent.

On the other hand, the willingness to preserve a given X may come from a premise that X bears negative value. Of course, preservation of something evil doesn't aim at prolonging that evil (not in most cases at least). In this case preservation usually serves as testimony or functions as a caution. A straightforward example is a survivor's tale of an atrocity, genocide or concentration camp.

Any combination of the above might be compounded by artist's awareness of the perishability of the object in question. If – speaking generally – things vanish and even memories of them fade away, then portraying them in a work of art can preserve them well beyond their limited time. We can imagine, of course, a creative act performed for the sake of pure representation and with no intention of preserving anything (or even with a clear intention of *not* preserving, e.g. when an author deliberately destroys her own work of art, or when she purposefully uses material or medium which don't last – in this case the lack of lasting may be a part of the artistic concept itself). Yet, the very act of capturing something amounts to preserving it, however the timespan of preservation. What matters is not the time that the work of art survives (nothing will be remembered forever, after all) but the fact that artistic representation of any given object "elevates" it on a new plane of existence. It opens up the object to a new dimension of being. In this

The argument

regard, artistic creativity acquires quasi-ontological power: it provides "additional" existence to things. Such added existence may well last longer than their "original" existence. This quasi-ontological, or, better, cosmological, aspect of artistic creativity is the core philosophical question in this chapter.

Perishability itself can take many forms, including the usual disappearance and ordinary obliteration, just as it happens in our world in which nothing is eternal. Human beings and memories of them die. Languages, discourses, and manners of portraying the world become dated, obsolete, and then extinct. No human concepts, institutions, laws, tales, or systems of values last forever, and all of them sooner or later slip into the abyss of oblivion. It goes without saying that the same holds for all physical artifacts and products of human hands, which vanish even more swiftly.

No beings are eternal, but some of them might cease to be even before their usual lifetime. Human beings can die young. Ideas, states, religions and all else can wither – or get cut – long before their blooming season. In such a case, artistic representation is somehow an ersatz of existence, a substitute for survival and the only erectable bridge over the precipice of nothingness. Also, things don't just die and vanish by themselves but are often deliberately eradicated. It applies to actual physical or intellectual entities and to mere memories.

The ancient Stoics weren't ignorant of all this. Marcus Aurelius is hard to surpass in his constant realization of the perishability of things. This leitmotif is one of the most persistent in his *Meditations*. "Where are they all now? Smoke and ash and a tale, or not even a tale."[269] "How many after being celebrated by fame have been given up to oblivion; and how many who have celebrated the fame of others have long been dead?"[270] "How many a Chrysippus, how many a Socrates, how many an Epictetus has time already swallowed up?"[271] Interestingly, Seneca explicitly employs the preservation theme, when he promises Lucilius that his name would be immortalized as the addressee of Seneca's letters. "The vast deluge of time will flow in upon us [...] What Epicurus promised his friend, I [...] promise you, Lucilius. I flatter myself that I shall have some favor with posterity, and can at least preserve for a time such names as I think proper to take with me. Our Vergil promised immortal honor to two persons and still makes good his promise:

> O happy friends! For if my verse can give
> Immortal life, your fame shall ever live"[272]

Seneca mentions the most obvious case of preservation: a name won't be forgotten (for some time at least) if it's recorded in literature. Obviously, and contrary to the common saying, no literature can provide true immortality (that's well above human paygrade), but there is no doubt that a name in the book can last longer than a name on a gravestone. Artistic creativity is capable of far more than that though. It can preserve whole languages, sensibilities, and ways of perceiving the world. This is actually, one may argue, what great art does best. The most eminent works of art, poems, novels and so on, are often just that: embodiments of a certain way of seeing the world which is thus preserved for future generations. It's many thanks to the works of Dostoevsky and Tolstoy that we know what the life in Tsarist Russia looked like. That world is preserved in their novels, while in reality it was long ago obliterated by time and Bolshevik revolution. On the other hand, artistic creativity captures human experiences, both glorious and gruesome. Anne Frank's *Diary of a Young Girl* preserves the experience of the Holocaust era and serves as a memento to us almost eighty years after the author perished in Bergen-Belsen. It will continue to do so when, in just a few decades, there will be no living human around to tell the story.

The big question is, of course, this: does the preservation theme agree with Stoicism? Can it be coherently expressed in the Stoic terms? I will argue that the answer is negative. There are three different steps, or partially interconnected layers of reasoning, that lead to that conclusion. Let's now go through them one by one.

[1] The first argument can be called the cosmological argument, and it unfolds as follows. The Stoic view of the universe is undergirded with the concept of eternal return. It's not an unequivocal idea, and it's open to vast interpretation, but the classical, orthodox picture is this (this is the view in which "transcyclical indiscernibility" or even "transcyclical identity" holds, to use Salles's terms[273]). The universe we live in is just one instance in an infinite series of universes that have been coming one after another for a past eternity and will be coming one after another for an eternity to come. There was neither an outset nor there will be an end to this sequence of worlds, there was no "in the beginning," there is no termination in sight. Each universe in this sequence has its own dawn and dusk. But after it comes to its end, a new iteration starts over, and everything repeats itself taking exactly the same course it took before. Everything that happens in our universe has already happened infinitely many times in its past iterations and will happen infinitely many times in the future ones. Every single trifle to a minutest detail sharp. You, dear reader, have read this book infinitely many times already, and infinitely

The argument

many times you have already wondered why **this** word is boldfaced. And you will wonder infinitely many times more since we have no ability to alter or divert this perpetual process. In the words of Nemesius:

> The Stoics say that when the planets return to the same celestial sign [...] the world returns anew to the same condition as before. [...] For again there will be Socrates and Plato and each of mankind with the same friends and fellow citizens; they [...] will encounter the same things[274].

What does it mean for the preservation theme? In the logic of eternal return, not a single fragment of the universe is prone to annihilation or oblivion. Certainly, everything becomes annihilated and melts into oblivion in the local sense, but nothing does so globally. Nothing ultimately disappears in the bigger picture, and nothing gets utterly forgotten because the universe repeats itself. Every petty piece of the world, every pattern and every particle of it recurs in its eternal pulse.

This negates the basic premise of the preservation theme. About everything that has occurred at least once we can be sure that it will reemerge infinitely many times, whether someone tries to save it from oblivion or not. Moreover, one may even say that within the logic of eternal return the very statement "something that has occurred at least once" is self-contradictory. Not a single object comes to be just once. Everything that happens in the present will not only happen in the future reiterations of the universe, but it has already happened in the past ones. Hence, all conceivable things are divided into just two groups: things that happen infinitely many times and things that don't happen at all. There is neither a need nor a possibility of transferring any item from one set to the other. Thus, any attempt at "preserving" something would be both in vain and redundant. To try to do it would be against the very principle of the universe and as such it would be – to employ Epictetean parlance – a doing of fools.

[2] The second argument can be called, roughly, the logico-psychological one. The reasoning is following. Even if we put aside the concept of an infinite sequence of universes and if we limit ourselves to the present world at hand, everything in it is still constant, monotonous and repetitive. In the world, as a Stoic perceives it, there is nothing new under the sun. The world is a good, old acquaintance that has nothing hidden up its sleeve to surprise us. Everything was, is and will be the same, following the same unchanged patterns. There is no alteration to these patterns, no clinamen to introduce novelty of any kind.

There is never anything new in human experience but rather the same old tale. As Seneca asks: "what is there to wonder at in bad men committing evil deeds? What novelty is there in your enemy hurting you, your friend quarrelling with you, your son going wrong, or your servant doing amiss?"[275] Everything is always the same in the department of mishaps that fall onto people. Here is Seneca again. "Have your servants left you? And is that all? Some have robbed their master, others have vilified him, others have betrayed him, others have trampled upon him, some have made an attempt on their master's life with poison [...] These, and all other mischiefs you can imagine, have happened to many."[276] And again: "What has happened to us has happened to every one before us and will happen to every one after us."[277] Particularly, there is no deviation in respect to death:

> Hippocrates after curing many diseases himself fell sick and died. The Chaldaei foretold the deaths of many, and then fate caught them too. [...] Heraclitus, after so many speculations on the conflagration of the universe, was filled with water internally and died smeared all over with mud. And lice destroyed Democritus; and other lice killed Socrates[278].

Monotony and repetitiveness are not limited to distresses only. They are indeed the most universal and common qualities of the world we live in. As Marcus Aurelius says, "everywhere up and down you will find the same things, with which the old histories are filled, those of the middle ages and those of our own day; with which cities and houses are filled now. There is nothing new all things are both familiar and short lived."[279] "All things are the same, familiar in experience [...] Everything now is just as it was in the time of those whom we have buried."[280] And "everything which happens is as familiar and well known as the rose in spring and the fruit in summer."[281] This monotony and predictability entail that it's not that important which fragment of the universe we experience and for how long. Everything that can be known can be deduced from a very limited experience. In the words of Marcus again: "He who has seen present things has seen all [...] for all things are of one kin and of one form."[282] "To have contemplated human life for forty years is the same as to have contemplated it for ten thousand years. For what more will you see?"[283]

How does the preservation theme look from this perspective? Consider the following example. In the final scene of episode 1 season 1 of the notorious HBO series *Girls* Hannah Horvath, a young wannabe writer, says that it seems to her that she might be "the voice of her generation, or, at least, a voice of a generation." This phrase, which is a cliché shared by thousands of aspiring artists, well illustrates our theme. "To be the voice of (a) generation" means, first, grasping the difference between one particular generation and others. Second, it means that the artist successfully expresses that difference and manages to tell the eternity about the particularity of her generation[284]. The very idea of doing this, however, is thwarted once we see it from the Stoic perspective.

Let's take the words of Marcus Aurelius:

> Constantly consider how all things such as they now are, in time past also were; and consider that they will be the same again. And place before thy eyes entire dramas and stages of the same form, whatever you have learned from your experience or from older history. For example, the whole court of Hadrianus, and the whole court of Antoninus, and the whole court of Philippus, Alexander, Croesus. For all those were such dramas as we see now, only with different actors [285].

If we agree to conceive the world in these terms, then the whole purpose of being a voice of (a) generation evaporates. To put it precisely: being a voice of (a) generation becomes both impossible and needless. It's impossible because in no particular generation is there anything special which differentiates it from any other. There is nothing new under the sun, everything was, is and will be just the same. Hence, the condition and the experience of every generation is identical to that of any other. Thus, there is nothing that could be used to define a generation and nothing for Hannah Horvath to write about. What's more, being a voice of a generation is needless. If all generations to come will be exactly the same, then a voice of the present generation won't offer them anything new, bracing or unexpected. Whatever Hannah writes, it will be of no use for future generations. They will be neither surprised by it nor they will learn anything from it. Everything that happens to her own census buddies is just a reiteration of what has already happened to the preceding generations (and just the same will relentlessly happen to generations to come). The universe is homogenous – or even Leibnizian – in the sense that the whole is reflected in every part, however minute. In other words, an artistic representation of any A is no lesson to any B, because $A = B$ (in saying this we again touch cosmology, since the idea of Stoic holism echoes here).

Obviously, "a generation" is just an example of "a fragment of the universe" which I used to define the preservation theme. The reasoning outlined above might be *salva veritate* repeated for any other entity. The conclusion is simple. In the Stoic universe, there is no need for an artist to preserve anything. Everything preserves itself. Everything is just the same old tale, which goes on without anyone's assistance. This undercuts the logic of the theme in question, making it incoherent with Stoicism.

[3] The position presented above is open to vivid criticism. How come, one may well ask, "everything was, is and will always be the same?" Our world is not that dull and boring! Things, places, events, people and stories do differ from each other, they aren't just a repetition of the same pattern. It's true that every generation – and every human being – is bound to be born and to die, but besides these shared limits they differ from all others in billions of particulars. It's an inexcusable oversimplification to turn a blind eye to this. There is no denying, for example, that the social, economic and political circumstances in which generations live do differ and do change dramatically. Why then do the Stoics turn down this diversity and focus on dullness and monotony instead?

This is exactly what my third argument addresses (it might be, crudely, called an ethical one). Even if there is something in the universe that stands out of the monotony outlined in [2], a Stoic is obliged to not acknowledge it. Why? Because her ethics requires her to do so. One of the cornerstones of the Stoic way of life is to take care to be never surprised, amazed, or caught off guard. It's a trade-off of a kind. If one wants to live like a Stoic, one has to forgo one's capacity of being amazed. For the Stoics, the human ability to be surprised is an ailment that should be eliminated. It's nothing else than a gate through which unrest, anxiety, and misery storm the mind. As such, this gate must be closed, locked and sealed at all times.

Diogenes Laertius refers to this idea as follows. "The wise man never wonders at any of the things which appear extraordinary, such as Charon's mephitic caverns, ebbings of the tide, hot springs or fiery eruptions."[286] Marcus Aurelius asks: "How ridiculous and what a stranger he is who is surprised at anything which happens in life."[287] Seneca writes a lot on this subject. First of all, he ridicules a person who gets surprised. "'I never thought it would happen!' How can you think that anything will not happen, when you know that it may happen to many men, and has happened to many?"[288] Accordingly, "Fabius was wont to say that the most shameful excuse a general could make was 'I did not think.' I think it is the most shameful excuse that *a man* can make. Think of everything, expect everything."[289] Also, "Nothing [...] should come upon us unexpectedly. The mind ought to be prepared not only against what usually happens but against whatever may happen."[290] And in particular: "Be prepared to submit to much. Is anyone surprised at being cold in winter? At being sick at sea? Or at being jostled in the street? The mind is strong enough to bear those evils for which it is prepared."[291] This approach is justified by the fact that a blow that comes unexpectedly is always more severe than a predicted one. "Unexpected accidents are apt to strike deepest. Novelty adds weight to calamity."[292] In a word, being surprised is profoundly nonstoic.

This might be further illustrated by the following metaphor. Imagine a child travelling on a plane for the first time. Everything would be new for her: the crowded and colorful airport, security checks, boarding, taxiing, the take-off roll, the ascent, the view, the experience of being above the clouds and weather, all told, for such a child everything is amazing and admirable. She might feel like she is inside a wonder which is displayed right there for her.

In contrast, a seasoned traveler has seen all this a thousand times before. She doesn't enjoy it any longer; it barely makes her yawn. It's worth less than a bored "Zeus... the same again!" The entire process of air travel is just a tedious necessity, transportation from point A to B, something that her job compels her to do, or an occasion to do some work. There is a world of difference between how she and the child perceive the same thing. They are indeed two opposite poles.

This difference reflects the discrepancy between the demands of the Stoic ethics and that of artistic creativity. Stoicism obliges us to always embrace the attitude of the seasoned traveler: whatever we do and whatever circumstance arises, we mustn't be surprised. On the other hand, artistic creativity originates – in a way – from the "child's mindset." It requires a dose of amazement and wonderment. Its level needs to be, so to speak, above average, whereas in Stoicism it needs to remain well below the usual limit.

Let's sum this up. There are three options. First, we may go orthodox in the understanding of eternal return, and we can interpret it as the reiteration of the universe as a whole. Such reading makes the preservation theme explicitly nonstoic (there is no need for a creative struggle to preserve anything, because nothing gets lost anyway). Second, we may limit ourselves to the present universe. In this case, the eternal return translates into the Stoic view of homogeneity and monotony. This makes our theme nonstoic as well: there is nothing exceptional that might be worthy of preserving. Finally, we may recognize that some of the phenomena of our world are indeed unique and cannot be inferred from or reduced to any general pattern. In this case, though, the Stoic ethical framework sets in and compels us to kill our sensibility to this. The *nil admirari* principle secures peace of mind but extirpates artistic creativity understood as preservation.

If there is, on the other hand, a counterargument that allows a shadow of a doubt, it's probably the following one. It's true that the Stoics reject amazement at any particular fragment of the universe, but they don't forbid amazement at the universe in general. They don't bar us from admiring its greatness, might, beauty, restlessness, and complexity. This again can be seen particularly in Marcus Aurelius.

This point may well open up another chapter of analysis, but it would involve a completely different conceptualization than I propose. After all, appreciation and admiration of the universe is one thing, while creating art in order to preserve its existence – is a whole new ball game. I assent that such an understanding of artistic creativity is possible, but, as mentioned in chapter 4, I don't take it on in this book. For the time being, we need to assume that the universe, of all things, preserves itself and thus the final counterargument doesn't refute the reasoning presented earlier.

8. The expressive theme

The expressive theme may be – to a degree – deemed a particularization of the preservation theme. The generic "fragment of the universe," which was to be preserved there, is now specified as the "self" of the artist. This is the subject of the present theme: I will now take on artistic creativity understood as an attempt to express the artist's self. It's a sub-case of what was discussed in the previous chapter, so we need to keep in mind that the previous train of reasoning (with all its ramification) applies here too. That's not all however. A new argument can be made, one tailored specifically to this theme.

We need to begin, though, with the basic notion of "the self of an artist." It's yet another complex and confusing concept to deal with it, but, fortunately, we don't have to discuss all of it. Only certain aspects of this concept are necessary for the purpose of this inquiry. First of all, I will rely on what was said in chapter 4 about the idea of subject. This book assumes the "traditional" view that there exists something that can be called "a subject" and that it can be coherently discussed. This subject – here goes the present argument – can be further specified as "self." To organize the discussion properly, we need to study two cases separately.

These two cases are not really just "cases," or even the two main concepts in the space of possible understandings of "self." They are way more, they are really two axes that help us organize the discourse and divide this chapter in two. Certainly, these two axes are to an extent interconnected, and the mere distinction between them is already an interpretation. But despite that, drawing this distinction is very useful, and it structures the argument clean.

The distinction is based on whether or not the artist's self is assumed to exist prior to the creative act. In the first variant, there is no prior existence of the self. The self is established only through the creative act. This is the case when the purpose of a creative act is not merely to express, but also to define the artist's individuality. In the second interpretation, the self-exists prior to the creative act and (to a degree) independently of it. In brief, in the former case, the creative act comprises both bringing artist's self to the existence and expressing it. In the latter, it stands for the expression of what is already there.

The first variant: artist's self is created through the creative act

In this interpretation, the self of the artist doesn't exist afore and independently from the act of expression. It's not something that sits there and patiently waits to be expressed. Quite the contrary: expression is an indispensable element which constitutes individuality. This idea can be illustrated with the following example. Imagine a poem by a distinguished author, a poem that is of significant and mostly unquestioned literary value. Further, imagine that this poem is rather a difficult one to understand. It's well-regarded as a great piece of literature, but it doesn't yield to an easy interpretation. Finally, let's imagine a naive reader who asks the author the blunt question: "Why haven't you written it in a less oblique way?"

There is a twofold answer to this. **First**, we may swiftly reply that there is no point in translating a poem into prose because the whole merit of a poem (and its very *raison d'etre*) consists in speaking indirectly. Remember what Emily Dickinson says in *[Tell all the Truth...]* about how truth should be expressed. Any "translation" of a poem into something "less oblique" or into "plain English" kills its elusive beauty (as I just did with Dickinson's lines). If we stretch our analytical hand too much into the matter of poetry, we risk ending up with mere chaff on our palm.

The key point, however, lies in the **second** answer. Here is the argument: translating a poem into prose is not only pointless, but also logically impossible. It's impossible to rephrase the content of a poem less obliquely because there is no content that exists separately from its oblique expression. "Content of a poem" isn't some well-defined being which just sits there and humbly waits to serve as material to be formed and presented to the world one way or another. It's a mistake to assume that there is some theoretical equality of status for all the possible ways of expression. It's a mistake to assume that the ways of expression which hadn't been employed are still open for consideration once the poem is written. There is no *what* in the poem that is separable from the way *how* it is expressed. The "content" of the poem comes into being when – and only when – the very words are typed.

This point of view is maintained by many authors, both artists themselves and those who studied the phenomenon of artistic creativity. Among the former, there was John Ashberry, who claimed that "if I did not write, I would have no idea of what I can write. I suppose that I write so as to find what I have to write."[293] Maurice Merleau-Ponty's words run along the same line: "My own words take me by surprise and teach me what I think."[294] Alphonse de Lamartine similarly: "I never think, my thoughts think for me."[295] More support for this view can be found in the writings of V. E. Frankl:

> Spiritual activity so absorbs the person [...] that he is not even capable of reflecting on what he basically is. The self does not yield to total self-reflections. [Thus] [...] human existence is basically unreflectable, and so is the self in itself. Human existence exists in action rather than reflection[296].

This standpoint is reflected in a particular example of emotion in Croce's and Collingwood's concept as reported by Stephen Davies:

> Through the articulation of inchoate feelings and impulses, the artist comes to express a particular, unique emotion, thereby bringing it to their conscious awareness. The emotion is constituted through the act of expression, having no prior identity; [...] [it] achieves its particular character through the manner of its expression[297].

Finally, to herald an author I will rely on more soon, Richard Rorty asserts:

> About two hundred years ago [the quote comes from a book published in 1989], the idea that truth was made rather than found began to take hold of the imagination of Europe. [...] At [...] the same time, the Romantic poets were showing what happens when art is thought of no longer as imitation but, rather, as the artist's self-creation[298].

In saying this, I've shifted from talking about the absence of radical and translatable content of a poem to the absence of artist's self. But the two are of course not unlike each other, especially in this context. This was the very reason to build the analogy with a poem. The first variant of the expressive theme is undergirded with a specific dynamic: a dynamic of

The argument

coming into being which consists in the act of expression. Nothing is static in this picture. A work of art spurts out and acquires its meaning and shape in this very leap. As such, it cannot be described in a static framework.

The Stoic framework, however, is just that: it's quite static. It's not a dynamic one, certainly not one of *Sturm und Drang*. Of course, a Stoic progressor develops her Stoic powers *over time* and tries to constantly evolve towards the ideal[299]. Yet, the ideal itself, once acquired, is static. It's an ideal of stillness, solidification, or – as some would even add – petrifaction. This might be argued for on two levels.

First, one of the basic premises of the Stoic ethics is – quite explicitly – drawing a clear and safe boundary. Stoicism entails shielding, putting up a barrier which resembles the immunological barrier within a living organism, or, on a different scale, a membrane surrounding a living biological cell. This, of course, is in order to be immune against the slings and arrows of outside fortune. To be safeguarded, self-protected and self-sufficient, to find safety behind an insurmountable fence – these are the goals the Stoics strive for. This picture can hardly be reconciled with the concept of creating one's self (or even *oneself*) through the act of artistic expression. The Stoic ideal is about sealing and securing the gate rather than sending scouts and emissaries into the vast external fields. It's about closing off and fencing in rather than about establishing the self in an outward process.

In Epictetus's own words this picture is outlined as this:

> Those who occupy a strong city mock the besiegers. "What trouble these men are now taking for nothing? Our wall is secure, we have food for a very long time, and all other resources." These are the things which make a city strong and impregnable: but nothing else than his opinions makes a man's soul impregnable [300].

Seneca presents it in the following way:

> "What then? Will there be no one who will try to do an injury to the wise man?" Yes, someone will try, but the injury will not reach him [...] Even when powerful men, raised to positions of high authority, and strong in the obedience of their dependents, strive to injure him, all their darts fall as far short of his wisdom as those which are shot upwards by bowstrings or catapults, which, although they rise so high as to pass out of sight, yet fall back again without reaching the heavens. Why, do you suppose that when that stupid king clouded the daylight with the multitude of his darts, that any arrow of them all went into the sun? Or that when he flung his chains into the deep, that he was able to reach Neptune? Just as sacred things escape from the hands of men, and no injury is done to the

godhead by those who destroy temples and melt down images, so whoever attempts to treat the wise man with impertinence, insolence, or scorn, does so in vain[301].

In more concise words: "So does a huge wild beast turn slowly and gaze at yelping curs, so does the wave dash in vain against a great cliff."[302] Epictetus also explores the idea of stone impermeability. "Stand by a stone and revile it; and what will you gain?"[303] Similarly Marcus Aurelius: "Be like the promontory against which the waves continually break, but it stands firm and tames the fury of the water around it."[304]

Second, having set that safe boundary, the Stoics leave the outside world to chance, fortune or providence, and engage the full potency of moral power and spiritual exercise to keep the inside quiet, tranquil and unruffled. It's a commonplace picture that the Stoic ideal is one of peace and tranquility and that the goal of the Stoics is to secure a calm pool of internal stability from the churning and devastating storms of the external world. It's reflected in the language cliché. The "stoic" attitude to something (especially something adverse) means serenity, calmness, and ability to respond reasonably with no sudden gust of emotion interfering with our decision. And indeed, the Stoic ideal of happiness – at least in the mainstream interpretations – consists of some form of internal quietude. Stoic spiritual exercise is aimed at smoothing the ripples away from the surface of the internal sea. The aim is to turn it into, as Marcus Aurelius puts it, "calm, everything stable, and a waveless bay."[305] The goal is to impose (or enforce), a static status and prevent things from stirring dangerously, to prevent a deadly eddy or ebb, to prevent anything that might disturb the self-contained inner universe. This is the point where the famous term *ataraxia* applies: imperturbability and lack of commotion.

There is a lovely passage in Epictetus which pins down the idea of valorizing internal peace far above anything that the outside world can offer. "[I am] perturbed, trembling at every piece of news, and having my tranquility depending on the letters of others. Some person has arrived from Rome. I only hope that there is no harm. [...] From Hellas someone has come. I hope that there is no harm. In this way, every place may be the cause of misfortune to you."[306] In Seneca's account: "The higher region of the universe, being more excellently ordered and near to the stars, is never gathered into clouds, driven about by storms, or whirled round by cyclones. [...] In like manner a lofty mind, [is] always placid and dwelling in a serene atmosphere."[307] Or, similarly: "The mind of a wise man [is like] the region above the moon, perpetually fair and serene."[308] In yet another phrasing: "[sage's soul] avoids all storms, it stands on firm

The argument

ground in fair daylight."[309] And: "The joy of the wise man is firm and lasting. It has no connection with chance or accidents, it is always calm and easy."[310] In the words of Marcus Aurelius: "make yourself like Empedocles' sphere, 'all round, and in its joyous rest reposing,' and if you shall strive to live only what is really your life, that is, the present, then you will be able to pass that portion of life which remains for you up to the time of your death, free from perturbations [and] nobly."[311] Finally, a very similar interpretation can be found in Pierre Hadot:

> When the self has thus isolated and returned into itself [...] it can be compared to the "Sphairos" of Empedocles. [...] This term denoted that unified state of the universe when it is dominated by Love, as opposed to the state of division it is in when dominated by Hate[312].

I believe that this well demonstrates how and why the two models (the self of an artist actualized in the dynamic of creative effort and the Stoic ideal of imperturbable peace) are at odds with each other. Using a very broad brush, we might sum it up in the following image: the artist is to the Stoic as Plotinus' perpetual effusion is to the relatively fixed and stable Plato's ideas.

The second variant: artist's self exists prior to the creative act

The second case, or rather the second framework, relies on the assumption that the artist's self exists by itself, prior to and (at least in some measure) independently of the act of expression. In other words, in this model, the self is no longer necessarily intertwined with the creative act. It's rather the primal matter and primal cause of artistic creativity, kind of a safe and stable grounding that creativity roots in and draws its energy and meaning from. In particular, it's possible that the self exists but isn't expressed at all. This constitutes a clear difference between the current variant and the previous one since the previous case implied that if there is no expression, then there is no individuality whatsoever.

Let's now assume a more specific model. To do so let's turn to the ideas of Richard Rorty advanced in his famous book *Contingency, Irony, and Solidarity*[313]. Its second chapter, "The Contingency of Selfhood," contains a seminal analysis of the poem *Continuing to Live* by Philip Larkin[314]. Rorty begins by pointing out that the poem pins down exactly what "fear of death" means (or, to be precise, what it meant to Larkin). "There is no such thing as fear of inexistence as such," says Rorty, "but only fear of some concrete loss."[315] The question is, a loss of what? The answer is: the loss of our "individual sense of what was possible and important."[316] We fear that we lose that "what [makes our] *I* different from all other *Is*."[317]

In other words, we are talking about the set of idiosyncrasies that define the unique self of a specific human being. The fear of death in turn – in Rorty's reading of Larkin – is the fear that these idiosyncrasies expire.

Obviously, in the plain sense, when a human dies the idiosyncrasies defining her individuality die as well. But this isn't the final word we can have in the matter, because a human can become a poet. The Rortian sense of "a poet" is wide and includes anyone who tries to advance a new language to describe the world, including Socrates, Jesus and Einstein just as well as Shakespeare and Larkin himself. A poet is someone who employs her creative pursuits to procure an afterlife for her set of idiosyncrasies. The uniqueness of the poet's self can last well after her death unless she failed to properly express it. Such failure is exactly what a poet fears. This is what the abstract "fear of death" means in her particular case[318].

But what constitutes this "unique self" that a poet strives to save from oblivion? (N.B. Notice that the view on the "self", which follows, suits our general minimalistic agenda. It avoids entanglement in colorful but risky metaphysical theories of the "self." Quite the contrary, it follows a simple and down-to-earth path, with as few tacit assumptions as possible.) Rorty's view is that there is a certain human trait common to all people without exceptions. This trait is our vulnerability to suffering. No human is (or has ever been) immune to it, and no one who is free from suffering now can be sure that she won't suffer in the future (except for those who are dying anesthetized and hold no belief in hell or purgatory). This trait is truly and universally human, although not exclusively human: we share it with thousands of other animal species. This last insight serves as a foundation for attempts to extend the scope of the liberal hope beyond the human domain (with Peter Singer as the hallmark author). For the time being tough, we will set our lesser siblings aside. Rorty argues that proneness to suffering is the single (and the only philosophically weighty) quality that unifies us all, without exception, and regardless of gender, sexual preference, nationality, religion, social status, political, or philosophical views. We are all in the same boat when it comes to suffering. This serves as the backbone of human solidarity which Rorty discusses in the final chapter of his book[319].

All humans are vulnerable to suffering, but they don't share all the different ways of suffering. Obviously, there are some pains that are common to us all. We can all suffer in the plethora of modes that our biology generously bestows on us. We are all prone to physical pain, hunger, disease and so on. And yet, there are manners of suffering which are unique to single individuals. Each and every one of us has her own set of phobias and traumas. Each and every one of us can feel pain and humiliation in her own, private and unique way (the Western culture knows the epitome of this in the idea of "Room 101" in Orwell's *1984*). These individual modes of vulnerability, the "particular varieties of pain and humiliation,"[320] as Rorty puts it, are exactly what defines our unique self (in Rorty's view). The general disposition to suffer is the bedrock of human solidarity, while the particular shades of vulnerability provide the principle of individualization. Every *I* is defined by the particular pattern of its possible suffering.

As I already mentioned, this understanding of "self" is minimalistic, safe and free of any particular metaphysical commitments. All I rely on is the elementary experience of suffering, known to everyone and irrefutable on the pre-philosophical, everyday-life level (it might be argued that any philosophy is relevant only as long as it doesn't undermine experiences as direct as pain – Kant might be interpreted in these terms[321]). Besides that, this approach is universal and inclusive. It can easily dovetail with many more specific theories of "self."

All of that being said and settled, we can now ask the essential question: is all this consistent with the Stoic doctrine? The answer appears to be negative, and the justification is as follows.

First of all and in the most general terms, the discussed Rortian understanding of the "self" is significantly different than the ancient understanding of it. Allowing some oversimplification here, we may say that in the ancient world "self" had much more of a prescriptive tinge than it has for us in the 21st century. The very idea of a universal "norm" for a human being is very problematic to us today, in the philosophical, ethical, political and practical domains alike. Any "ideal" form of human life needs to be highly individualized. In our contemporary, post-Romanticism world this is much more important that it – apparently – was for the ancients.

This general remark requires a detailed and precise explanation. In particular, we need to know more about how it can be expressed in the Stoic terms. This can be discussed in five points.

[1] There is the line of thinking that goes under the "ontological" or "Heraclitean" headline, due to its appeal to Stoic cosmology. According to it, the universe is permeated by Logos, the cosmic and all-reaching Reason, which permeates everything and is present in everything. No two parts or two particles of the universe are disconnected from one another. Everything is thoroughly knit together by the omnipresent Logos, the divine substance, the primary principle of the universe.

This reading, which uses terms like "knit together" or "connected," can be called the weak interpretation of Stoic ontology. The strong interpretation goes a step further and entails not only that all the things in the world are connected, but that they actually *are* the same. They are equal to each other and unified in the all-governing and all-sustaining Logos. On this reading Logos is everything and every particular thing is just a local and transient instantiation of it. Our universe is nothing else than an ocean of Logos, in Marcus' words, "constant a flux, both of substance and of time."[322] Certain spouts erupt here and there, now and then, taking the form of objects, places, animals, and humans. All human beings are essentially the same because they are fundamentally nothing else than instantiations of Logos. They thus lack ground to individualize and differ from each other [323].

Diogenes Laertius explains how that view was upheld by the early Stoics:

> The doctrine that the world is a living being, rational, animate and intelligent, is laid down by Chrysippus [...] Apollodorus [...] and [...] Posidonius. [...] The unity of the world is maintained by Zeno in his treatise *On the Whole*, by Chrysippus, [and] by Apollodorus in his *Physics*[324].

Epictetus presents it this way:

> But are plants and our bodies so bound up and united with the whole, and are not our souls much more? And our souls so bound up and in contact with God as parts of Him and portions of Him, and does not God perceive every motion of these parts as being his own motion connate with himself?[325]

In other words, we, humans, are all "from the same seeds and of the same descent from above."[326] In Seneca, we read: "All men descend from the same original stock, no one is better born than another [...] The universe is the one parent of all."[327] In Marcus Aurelius: "Of [the] common nature every particular nature is a part, as the nature of the leaf is a part of the nature of the plant"[328] And for a pithy summation: "All things are implicated with one another, and the bond is holy."[329]

[2] "Logos" can also be interpreted more figuratively, and emphasis can be put on other connotations of this ambiguous term. Here, the associations with "word" and "law" will be explored. In this view "Logos" is a universal principle of the universe, governing all levels of being, from the tiniest particles up to the motions of planetary systems, from the basics of the Pythagorean theorem to the mathematical sophistication of the string theory, from the behavior of the simplest bacteria to the intricacy of human spirit. This reading of Logos is again holistic and unifying. It's one

The argument

and the same Law for the entire universe, holding for everything and for everybody. The first, foremost and final obligation of a human being is to abide by that Law. This requirement is both a requisite and a sufficient condition for living a meaningful and flourishing life.

Whatever the details and specifics of this Law are, we need to remember its unifying power. The Law is fixed, it leaves no loopholes and no exceptions. All human beings are subjected to the same universal rule. The ancient Stoics would also readily add that this act of subjection is the ultimate and quintessential act which defines us as human beings. Everything else is a mere contingency that hardly matters. Hence, if we are defined by our subjection to the same Law-Logos, it follows that we are in effect all the same. There is no principle of individuation: every conceivable individuality would be immediately dismissed by the Stoics as negligible in the light of the universal Law-Logos. Since the latter is solely what matters.

Epictetus writes as follows on this:

> For how do we proceed in the matter of writing? Do I wish to write the name of Dion as I choose ? No, but I am taught to choose to write it as it ought to be written. And how with respect to music? In the same manner. And what universally in every art or science? Just the same. If it were not so, it would be of no value to know anything, if knowledge were adapted to every man's whim [330].

Zeller's explicitly remarks that in Stoicism

> the claims of individuality are ignored [...] The universal claims of morality are alone acknowledged; the right of the individual to act according to his peculiar character, and to develop that character, is almost ignored. The individual, as such, dwindles into obscurity[331].

[3] Besides Logos and Law, we can offer the following argument. Stoicism proposes a set of spiritual and mental exercises for living a good life. Importantly, they are the same for everybody: they allow little personal freedom and deviations. The formula of a content life has been – according to the Stoics – settled once and for all. It has little regard for the predilections of individuals. Thus, every adept of Stoicism is obliged to follow one and the same path, even if disavowing one's individuality is the cost. In loosely Foucaultian language this might be expressed as roughly: "there is no unique self in Stoicism, there are only techniques of the self."

[4] We may also recall what was said in the preceding chapter about the Stoic view of monotony, constancy, and repetitiveness of everything. If everything in the world has been and will always be the same, if there is nothing new under the sun, if all we know and all we experience is just a mere reiteration of what already happened in the past and to other

humans, if, moreover, in order to live happily we need to forgo any individuality, then no unique self is possible let alone admissible. (For a detailed exposition of this, see chapter 7.)

[5] We may also propose a new reading of the problem, which may shed some fresh light on it. This new reading starts off with the ideas of Stoic egalitarianism and cosmopolitanism. It is commonly acknowledged that the ancient Stoics opened the gates of philosophy to everyone: to Greeks, Romans, uncivilized barbarians, to freemen, freedmen, slaves, to men and women, as well as to the rich and the poor. The theoretical foundations of this were strong and simple: according to the Stoics all people are equal in their participation in Logos, however, the term be understood. In this vein, the ancient Stoics are credited by some scholars for laying the first foundations for the idea of general human equality and universal, undeniable human rights (although this particular interpretation is open to debate).

Yet, it can be argued that this venerable idea has a troublesome consequence, which somehow takes root in the Hegelian logic of thesis and antithesis, or, more precisely, in the fact that every unification on the basis of a shared quality X entails exclusion of those who lack X. Let's take a few examples. First, we can imagine the Greeks of the classical era, with their distinction of "us" versus "barbarians" (a distinction rejected by the Stoics). Anyone who spoke Greek and shared other characteristics of a free Greek male was counted as one of "us" as opposed to one of "them," the inhuman barbarians. Second, we have St. Paul, who abolished this logic by proclaiming famously that "There is neither Jew nor Gentile [...] for you are all one in Christ Jesus."[332] This can be interpreted in terms of Christian universalism: ethnic differences don't matter for the apostles of the new faith, and every human can become a Christian. Alas, the often overlooked, darker side of the coin is quite disturbing: everyone who rejects "being in Christ Jesus" falls short of being human. The circle of "humanity" is narrowed to only those who convert.

This mechanism recurs throughout history, sometimes with catastrophic consequences, as when being "Aryan" or "German" was used to define "us" against "them," the subordinate races, or when being "devout follower of the line of the Party" was used to define "us," against "them," the despicable and disposable enemies of the people. In a like manner, the Stoic emphasis on universalism and egalitarianism produces its own backlash: in order to illuminate what people share (i.e., that we are all equally capable of living contentedly) all diversity and individual differences must be kept in shadow. On this reading, the explicit claim that

The argument

the gate of philosophy is open to everyone is inseparably followed by an implicit impulse to deny – or at least trivialize – all individuality.

For all the above reasons we can see that Stoicism, as a philosophy of life, is tailored for humans in general, rather than for a specific, individual human being. This point alone puts it at odds with some part of our modern sensibility. The path that the Stoics designed is just the same for everyone, there is no room to roam around, there is no space for personal deviations. Thus, there are no "unique selves" that would crave for expression. There are no unique, irreplaceable personal cosmoses that would be extinguished with the death of their bearers. Everybody is equal to another, but not in the sense the liberals would like to embrace, i.e., in the equality of rights and opportunities, but in the sense, a totalitarian Big Brother would love to enforce, i.e., the sameness of mind, sameness of goals, sameness of fears. Thus, in Stoicism, we can't really talk about "expression of the self," because there is nothing particular to express in this desert landscape (to rephrase Quine[333]).

These are the arguments that put the expressive theme at odds with Stoicism. Are there any counterarguments to this reasoning? Yes, there are as follows.

[A] The first and the most important counterargument is simple: the arguments [1] - [5] commit the fallacy of presentism. In other words, they rest too much on applying our contemporary understanding of "self" to ancient philosophy. The 20th-century concept of individuality, described in Rortian terms, gets separated from the context it belongs to and is collated with the conceptual grid of Stoicism with its fundamentally different background and frame of reference. This can be seen as unacceptable on principle.

My reply to this is simple. As I declared in the Introduction, presentism is the methodology of this book. I take it as settled that it is acceptable. Everyone who doesn't agree that ancient ideas might be legitimately evaluated from the contemporary point of view needs to dismiss not only this chapter but the whole book altogether.

[B] An interpretation can be made that Stoicism was the first philosophy in the West that made egalitarianism one of its cornerstones. It did so, as I argued, at the cost of trivializing human diversity. Yet, one may argue that this price was necessary only at the pioneering stage. Birth pangs are always painful, but do we have to feel them forever? Why can't we reasonably expect that it is possible today to be *both* egalitarian and open for diversity?

[C] On a different note, one might rightly wonder whether the Rortian framework, as referred to above, doesn't raise Stoics' eyebrows? That framework is based on the idiosyncrasies of suffering. This conflicts with the Stoic notion that suffering is not something to be dwelled on, let alone emblazoned on the banners of one's self. Suffering is the enemy: it's to be combated, not contemplated. Thus, the idea of using it to define "self" might seem dubious in Stoicism.

[D] Finally, there are some passages in the ancient Stoics that indicate that they did, in fact, allow for individuality of some kind. Among them are the following. First, Epictetus says: "Man, consider first what the matter is […] then your own nature also, what it is able to bear. If you are a wrestler, look at your shoulders, your thighs, your loins: for different men are naturally formed for different things."[334] In the words of Seneca:

> You must decide whether your disposition is better suited for vigorous action or for tranquil speculation and contemplation, and you must adopt whichever the bent of your genius inclines you for. Isocrates laid hands upon Ephorus and led him away from the forum, thinking that he would be more usefully employed in compiling chronicles. For no good is done by forcing one's mind to engage in uncongenial work: it is vain to struggle against Nature[335].

Marcus Aurelius likewise: "[other] persons have their peculiar leading principle and follow their peculiar movement."[336]

In summary, the expressive theme is a particularization of the previous theme, hence all the Stoic disinclination to the preservation theme applies here as well. But a brand new cluster of objections springs up when we narrow ourselves to the expression of self. Stoicism is inimical to it on two grounds. First, because Stoicism upholds the static picture rather than a dynamic one, second because Stoicism is more focused on universal principles than on individual differences. Yet, this answer is not indubitable: a small battery of counter-arguments ([A] – [D]) can be raised, and some of them are not easy to quash.

9. The cognitive theme

The cognitive theme is the paradigm of understanding artistic creativity as a means of cognition. In other words, it's about artistic creativity employed to gather knowledge about the world. Obviously, this is a very general idea, and it requires explanation and examples.

One thing I want to avoid is sinking in the boundless topic of "cognition" itself. Fortunately, not all aspects of the theory of knowledge are relevant here. The ancient Stoics significantly contributed to the advance of epistemology, but this is neither the subject matter of this book nor is it essential in the cognitive theme. In this chapter "cognition" doesn't stand for the theory of knowledge as such (nor for advancing it), but rather for collecting usable data and deepening that kind of understanding of the world which serves as the base of ethical judgments. Let me recall Lawrence Becker's words: "Sages must know [...] about things relevant to [...] [their] endeavors [...] [This includes] both theoretical and practical knowledge – about oneself, about others, [and] about possible physical and social environments."[337]

In Stoicism, gathering relevant information about facts is an initial and necessary condition of an ethical reasoning – I will discuss it in detail later in this chapter. This "practical" approach is the core of how I understand "cognition" in this chapter. The intricacies of epistemology, the subtleties of cognitive science, as well as abstract concepts detached from daily life, distant planets and other rare earth elements – all of this won't occupy my attention.

Obviously, there are branches of knowledge in which we can't really speak of actual cognition through artistic creativity. Neither motion of protons, nor gravitational waves are good targets for cognition through art. We don't usually associate artists with the laboratories of high-energy physics or astronomical observatories, although one can reasonably argue that this lack of association is a rather recent invention (rewind two centuries back and we get Goethe, who authored both literary and scientific works, like *Theory of Colors*, and who was, presumably, one of the last great authors before the roads of artists and scientists ultimately forked). We can agree that today's artists – in our sense of the term – readapt and metaphorize concepts from the scientific field (e.g., *Elementary Particles* by Michel Houellebecq) rather than contribute to the actual scientific research. Does it undermine the cognitive theme, though? Certainly not, because, as it happens, high-end scientific discoveries and high-tech technological inventions aren't critical for our ethical judgments and daily decisions. Certainly, if one happens to be an amputee, it's crucial for her to know whether or not the science of her time is able to provide her with a functional artificial limb (future reprints of this book can replace this with "whether or not it is able to make her limb regrow"). But it's not essential for her to understand all of the science of her prosthesis. In the same vein, the highly mathematized laws of particle physics or the location of calderas on the surface of Io undoubtedly are knowledge, but not the kind of knowledge that is necessary to live an ethical life. And, as it happens, it's not the kind of knowledge that we usually obtain through art.

What kind of knowledge is, then, relevant to the cognitive theme? The knowledge that an artist pursues might be the knowledge of how society works, a theme that literature has pursued at least since the times of Homer. This may include a general description of the social world, as well as more specific insights, such as the presentation of role models of virtues deemed honorable in a given culture (e.g., Achilles or Odysseus). This implies that creative effort might help to get a grip on the values that are valid in a particular place and time.

Homer is just the beginning of a long sequence of epic literature (as Western culture knows it) which attempts to discover and describe the social world in its entirety. We can mention the classical prose of the 19th century, with Tolstoy's monumental works and Balzac's *Human Comedy*. There is also Zola's naturalism, which can be, from this viewpoint, read as an attempt to tear off the appearances and uncover what the world is really like. In Zola's case, uncovering the true essence of the world happens through unwrapping the softening, soothing and mollifying veil, the veil which makes the world appear less brutal and less horrifying.

The effort to unwrap and demythologize might take other forms as well, like when the "real" character of the world is brought to light from under a cover of ideology, e.g., the ideology of slavery, as in *Uncle's Tom Cabin*. The cognitive theme might be focused on investigating the walks of a life lived in a changing world, like in Lampedusa's *The Leopard*, or in a society that has undergone a revolution, like in Rybakov's *Children of the Arbat*. The cognitive theme might be particularly beneficial in these cases, since the situation of a profound social transformation usually leaves no way of life unturned, resulting in a substantial need for an inquiry into the new situation. One may also argue that this is the case when artist's intuition is especially useful since it's able to recognize the new patterns of life much earlier than scientific studies do. Furthermore, it's not necessary for such a transformation to have taken place in the real world. An artist herself can conjure up a world and then investigate what a life would look like in it. In particular, this might be a dystopian vision, pursued in order to analyze what and why may go wrong, as in Huxley, Orwell, or in *Black Mirror*. Usually, such an approach magnifies some phenomena which are already there and thus makes them perceivable more easily (e.g., early cases of photo manipulation for propaganda purposes turned into a full-blown doctrine of mutability of the past in *1984*). Finally, the cognitive theme might refer to the study of a world in which a social transformation has gone bankrupt, and an ideal once pursued failed to produce a fruitful change. This is the case of already mentioned *Elementary Particles* by Michel Houellebecq.

On the other hand, the cognitive theme doesn't have to be concerned with the society as a whole. The above list of examples, which certainly doesn't exhaust the topic, needs to be complemented by another equally important and equally thumbnail list. The cognitive theme can be focused on how a mind of an individual human works – which is just as broad an area of inquiry. In John Madden's *Shakespeare in Love* (discussed already in chapter 6) there is a wager as to whether a theater play can show the truth of love. It's settled by Queen Elizabeth in favor of young Will Shakespeare, and we can concur with her that *Romeo and Juliet* does indeed provide us with some understanding of what it means to be in love. Consequently, and committing one more oversimplification, we might assert that *Titus Andronicus* forwards our understanding as to what it means to be carried away by lust for revenge.

The creative effort of an artist might also aim at hidden aspects of human psychology and may attempt to investigate the depths that are inaccessible to laymen (and this, one might argue, is where the cognitive potential of art is at its greatest). Marcel Proust springs out as a classic example. The cognitive theme can be employed to study a human being experiencing an absurd situation (e.g., *The Wall* by Jean-Paul Sartre), an oppressive one (e.g., again, Orwell's *1984*) or simply an unusual one (e.g., *Robinson Crusoe* by Daniel Dafoe). Art can help us understand a situation which is deemed illicit in our social circumstances (Nabokov's *Lolita*) or when we experience the profound technological transformation of the world, which leaves no social rule unchanged (like in the world envisioned by Arthur C. Clarke in his *Space Odyssey* series).

Obviously, these examples barely scratch the surface of how the cognitive theme can feed us with facts of life. Also, I don't claim that any of the mentioned works were created solely for the sake of cognition – this would be indeed a ridiculous assumption to make. Furthermore, it's interesting to note how closely bordered the cognitive theme is to both the preservation theme (chapter 7) and the didactic theme (chapter 13).

That said, we can turn to the central question: is the cognitive theme coherent with Stoicism? I will argue that the answer is affirmative. The general line of the argument is that acquiring knowledge about facts is necessary for the Stoic goal of achieving a good, full and content life.

In everyday, non-philosophical parlance Stoicism might be (and sometimes is) pegged as a "sober" or "realistic" philosophy of life. The Stoic approach to reality is based on proper analysis of every situation, circumstance and condition one happens to face. All Stoic ethical reasoning relies on the prerequisite knowledge of facts. Only upon that knowledge practical reasoning is exercised, and from it, all actions follow.

The Stoics were materialists and rejected Plato's transcendence (in Giovanni Reale's terms: they rejected the "second voyage"[338]). They held that everything that exists belongs to this world and, to speak Kant, everything we can hope for also belongs to it. The Stoics sought neither a mystical refuge nor a solace in the hereafter. As the convenient formula goes, the difference between religion and Stoicism is that the former is about the afterlife, while the latter is about earthly life[339]. Stoicism is entirely concerned with our present life, not with what lies beyond the grave, not with any daydreaming. The aim of a Stoic is to secure her salvation here: in this life, on this earth.

A Stoic seeks bliss and fulfillment in the proper application of her agency. In order to apply it properly she must "follow the facts,"[340] she must follow the principle of *memento mundi*[341] or *facta sunt servanda*. She must acknowledge the world as is, without sugarcoating and without deluding herself with pleasant fairy tales. The facts must be acknowledged and cannot be denied. Before any ethical reasoning commences a Stoic must obtain, to the best of her ability, the proper entry data, that is, she must obtain knowledge of initial conditions and all pertaining facts. But where do this data come from? Can cognitive theme of artistic creativity be of help here? If it can serve as an input device, providing the relevant knowledge about the facts, then it is not only consistent with the Stoic framework but may be highly useful to the Stoic ends.

This general reasoning translates into a few specific arguments, which I will now present one by one.

[1] As every handbook asserts, one of the chief Stoic principles is about living in agreement with nature. However, there are substantial reasons which undermine our today's confidence in the concept of "nature." Those reasons are mentioned in the Introduction[342] and they make it doubtful whether the 21st century Stoicism still can and should draw its ethical norms from nature or otherwise rely on it. One interpretation of this problem is particularly informative in regard to the cognitive theme. It's the interpretation proposed by Lawrence Becker[343] and the gist of it is this: "consistency with nature" should be read as "consistency with facts." Such an approach, although streaked with a tautological undertone, cannot be easily dismissed. In fact, if faced with a choice, the Stoics would indeed opt for the ethics pursued in accordance with facts rather than against them. Nothing, in fact, is more anti-Stoic than going anti-factual.

If we adopt this view, our argument attains its full meaning. If the original Stoic framework was closely associated with the principle of "following nature" and if we agree that this principle may be translated into "ethical judgments shall not be based on counterfactual statements," it follows that it's vital for a Stoic to know what the facts are. Consequently, if art can lend a hand in getting to know these facts (as it does in the cognitive theme), it's more than welcome in Stoicism. The most obvious source of our knowledge of facts is science, but art is the other side of the coin which allows us to explore what science isn't qualified to handle. And indeed, art and science can harmonize nicely and deepen our understanding of the world together. To paraphrase the opening of Pope John Paul II's 1998 *Fides et ratio* encyclical, we may say that "science and art are like two wings on which the human spirit rises to the contemplation of truth."[344]

In Lawrence Becker's own words: "[ethical inquiry] cannot begin until all relevant description, representation, and prediction are in hand, all relevant possibilities are imagined, all relevant lessons from experience, history, practice are learned – until, let us say, the empirical work is done."[345] Based on what we discussed, there is strong evidence that artistic creativity can be very helpful in this work.

[2] One of the Becker's interpretative concepts is particularly relevant to the cognitive theme. It's called the "Axiom of Futility" and the original formula is as follows. "Agents are required not to make direct attempts to do (or be) something that is logically, theoretically, or practically impossible."[346] In other words, a Stoic should neither wish nor strive for anything impossible – this is a crucial premise of the do-not-deny-the-facts attitude. Obviously, as Becker rightly points out later on, "impossibility" has levels. There is the basic trio of logical impossibility (2+2=5), theoretical impossibility (travelling faster than light) and practical impossibility (the United States losing a war against Iceland), but this doesn't exhaust the picture.

Let's take a military example (the ancients would approve). Imagine a commander who dispatches a unit of soldiers to a section of the battlefront, knowing full well that it's impossible to hold it up. If this commander happens to be Stoic, she, certainly, can't expect the mission to succeed. Similarly, if the soldiers know that they are on a suicidal mission and if they follow Stoic ethics, they won't expect to fulfill the task (as it would mean wishing for an impossibility). But does it automatically imply that the commander shouldn't have given the order or that the soldiers should incite a mutiny and abandon the mission? Definitely not. And by saying "definitely not" I mean neither the martyrological misinterpretation of Stoicism (I will explore it more in point [3]), nor the false notion that to obey an order is the highest duty of a Stoic. The reasoning turns the other way. To be engaged in a given section of the battlefront is a first-order objective[347], but it can simultaneously be a part of a broader plan and an instrument to achieve a goal of a higher order. This higher goal could be defined as, e.g., "to pin down enemy forces here, to allow for a launch of an offensive there." In this case, losing a battle or giving up a section of the front means neither that the war was lost nor that the higher objective wasn't met. Furthermore, as the history of wars teaches us all too well, soldiers sometimes fight to the end, despite being perfectly aware that their mission is in vain. This is also acceptable in Stoicism (but importantly: it doesn't imply that a Stoic *must* always fight to the end – again, see the discussion of the martyrological misinterpretation in point [3]). To give a testimony to future generations, to be acknowledged as a hero, to prove that one's cause is right by sacrificing one's life – these kinds of goals are just as legitimate in Stoicism as the plain practical goals. In sum, one has to be particularly cautious when appealing to the Axiom of Futility. It's true that a Stoic mustn't desire impossible things, but this formula mustn't be oversimplified.

In every project, it's better to be aware of its feasibility than not to be aware. This holds for every endeavor and every commitment. If artistic creativity can go hand in hand with science in expanding our knowledge on what's possible and what's not, it's all the more reason to assert that the cognitive theme is consistent with the Stoic framework.

[3] Alongside the ascetic misinterpretation (chapter 6) and the conservative misinterpretation (chapter 10) there is another common misunderstanding of Stoicism which can be dubbed the **martyrological misinterpretation**. It's less seminal than the previous two, and I will discuss it in less detail. Yet, it still sheds light on our problem in question.

The martyrological misinterpretation of Stoicism assumes that the core premise (and the core consequence) of Stoicism is to cling to fixed laws and tenets, regardless of the price and ramifications of doing so. In other words, the martyrological misinterpretation is a fetishization of steadfastness, it's a distorted understanding of firmness. It's the virtue of constancy gone awry. To follow it is to adhere to decisions once made without taking into account that circumstances can change. In the extreme case, it means blind devotion to one's principles up to the point of sacrificing one's life – which is often an act of foolishness as well as an act of heroism[348].

The argument

Epictetus tells an excellent story to illustrate this.

> One of my companions [...] for no reason resolved to starve himself to death. I heard of it when it was the third day of his abstinence from food and I went to inquire what had happened. "I have resolved" he said. "But still tell me what it was which induced you to resolve, for if you have resolved rightly, we shall sit with you and assist you to depart, but if you have made an unreasonable resolution, change your mind." "We ought to keep to our determinations." "What are you doing, man? We ought to keep not to all our determinations, but to those which are right." [...] This man was with difficulty persuaded to change his mind[349].

It's clear that Epictetus himself was well aware that his teaching could be martyrologically misread. To avoid this pitfall, we must keep in mind that constancy is indeed a value within the Stoic system, but it's an auxiliary value, not the ultimate one. Firmness is a right thing, but only firmness about the right thing.

How does this relate to the cognitive theme in artistic creativity? The connection is direct: the more facts we know, the easier it is for us to avoid the martyrological misinterpretation. Being aware of the explicit and implicit rules that govern the world always makes it easier rather than harder to avoid mistakes. The more we know about the world, the more aware we are of the specific traps that can lead to martyrological situations. Specifically, we are particularly prone to falling for the martyrological misinterpretation if we are blind to the dynamic character of the world and if we don't take into account the relentless Heraclitean flux and transformation of the universe. Most of the situations we face are not settled once and for all but are subject to change. To fail to comprehend this, to be undersensitive to change, to perceive the circumstances as immutable – these are major risk factors. Artistic creativity can help us avoid them.

[4] There is a commonplace "the world is a stage" topos in the Western culture. In the words of a man who is traditionally acknowledged to have understood it better than others:

> All the world's a stage,
> And all the men and women merely players[350]

This metaphor is so common that it's become a platitude. The core concept is clear: the world, and particularly the human world, is a stage (or a theater) in which particular humans play roles. As we will see in the next chapter, the Stoic interpretation of this is ambiguous and there are at least two competing readings of it. But both of them dovetail on the crucial issue: when we play a role, we are obliged to play it to the best of our ability. Importantly, this obligation isn't an obligation ordered or prescribed by someone or something. It's rather a logical necessity. The idea that a role should be played the best way possible is, in a way, encoded in the concept of a role itself. The Stoic rules of applying practical reason don't allow to simultaneously accept one's role and refuse to play it well. This approach makes the world-stage metaphor highly useful for the modern reading of Stoicism since it allows us to talk about "obligation" without explicit reference to any superior power (nature, Reason, God, or anything else).

In order to play a role the best way possible, it is necessary to know what it means to play it well. Whether we are to play a political leader or a junkie living in squalor, a rock star or a castaway, we must be able to distinguish a dazzling performance from a disappointing one. And this is where the cognitive theme sets in. As discussed earlier and despite what some hold, knowledge doesn't come exclusively from science. Art and the creative efforts of artists can surely teach us a lot on the rules of particular human roles. Thus, the cognitive theme, taken in the sense here described, is consistent with Stoicism.

10. The revolutionary theme and the conservative misinterpretation of Stoicism

> One has renounced grand life when one renounces war. In many cases [...] "peace of soul" is merely a misunderstanding [...] "Peace of soul" can [...] be [...] the beginning of weariness, the first of the shadows which evening [...] casts. [...] Or unconscious gratitude for a good digestion[351].
>
> Friedrich Nietzsche

The present theme, which I will, somehow exuberantly, call the revolutionary one, is in a way complementary to the preceding one. While the cognitive theme was about the understanding of the world as it is, the revolutionary theme is about changing it. It's a paradigm of understanding artistic creativity as a way of transforming the world.

In the previous chapter the outcome was quite straightforward and uncontroversial: employing creative effort to cognize the world is contributive to the Stoic cause. But what will happen when we switch from mere cognition to action? The question is ambitious: is attempting to change the world consistent with Stoicism?

The argument

In order to properly outline this problem I will stick to the framework proposed in the previous chapter: the concept of the world as a theater in which individuals play various parts. Some play slaves while some play presidents, some play the poor and some play the rich, some play loony artists and some play law-abiding citizens. The essential point is that we haven't assigned our roles ourselves. We didn't decide who plays what. Humans are required to play their parts but have no influence on making the assignments[352]. Who then, we may ask, assigns them? An orthodox ancient Stoic would promptly answer that it is "nature," "universal reason," or "fate" (this would vary by particular author and interpretation), but from our point of view, it's not critical to specify this. The crucial idea consists of two points. First, it's not us, humans, who assign, but somebody (or something) else[353]. Second, the assignments of the roles are fixed and immutable (within the classical reading of the metaphor). If one happens to be a slave, a soldier, a president, or a cursed poet – she must, she should, and she will remain in this role. There is no other option allowed.

The statement that the assignment of the roles has been made not by us can be translated into Stoic technical idiom as "it is not in our power to decide who receives what role." This phrasing raises a question: what then *is* in our power in this respect? The traditional answer is that it is in our power to not deny the assignment, to accept and embrace it, to fulfill what it compels us to do, and to do it to the best of our ability. We don't decide what we are ordered to play, but it's up to us to play it the best we can. If we happen to be slaves, then we must be obedient and do the work we are forced to do. If we are presidents we must preserve, protect and defend the constitution. If we are rich, we must use our riches in the most beneficial way available. And so on.

This traditional reading can be put in the following nutshell: accept assignment and act ably. Epictetus describes it as follows:

> Remember that you are an actor in a play, of such a kind as the author may choose: if short, of a short one, if long, of a long one. If he wishes you to act the part of a poor man, see that you act the part naturally, if the part of a lame man, of a magistrate, of a private person, do the same. For this is your duty, to act well the part that is given to you, but to select the part, belongs to another[354].

In another passage:

> The wise and good man [...] is attentive only to this, how he may fill his place with due regularity and obediently [...] A prince or a private man, a senator or a common person, a soldier or a general, a teacher or a master

of a family? Whatever place and position [...] I will die ten thousand times rather than desert them [355].

This approach is in sharp contrast with a wide range of examples of artistic creativity employed to do something dramatically opposite, i.e., inducing a change in the world. The most obvious case is all the art associated with revolutions and social changes, both these which actually happened and those that were merely postulated. As to the former one, Vladimir Mayakovsky is a great example. Remember his famous 1918 poem *Left March* and its final stanza in particular[356]. If the revolutionary message could be any more explicit, it is so in his *Our March* where the call for revolution – the new deluge and cleaning up every corner of the earth – is clear and present[357].

On the other hand, we have a gamut of examples that can be derived from the 1960s and 1970s counterculture. Think, for example, about John Lennon *Imagine*. The juxtaposition of the two authors, Mayakovsky and Lennon, reveals one more divergence. One artist might call for a change and actually see it happen, while another may never witness what he calls for. One can argue that the vision advanced by Lennon is practically infeasible: an ideal of a world with neither borders nor murderers is far too utopian to ever come true. But certainly, it doesn't make *Imagine* worthless or irrelevant (as a matter of fact, it may even make the song *more* appealing). Practical futility doesn't diminish the artistic merit.

Furthermore, this futility may well turn out to be no futility at all. Artistic creativity doesn't have to call for change in full voice. It may carry out the painstaking, preliminary work, it can create conditions which make new things conceivable. It can, among all else, shift the Overton window, changing the rules of discourse to include new ideas and question old ones. As the popular quip goes, abolition of slavery was once a crazy liberal idea. The zeitgeist changed: this once "crazy idea" turned into a predominant one. It didn't happen without the contribution of various artists who paved the way for this change (the mentioned H.B.Stowe is an obvious example). This scenario is almost a commonplace: an idea is unthinkable or "forbidden" at the outset, then it's advanced by a breakthrough book (or other work of art) which makes it expressible and debatable. Then, over time, it gets more and more traction, becomes a mainstream idea and turns into a policy. Finally, it seems unthinkable to even express the opposite of it, and it seems unimaginable to turn back time.

This provides context to Lennon's lyrics. Merely envisioning a new world might be just as revolutionary as a direct call for overthrowing the existing

The argument

status quo. Another example of this, one which directly sticks to the world-stage metaphor, is the subversive pattern in art. In it the creative efforts aim to reveal that certain social roles are mere conventions, products of custom and tradition. Let me recall what the illiterate Capulets' servant says in *Romeo and Juliet* when he is ordered to go around town and deliver invitations to the evening's reception:

> Find them out whose names are written here! It is written, that the shoemaker should meddle with his yard, and the tailor with his last, the fisher with his pencil, and the painter with his nets; but I am sent to find those persons whose names are here writ, and can never find what names the writing person hath here writ[358].

This passage was probably meant by Shakespeare to entertain his groundling audience by making the servant sound funny. But this joke can be seen as an early forerunner of subversive art. Today its most vivid expressions can be found in the areas associated with gender and sexual issues. Artistic creativity is one of the most useful means of displaying that gender, and sexual identities are not fixed and immutable, but rather performed and malleable. Performances by drag queens and kings are a clear example, alongside with movies (and musicals) like *Priscilla, Queen of the Desert*.

There are also currents in contemporary art that express their call for social impact and political relevance by directly opposing the *l'art pour l'art* model. The concept of "art for the sake of art" claimed total independence for artistic creativity and advanced the idea that art should be completely detached from earthly business. This ideal of disengagement, however, can be criticized as a shameful act of evasion, withdrawal, and abdication of responsibility. It can be considered an outcome of slave mentality: the inability to act not only unopposed but praised as a virtue. If art wants to be significant, one can argue, if art wants to be treated seriously, if art wants to retain its eminent position, if it doesn't want to be easily and effortlessly discarded as a mere quibble, then it must strive for social influence and political meaning. An example of this is Artur Żmijewski's 2007 manifesto *Applied Social Arts*. It considers the problem of what should be done in response to the fact that the overgrowth of art's autonomy has led to its excessive alienation. Here are the manifesto's recommendations:

> **1.** [Art should] instrumentalize its own autonomy and thus regain control over it. [...] **2.** [Art should] encroach upon other fields, such as science or politics, as a way of proving oneself. [...] **3.** It is also

worth trying to keep statements by reviewers from being treated as decrees[359].

The whole purpose is clear – the possibility of political engagement. As the manifesto says, "instrumentalization of autonomy makes it possible to use art for [...] serving the cause of [...] political action."[360]

On a bit different note, I'm well aware that I completely set aside the problem of *efficiency* of artistic creativity as a means of changing the world. Artistic creativity can indeed lay the foundations for lasting and profound change, but still, it can be argued that if one's chief goal is to induce change, then artistic creativity isn't the most promising way to accomplish it. As Andrei Voznesensky wrote in his 1988 review of a book on Anton Chekhov:

> Readers in the Soviet Union now have not the time nor the ear to catch Chekhov's subtleties. [...] There are demonstrations in the streets and vehicles rumble past loaded down with the newest Soviet rockets. Who has time for *The Cherry Orchard* when the orchards near Chernobyl are turning black?[361]

This is a huge topic, but I won't address it here. My subject matter isn't finding out what the best way to change the world is but whether it is stoical to wish for such a change.

Finally, the revolutionary theme can be aimed not at a transformation in the socio-political status quo but at a change in the artistic realm itself. To change the rules of the artistic discourse and to change the boundaries of what is deemed "art" – this has been the Holy Gail of all avant-gardes. A neat example is the famous *4'33"* by John Cage: a musical score which consists entirely of silence. Another example: "The distance from this sentence to your eye is my sculpture," the 1974 concept of the Fluxus artist Ken Friedman. Such instances of artistic creativity are included in the revolutionary theme, and it is so for two reasons. First, a change in the domain of art counts as an actual change in the external world. Second, as history teaches us and as it's implied by the very term "avant-garde," a change in art often heralds and a change in the extra-artistic realm.

We can now confront the main question: does the revolutionary theme agree with Stoicism? Given the discussion of the world-stage metaphor in the preceding chapter, it might seem that the answer is pretty clear and plainly negative. No, the answer would go in the first place, an aspiration to inflict a change in the world is not the Stoic way to go. As explained before, we do not decide who plays what role on the world stage. Our part is to accept the roles and play them as ably as we can. We have neither power nor authority to change it. The division between things in and not

The argument 75

in our power seems to support this interpretation: it is not up to us to decide who plays what. What is up to us is to accept the role we find ourselves in, to play it, and to intend to play it well.

This argument seems logically coherent. Yet, I will argue that it's not our final word in this matter. It's rather a premature answer, which doesn't hold in more detailed analysis. Before I offer my reasons for that, however, I want to underline again how important and far-reaching this problem is. Asking whether the revolutionary theme in artistic creativity is consistent with Stoic ethics is nothing short of asking the great question whether an attempt to change the world is acceptable from the Stoic standpoint. It's one of the key issues for interpretation and overall evaluation of Stoicism.

I will use the term "conservative misinterpretation of Stoicism" for the idea that it is essentially nonstoic to wish for a change in the world. As already said, this answer is preliminary and, as I will argue for, it is misguided. It's quite common, however, just as the ascetic misinterpretation is. Thus, before challenging it, I will explore it closer, and I will go through the reasons behind its popularity.

First of all, the word "conservative" is used in its broad meaning. In arguing that the conservative reading of the Stoic ethics is a misinterpretation of it, I don't mean to deliver any political message or to argue that political conservatism as such is misguided. Quite the contrary, my intent is to disentangle Stoicism from explicit political commitment. Stoicism is politically unbiased, and its followers can espouse whatever political view they want. I argue that Stoicism can conform to a wide variety of worldviews. Thus, in using the word "conservative", I will rest chiefly on its basic etymological sense which the Oxford English Dictionary defines as "characterized by a tendency to preserve or keep intact or unchanged," or "[something] that conserves, or favors the conservation of, an existing structure or system."[362] The "structure or system" I will refer to is the world in general, and thus we arrive at the working meaning of "conservative" as, roughly, "willing to preserve, sustain and support the present condition and status of the world."

The general premise of such understanding of conservatism might be compressed to the following, painfully simplified, formula: everything is good the way it is. Whatever has been established and settled, has been established and settled for good. There is no need to alter or ameliorate anything. The best is the enemy of the good. Change is a threat, not a hope. Moreover, at the end of the day it turns out that bringing about any change in the world is above our human paygrade: we are impotent to do it, we have no authority to do it, and if we try nevertheless, a disaster will result. We are not supposed to undertake any reforming or revolutionary endeavor. To try to amend the world would mean ungratefulness to the power greater than ourselves (however we understand it) which set the world on its track. And this higher power surely took great pains to do it properly: hence, everything is good the way it is.

The conservative misinterpretation of Stoicism can take one more, worrying form: it can slip into giving up. It can turn into a debilitatingly passive compliance with whatever fate brings. It can deteriorate into a belief that the ultimate virtue and obligation of a human is to dully adapt to whatever happens. It can devolve into a belief that slavish obedience is the foremost and noblest human capability. In other words, the conservative misinterpretation blazes a dangerous trail for a pejoratively-edged fatalism and resignation. It fosters pessimism-paralysis and invites, as Ivan Goncharov would put it, the "Not to be" answer to Hamlet's question. In his 1859 novel *Oblomov*, Goncharov depicts an extreme case of this: the protagonist is virtually incapacitated by his unwillingness to take any practical action.

> Lying down was [...] his normal state. When he was at home – and he was almost always at home – he was lying down [...] [His] study struck [...] by its neglected and untidy condition.. [...] Everything was so dusty and faded and devoid of all traces of human presence[363].

My core argument in this chapter is that the conservative misinterpretation is, as the name implies, a distortion and misreading of Stoicism. Yet, before presenting arguments against it, I will do justice to the arguments in favor. There are indeed some, yet I will argue that they are less convincing than the arguments against. I'm not in the habit, however, of disproving something by ignoring it, thus the arguments in favor are as follows.

[1] The traditional reading of the world-stage metaphor provides the first argument: on the world stage we are not the ones to decide who plays what role. Our task is to merely accept the preordained assignment and fulfill the roles doled out to us. The ancient Stoics used the example of slavery: "if someone is a slave then she mustn't revolt but must be obedient and do her slavish duty." This leaves little doubt in the matter. What is, after all, more conservative than inferring an obligation to be a slave from the very fact of being one?

[2] The second argument comes from the division between things in and not in our power. If this idea is misunderstood, it can be easily turned into an excuse that "virtually everything in the world is not up to us, thus a Stoic shouldn't care about anything and should 'let everything go'." As

presented with the example of Mr. Oblomov, this is also a form of conservative misinterpretation.

[3] Besides the division into things in and not in our power, many other traditional Stoic concepts are prone to the conservative misreading. These concepts are, for example, eternal return, determinism and, above all, nature. Unfortunately, it would be too digressive here to discuss all of the details of their conservative tinge. In the Introduction[364], I summed up the arguments for which I hold that the Stoic appeal to nature is highly misleading today and – to speak very generally – a similar line of reasoning applies to mentioned eternal return and determinism. They are all liable to conservative misinterpretation.

[4] The ancient Stoics were fortunate to have a safety net we no longer possess; a safety net which – to an extent – kept them from falling into the trap of conservative misinterpretation. In the 21st century, we lack that defense line and therefore the conservative misreading is much more of a danger to us. What's that defense line? An ancient Stoic, if accused of excessive passivity, could say the following: "Yes, in principle, we, the Stoics, are obliged to accept and submit to the social and political order we happen to live in. Yet, not to every order, but only to just and rational one. If we happen to live under a cruel dictatorship, in which the natural and rational norms of social life are violated, then we are obliged not to be obedient but to overthrow the tyrant. We never espouse unconditional surrender. We submit to the order of the world, but only on the condition that it's natural and rational."

Alas (and keeping in mind our diminished trust in the principle of "following nature") we, the citizens of the 21st century, cannot abstract from our historical experience. That experience teaches us the distressing lesson that the concepts of "natural" and "rational," when applied to social systems and political orders, turn out painfully arbitrary and mostly rhetorical. Given that historical perspective, we need to be quite skeptical about any alleged noncircular "metaphysical" or "absolute" justification of any system of political power or social order. This skepticism undermines the safety clause of "unnatural and irrational cases excluded." The principle "accept all political systems but the unnatural ones" gets reduced to the crude "accept all political systems." The bottom line is that the ancient Stoics were more protected from the conservative misinterpretation than we are. Thus, we must be particularly aware and careful about its dangers.

[5] One may hold that the risk of falling for the conservative misinterpretation is a consequence of one specific Stoic spiritual exercise

in particular. The exercise is as follows: "In every mishap and every misery comfort yourself with the reminder that you aren't the only one subjected to it. Quite the contrary, there have been flocks of other humans struck by the very same suffering that agonizes you." Noble in its goal and excellent in efficiency, this technique relies on a premise which is strikingly conservative: an assumption that, in the words of Marcus Aurelius, "all things such as they now are, in time past also were [...] for all those were such dramas as we see now, only with different actors."[365] It is conservative after all to assume such constancy in the world.

[6] The conservative misinterpretation has been defended by some Stoic scholars. Ben Kimpel is one example. "If, for example, a human being were in slavery to the Romans, he would live worthily as a slave, when he accepts such a status as a slave and does what is consistent with the 'nature of a slave.'"[366] This passage can be read on a few different levels. Formally, it doesn't imply that human beings are obliged not to revolt. On the other hand, the very phrasing of this sentence, the use of notions like "nature of the slave" is in itself conservative because it reproduces a discourse of submission and obedience. Kimpel associates the notion of slavery primarily with "living worthily as a slave." About any possible emancipation, no notice is taken.

This set of arguments in favor of the conservative misinterpretation is countered and – in my judgment – surpassed by a battery of arguments against it. The arguments I will now turn to reject the conservative misinterpretation and argue for possible consistency (or at least coexistence) between the revolutionary theme and Stoic ethics.

[1] The first argument rests on how the world-stage metaphor may be re-read. Let's return to the core idea: "All the world's a stage / And all the men and women merely players."[367] Some are beggars and some choosers, some are kings, and some are philosophers. The assignment of the roles is not up to us: we do not decide who plays what. The only thing which is in our power is to accept the assignment and toil to play our role the best we can. Call this the traditional reading of the Stoic metaphor of the world stage.

This traditional reading, however, sparks some doubts. The most blazing one is that there is a strong conservative bias implied by the very language used. Any counteraction, subversion or rebellion is excluded almost by definition. Doing so would amount to opposing what Nature and Reason have authorized. It would be an act of ultimate ungratefulness and irrationality. A slave is a slave, and will be one, and to oppose that is madness.

The problem is that this rhetoric sounds dated. Furthermore, this traditional reading is intrinsically inconsistent. For example, certain roles are indeed immutable and unchangeable by definition, like being someone's father or an heir apparent to the throne. But many roles are changeable or elective. One can renounce American citizenship and apply for Ecuadorian citizenship, one can be elected to the office of the president and then resign it, and one can choose to befriend one person rather than another (as the saying goes, we do not choose our family, but we do choose our friends). In brief, some social roles are fixed, but other can be adopted, adapted or abandoned[368]. Doesn't it make the traditional reading of the world-stage metaphor oversimplified and lopsided[369]?

This is why we may want to consider re-reading it. The traditional approach is expressed by just one principle, namely, "play your part well." A possible new reading would rely on two principles. First, "it is pointless to question the rules of a role," second, "remember that you can switch roles."[370] There is (contrary to what may seem) significant common ground between this interpretation and the traditional reading. This common ground is that under no circumstance it makes sense to play any role against its rules. Whatever role we play, whatever we do and whoever we are, it is purposeless to undermine the rules while playing. If we happen to be rich, presidents, or soldiers and if we decide to accept these roles – we must take them as they come, with all the limitations and obligations they impose upon us. To be a president, but a bad one, neglecting and ignoring her duties, it is as nonstoic as it gets.

The traditional interpretation exhausts itself in the simple bottom line that we must play whatever role fate has bestowed on us. Rebellion is pointless. The novelty I propose is that pointlessness consists not in rebellion against the assignment itself but in rebellion against the rules of specific roles. It's fixed what it means to be a good president or a good soldier, but – at times at least – we may have some choice between them. The world-stage metaphor may be read as an alternative. The scripts of the roles, their "content" (what it means to play such-and-such role) and the evaluation criteria (what it means to play it well) are givens. We can't negate the details and specificity of roles that are available to us, but, if we have a latitude in choice, we can make the choice. That choice is always an either-or and all-or-nothing one (here the fixation of the roles holds). No one has the authority to undermine what it means to be a good president or soldier. Yet, if we are fed up with being either one, *and* if the situation permits, we can resign the office or cease our military career[371].

I realize that this is quite a novel reading or even a major amendment to orthodox Stoicism. I hold, however, that we need to seriously consider it in the 21st century discussion of this philosophy. We need to open this line of thinking in the context of the "paradigm of reinterpretation" discussed in the Introduction. If we want not just a study of ancient Stoicism but a genuine attempt to make the Stoic philosophy relevant today, then we need more than just to repeat the Stoic message verbatim. We need to try to translate it into the contemporary idiom and conceptual network. As I have already proposed elsewhere[372] and as I will continue to argue for, a fresh reading of the world-stage metaphor appears to be one the viable options on the table.

It isn't, however, completely out of tune with what the ancients had to say. We can trace passages in their works which suggest that they were more open to this reading than we usually tend to think. For instance, let's turn to Epictetus. "In the Saturnalia a king is chosen by lot, for it has been the custom to play at this game. The king commands: [...] 'You drink' [...] 'You mix the wine' [...] 'You sing' [...] 'You go' [...] 'You come.' I obey [so] that the game may not be broken up through me."[373] Isn't it surprisingly similar to the view I proposed earlier? I follow the commands of the Saturnalia-king *as long as I don't want to break up the game*. If I decide that I'm done with the revels, I'm free to leave the party.

In Seneca's *On Tranquility of Mind* we read:

> He is not able to serve in the army: then let him become a candidate for civic honors. [...] Is it dangerous for him even to enter the forum? Then let him prove himself a good comrade, a faithful friend, a sober guest in people's houses, at public shows, and at wine-parties. [...] See what a wide extent of territory, what a number of nations present themselves before you. Thus, it is never possible for so many outlets to be closed against your ambition that more will not remain open to it[374].

The traditional reading of this passage focuses on the "inhibition part," i.e., on how we can be denied a certain way of life (a soldier, a politician, etc.). Yet, the "wide extent of territory" part suggests a quite different reading: no matter what we are denied, there is always plenty of jobs, tasks, and walks of life that are open to us. Seneca underscores the vast possibilities – "wide extent," "number of nations" – that are available to us. We may choose from them even if we are denied a career of a soldier or in public service. Our leeway is greater than what the conservative misinterpretation holds.

[2] The traditional reading of the world-stage metaphor may be dangerous in practice, for there is a tinge of the Nuremberg defense in it. The concept "we have no authority whatsoever in the assignment of our roles" effectively translates into a concept that whatever we do we simply

The argument

follow superior orders and subordinate ourselves to pre-ordained decisions. With all the consequences that follow.

The traditional reading relies heavily on an elusive and superhuman higher power which had assigned the roles (it's "Logos," "universal reason," "nature," or "fate," depending on the interpretation). It takes the responsibility off human shoulders and dispatches it somewhere to the vague beyond. Thus, embracing this view means abdication from responsibility for ourselves, for our deeds, and for the world. Perhaps for the free-spirited Stoics of antiquity, this could have been acceptable, but for us, it should set off all master alarms. After the experiences of Auschwitz, Kolyma, and Rwanda we know well the results of such an escape from responsibility. We also know that this is something we can no longer consent to. We, humans, are the only ones responsible and in charge.

[3] In chapter 6 I argued against the ascetic misinterpretation from the position that there are far more attitudes and ways of life accessible to a Stoic than it is usually asserted. One of the justifications for this was that Stoicism is about exercising and enjoying one's agency, which translates into flourishing in terms of available resources and striving to actualize one's goals and upholding one's values. Seen from this perspective, Stoicism (and modern Stoicism especially) is about "how" to attain one's goals rather than "what" these goals are supposed to be. On this reading, it may turn out quite a "liberal" philosophy. In particular, reshaping and transforming the world don't have to be essentially incompatible with it.

Stoicism, as I argued in chapter 6, doesn't define for us the specific values to uphold and goals to pursue. It doesn't free us from responsibility for selecting them. Stoicism isn't a magic box that we can feed with input data and obtain readymade answers in the output. All of this undermines not only the ascetic misinterpretation but the conservative misinterpretation too.

Lawrence Becker seems to support this line of thought. He asserts that in Stoicism we don't have to "pursue any one particular version of the good life[375]." He underscores the lack of uniformity in this regard and reminds us that "the stoics of antiquity were as diverse as plebeians and aristocrats, rhetoricians and physicians, career soldiers and career poets, apolitical logicians and political advisers, slaves and emperors. [...] In principle, the diversity of possible stoic lives [...] is very great."[376]

[4] The great Stoic division between things in and not in our power appears to be, as I remarked already, grist for the mill of the conservative misinterpretation. This division seems to shove disturbingly many things

into the abyss of the "not in our power" category, which entails that "nothing can be done about them," which in turn entails the conservative position. We may argue, however, that such understanding of this division is not the only one. There is another reading of it possible, one which greatly extends the Stoic domain of activity and is less prone to the conservative misinterpretation.

The conservative application of the division goes along the following line. First, divide all the things of the world into what is in your power and what is not. Second, let go of the latter and embrace the former. This order can be reversed, however. Let's think about it this way. First, define your values, goals, and commitments, and only then decide what in them is up to you and what is not. Then strive towards your goals and follow your values *through* that which is in your power. In Epictetus' words: "Every thing has two handles, the one by which it may be borne, the other by which it may not."[377]

This reading is less conservative because it is less exclusive. Much more things, projects, goals, and values can fit into the Stoic realm of within-our-power activity. In particular, a goal defined as "to try to change world" is no longer so easily written off as "not in our power." The "in our power" handle of this ambitious project can be grasped firmly. In order to try to change the world, we can try to write a book in which we would advance a better version of the world (or just a new interpretation of Stoicism). We can decide to join a street protest. We can prefer voting this way rather than that way. Finally, we can try to transform the world through our artistic pursuits.

[5] Another argument against the conservative misinterpretation is a refutation of one previous argument in favor of it, namely, the argument that Stoic naturalism entails a degree of conservatism. The point is that the "naturalism entails conservatism" view isn't diachronic and is thus misjudged.

Stoicism originated in pre-Hegelian times while it's only after Hegel that the historical perspective truly became part of Western thinking. Hence, a post-Hegelian interpretation of Stoic naturalism is less bound to produce conservative consequences than a pre-Hegelian one. In other words, even though there was no historical perspective in the ancient Stoics, they didn't hold that nature was static or stagnant. They maintained a picture of a dynamic, constantly re-growing and self-transforming natural world. It is only our post-Hegelian point of view that "makes us" read conservatism into ancient Stoic naturalism.

[6] Finally, an unorthodox, socio-economic argument can be brought in, mirroring and complementing a similar argument used against the ascetic misinterpretation. Imagine that a Stoic possesses a laptop and that laptop irreparably crashes the very day its warranty expires. If she is a follower of either ascetic or conservative misinterpretation, she is unlikely to attend a street protest and carry a banner reading "Bloodthirsty computer moguls! Stop planned obsolescence! We demand laptops that last decades!" If she espouses the ascetic misinterpretation, she wouldn't support such protest because she would be content that her laptop had lasted these mere two years it had. Consequently, if she espouses the conservative misinterpretation, she wouldn't support such protest because what has once been established (e.g., that laptops must work no longer than their warranties last) must be so for ever, and hence, all protest is pointless. Thus, fuel for progress is cut off, and the development of society is impaired. This is a common ground shared by the ascetic and conservative misinterpretations. No change in the world shall be demanded (conservative part) because we are obliged to be satisfied with what we already have (ascetic part).

This argument may seem digressive but let's not overlook that the ancient Stoics themselves paid significant attention to the social aspect of their philosophy. In fact, they used to attack the Epicureans with an argument that "an Epicurean state must fail."[378] This argument can be spelled out as follows: "due to Epicurus' advocacy of seclusion and disinterest in any political or social activity, his followers are inherently unable to form a lasting society of any kind." This argument is para-Kantian in a way. From the Stoic point of view, it was a flaw of Epicurean philosophy that it couldn't be "adopted without a contradiction as a universal law." But if it's so, why can't we apply the same standard to the Stoics themselves? Let's note that if we assume the conservative misinterpretation, then a Stoic state must fail too. Its inability to develop and progress would debilitate it – this proves even more serious liability in the contemporary world than in antiquity.

In sum, the final evaluation of the conservative misinterpretation is not unambiguous. There are arguments in favor and against it. As I have discussed, however, there are reasons to believe that the latter may outweigh the former. This happens not without certain ambivalence, but I believe that I've shown how the 21st century reading of Stoicism can go beyond the limits of the conservative misinterpretation. Consequently, the revolutionary theme of artistic creativity may dovetail with the Stoic framework.

11. The axiological theme

The axiological theme is in some respect complementary to the revolutionary theme. The revolutionary theme, analyzed in the preceding chapter, was a paradigm of understanding artistic creativity as a means of reshaping the world. However, someone who intends to reshape the world doesn't do so, in most cases at least, for the pure joy of a makeover[379]. There is usually a bigger goal in play which might be summed up (in most cases at least) as "to make the world a better place." Certainly the details of how to do it vary hugely in scope and specificity of aims. There has never been any lasting consensus about them, nor it is imaginable that such consensus ever appears. But despite that, we can agree on one point. If someone wants to transform the world, they usually want to transform it for the better (according, of course, to their own understanding of "better"). Attempting such transformation by means of artistic creativity is the subject matter of this chapter.

Why "axiological theme" and not "aesthetic theme?" First of all, "axiological" refers to the order of value while "aesthetic" refers to the order of beauty. "Beauty" could serve well in most contexts for this chapter, but not in all of them. The interrelationship between "valuable" and "beautiful" is a major problem in itself and we can't interchange the terms *salva veritate*. Furthermore, if we settled on "beauty" then we would have to talk in terms of "artistic creativity which produces beauty." Such notion though sparks immediate problems. In particular, "producing beauty" is too narrow a concept, because there are works of art which are valuable but which defy (sometimes purposefully) the idea of beauty. One example is Damien Hirst's artworks which exhibit dissected animal cadavers preserved in formaldehyde. Thus, the axiological discourse of value is more fitting for this analysis than the aesthetic discourse of beauty.

That being said, the axiological theme is a framework of understanding artistic creativity as a means to increase the overall value of the universe. This is achieved by bringing a new object of positive value in it. In plain English, it stands for a case when an artist makes the world a better place by bringing a valuable work of art in it.

It's beyond the scope and beside the point of this chapter to immerse in the infinite debate over the definition of "value." Fortunately, reliance on artist's subjective perspective can relieve me from this concern. In other words, I don't refer to the objective value of a given work of art (and thus I don't have to inquire if and how objective value is possible) but to the artist's assumption that what she makes has value. This assumption is largely justified since an act of artistic creativity is in most cases

The argument

accompanied by artist's (implicit or explicit) belief that her work makes sense and is of value. (Needless to say, we are talking of artistic value, not utilitarian or economic.)

I started the chapter by drawing a connection between the revolutionary and the axiological themes, now I can highlight the difference between the two. The revolutionary theme focuses on bringing about a concrete social or political transformation. In the axiological theme, the emphasis is on the work of art itself. What matters is not the practical, provocative, or political potential of the artist's work, but its purely artistic merit. The artistic value itself is – in artist's intention – the value she adds to the universe. Producing an inspired poem, a momentous movie, or a remarkable performance provides new value to the world not because of political or social ramifications, but *by itself*. Weren't the concept of "beauty" so burdened with mentioned interpretative problems, I would simply say that within the axiological theme an artist makes the world a better place by producing beauty.

Certainly, in saying this, I make an assumption that although a work of art admits of social, political, practical, psychological, theological and other types of explanations, it cannot be fully reduced to them. There is always a residue that can't be exhausted by a reductive effort: i.e., the artistic value, which is autonomous and can (and should be) considered independently of all other values. This is *a* possible position in aesthetics, but I'm well aware that there are other positions which claim the contrary. These other viewpoints are that the artistic value never exists just for itself, or at least that *ars ancilla est*, i.e., artistic value is less relevant than the political or social dimensions of art. Nevertheless, the position I chose is perfectly legitimate and I have every right to hold it.

Let's now turn to the chief question: how does the axiological theme look from the Stoic perspective? Once we raise the question, we immediately confront the key issue: in the Stoic view, the universe itself is by default excellent. It is intrinsically and absolutely perfect. An orthodox Stoic wouldn't refrain from an even stronger, Leibnizian statement that our world is the best of all possible worlds. Let's dig deeper into this.

There are a few types of arguments which support the Stoic view on the excellency of the universe. First of all, excellency might be inferred from its purposeful, rational organization in which everything is well tuned (remember the discussion in chapter 8). In the words of, respectively, Diogenes Laertius and Epictetus, the universe is "a living being, rational, animate and intelligent,"[380] while "plants and our bodies [are] bound up and united with the whole."[381] Everything is permeated with rational purpose, and nothing is left to chance. As Marcus Aurelius says, "all things are implicated with one another, and the bond is holy,"[382] and also, as his states in the famous passage, "of [the] common nature every particular nature is a part, as the nature of the leaf is a part of the nature of the plant."[383] Seneca paint this picture with even a bigger brush:

> You are about [...] to enter a city of which both gods and men are citizens, a city which contains the whole universe, which is bound by irrevocable and eternal laws, and wherein the heavenly bodies run their unwearied courses. You will see therein innumerable twinkling stars, and the sun, whose single light pervades every place, [and] who by his daily course marks the times of day and night, and by his yearly course makes a more equal division between summer and winter. You will see his place taken by night by the moon [....] you will see five stars, moving in the opposite direction to the others, stemming the whirl of the skies towards the West. On the slightest motions of these depend the fortunes of nations [384].

Interestingly, in one version of the argument, the excellency of the universe is exemplified in the universal equality of human beings, who are "from the same seeds and of the same descent from above."[385] As Seneca puts it, "the universe is the one parent of all"[386] and thus "no one is better born than another."[387]

The constancy and immutability of the world also bespeak its perfection. "So many rivers, so many showers of rain from the clouds, such a number of medicinal springs do not alter the taste of the sea, indeed, do not so much as soften it."[388] On the same note, human actions fall short of inflicting any change on the course of nature. "Do you suppose that when that stupid king clouded the daylight with the multitude of his darts, that any arrow of them all went into the sun? Or that when he flung his chains into the deep, that he was able to reach Neptune?"[389] Another argument comes from the universe's potency and might, which is manifested particularly in its destructive powers and their insidiousness. By no means paradoxically, apprehension of these fatal forces can prove the magnificence of the universe:

> We are never safe. Even in the middle of our pleasures [fortune] gives cause to mourn. War is stirred up in the calm of peace, and the means of security converted into fear. The serenity of summer is often changed into sudden tempests [...] Diseases fall upon the most temperate [...] Chance is continually making choice of some new evil to remind us of her power [...] Whatever by a long continuance of much labor [...] has been scraped together and raised on high is scattered and demolished in one day. Nay [...] a day and not rather an hour, a moment suffices for the overthrow of empires [...] Destruction comes on amain [390].

There is also the argument from the universe's abysmal spatiotemporal dimensions. Marcus Aurelius prompts us as follows: "look to the immensity of time behind you, and to the time which is in front of you, another boundless space."[391] "Asia, Europe are corners of the universe, all the sea a drop in the universe, [Mount] Athos a little clod of the universe. All the present time is a point in eternity."[392] Also, "constantly contemplate the whole of time and the whole of substance, and consider that all individual things as to substance are a grain of a fig, and as to time, the turning of a gimlet."[393] Another argument appeals to the universe's consistency with its own laws, its coherence and the persistent succession of things. "There is no harm to the elements themselves in each continually changing into another [...] Nothing is evil which is according to nature."[394] "By Nature's command, it is that so many changes and revolutions happen in her kingdom. Clear weather succeeds the clouds, and when the seas have awhile been calm, fresh storms arise. Different winds blow in their turns, day succeeds night, part of the heavens rise above, and part sink beneath the horizon. The eternity of things is made up of contraries."[395]

The excellence of the universe might also be deduced from its clarity and immaculacy. "The Pythagoreans bid us in the morning look to the heavens that we may be reminded of those bodies which continually do the same things and in the same manner perform their work, and also be reminded of their purity and nudity. For there is no veil over a star."[396] As Seneca argues, the pattern of things which are "near to the gods [...] [is] sublime, well-ordered [...] proceeding in a regular and harmonious course, tranquil, beneficent."[397] Finally, the basic experience of the beauty of the universe was not foreign the Stoics. Seneca says that his eyes are never bored by the immense spectacle of things[398] and in a similar vein, but even more exuberantly:

> I can raise my eyes from the earth to the sky in one place as well as in another. The heavenly bodies are everywhere equally near to mankind [...] I am allowed to gaze on the sun and moon, to dwell upon the other stars, to speculate upon their risings and settings, their periods, and the reasons why they move faster or slower, to see so many stars glittering throughout the night[399].

The Stoic concept of the excellency of the universe has direct ramifications for our matter. If the world is perfect just as it is, then there is no room and no need for artistic creativity to add anything to it. Thus, the axiological theme is incompatible with Stoicism, in a twofold way to boot. Adding any extra value to the world is both impossible and unnecessary.

This reasoning requires a few comments. **First**, the gist of the argument can be expressed as follows: infinity plus infinity equals infinity. Or, in a different view, a full glass will not become any fuller if we pour some extra water in it. If the Stoics grant the highest possible value (excellency) to the world itself, then there is no possibility to add anything more to it. If the world is perfect by itself, and if this perfection admits of no further degrees of improvement, then nothing more can be added. This refutes the logic of the axiological theme.

Second, from the concept that the world is excellent by itself it also follows that there is no *need* to improve it. And if it is so, all such efforts are essentially groundless. After all, why would an artist toil to create something valuable, if she knows in advance that it makes zero difference? The universe is just as excellent without her work as it would be with it. The psychological drive of artistic creativity is undermined: why exert oneself if it changes nothing?

Third, one of the premises of artistic creativity is the painful experience of imperfection, misery, evil or ugliness of the world. This experience might invite counteraction: an artist may try to patch and improve what she perceives as flawed. In the excellent Stoic world, however, this primal experience of misery is absent. Thus, this particular inspiration to create is removed.

Fourth, the idea that the universe is excellent is often (but not always) accompanied by some form of reference to Reason, Logos, or Nature, interpreted as the prime substance or governing principle of the world. Its authority guarantees and seals the overall perfection of the universe. On this reading, the axiological theme is, again, clearly purposeless. How could creative effort of a mere human being amend that what has been commanded by Nature or godlike Reason itself? Such an attempt might be seen as an act of ingratitude, disobedience or even a blasphemy against the ruling Principle of the universe.

In sum, the axiological theme of artistic creativity can't be agreed with Stoicism. The Stoics hold that the universe is perfect in itself and such position makes the axiological theme redundant. In an excellent world there is, by definition, neither room nor need for improvement. Moreover, living in such a world rules out the baseline experience of misery, and thus the axiological theme loses the grounds it is rooted in.

12. The autotherapeutic theme

> Does anyone wish to be miserable and unhappy?[400]
>
> Socrates in Plato's *Meno*

This chapter applies yet a different take on the idea mentioned above that one of the possible roots of artistic creativity is the experience of misery. In the axiological theme, I referred to this in terms of certain deficiency of the universe as a whole, and I juxtaposed it with the Stoic idea of its excellence. This experience, however, can be represented in a much narrower scope. Instead of the cosmic, grand scale debate of "excellency of universe" versus "misery of being," we can zero in on the very personal experience of discontent, anguish, and suffering. This is something that every human knows from their own life, and I don't believe there is a single reader who doesn't – whoever has gotten that far into a book on Stoicism surely knows what we are talking about. I explored it in detail in chapter 3. Just replay *My Gypsy Song* by Vysotsky, the song about the bottom-of-the-soul sorrow, the inexplicable nostalgia and the gut feeling that things are just not right.

The difference between the axiological theme and the autotherapeutic theme is clear. While in the former artistic creativity was a way to attempt improvement of the universe as a whole, in the latter the goal is far less ambitious but much more attainable. Artistic creativity is seen as a remedy to the ailments and ills of a particular life, namely, the life of the artist herself. It's a remedy to the personal experience of meaninglessness of life, to the experience of, as Prince Hamlet would put it, "being out of joint." In other words, in the autotherapeutic theme, the artist produces not only the actual work of art but also simultaneously produces (or restores) the purpose and meaning of her own life.

Nietzsche brings up this theme in *The Birth of Tragedy* where he claims that "at a point when the will is in the highest danger, art approaches, as a saving, healing magician. Art alone can turn those thoughts of disgust at the horror or absurdity of existence into imaginary constructs which permit living to continue."[401] Abraham Maslow advances a similar view when he discusses creative efforts in terms of "self-actualization." He says that even in a situation where all the basic needs of a human being are taken care of, "we may still (if not always) expect that a new discontent and restlessness will soon develop unless the individual is doing what he is fitted for. A musician must make music, an artist must paint, a poet must write, if he is to be ultimately at peace with himself."[402]

Needless to say, the autotherapeutic theme is commonly admitted to by artists, past and present. Jerzy Nowosielski, an eminent Polish religious painter, reportedly confessed that he "suffered continuously," with his only respites in the moments he painted. Ernest Hemingway famously replied "Portable Corona No.3."[403] when he was asked for the name of his therapist. Similarly, Goethe's *Sorrows of the Young Werther* can be convincingly interpreted as a proxy suicide. In the novel, Werther kills himself due to unfulfilled love, thereby curing the author's own amatory sickness. In the present day, the autotherapeutic theme of artistic creativity is employed in professional settings in mental health service. There is, for instance, writing therapy, drama therapy, and art therapy. As the American Art Therapy Association defines it

> Art therapy [...] uses art media, the creative process, and the resulting artwork to explore [...] feelings, reconcile emotional conflicts, foster self-awareness, manage behavior and addictions, [...] . A goal in art therapy is to improve or restore a client's functioning and his or her sense of personal well-being[404].

In order to properly evaluate this theme from the Stoic point of view, we need to notice a fundamental parallel first. Both the autotherapeutic theme and Stoicism as such aim at the exact same thing: curing the hurting self. It's no coincidence after all that Stoicism has been called an autotherapeutic philosophy. Essentially, it was never meant to be mere verbal or mental quibbling. The Stoics never meant to "philosophize" in the pejorative sense of hardly-graspable abstractions and practical uselessness. Quite the contrary, Stoicism has always wanted to be as practical and as useful as possible. It was designed to cure people, to ease the pains of human life. Some would even say that in this respect Stoicism is the best solution the Western thought has ever yielded. (This bold claim might be substantiated with several arguments; they are too digressive for now, though.)

This view is anything but surprising. As Foucault explains in *The Care of the Self*:

> A whole series of medical metaphors is [used by the Stoics] to designate the operations necessary for the care of the soul: put the scalpel to the wound; open an abscess; amputate; evacuate the superfluities; give medications [...]. The improvement [...] that one seeks in philosophy [...] increasingly assumes a medical coloration[405].

The autotherapeutic understanding of Stoicism seems almost unavoidable to Foucault. It's just short of a tautology, of an *ex definitione*

The argument

situation. It holds for virtually everybody and is *the* understanding of choice:

> The practice of the self implies that one should form the image of oneself [...] as one who suffers from certain ills and who needs to have them treated [...] Everyone must discover that he is in a state of need, that he needs to receive medication and assistance[406].

We can agree in this context that Stoicism and the autotherapeutic theme of artistic creativity share the same goal. The key question now is whether they can aid each other in its pursuit or are they doomed to thwart each other? There is no obvious answer to this, and I won't be able to provide a clear and clinching argument. Thus, I will examine both options that are on the table. I will first analyze a possibility that Stoicism and autotherapy through artistic creativity can support and strengthen each other. I will next turn to the other option, i.e., one in which the two endeavors can't go hand in hand.

The possibility of cooperation

In this view Stoicism and the autotherapeutic theme of artistic creativity can be pursued simultaneously. In saying this, I apply a kind of "presumption of cooperation" logic. Here it is. If tool A and tool B serve the same goal C, then whoever wants to work towards C may consider, unless proven otherwise, that A and B can be put to action together and that they won't foil each other.

In our case, this logic can be exemplified in two particular ways: first by employing the good, old concept of catharsis, second, by means of a certain Stoic technique which can be labeled "the broad (or cosmic) perspective" or "you are never alone." Let's go through them one by one.

[1] An encyclopedia defines catharsis as "a beneficial transformation of painful emotions through absorbed contemplation of a powerfully moving work of art."[407] The concept originates with Aristotle, who asserts in *Politics* (1341b-1342a) that

> music should be studied [...] with a view to (a) education (b) purgation [*katharseos*] (the word "purgation" we use at present without explanation, but when hereafter we speak of poetry, we will treat this subject with more precision) (c) for intellectual enjoyment, for relaxation and for recreation after exertion[408].

In a subsequent passage the philosopher remarks that "the purgative melodies [...] give an innocent pleasure to mankind"[409] while in *Poetics* (1449b) we read that "[A tragedy contains] incidents arousing pity and fear, wherewith to accomplish its catharsis of such emotions."[410] Unfortunately,

Aristotle did not fulfill the promise of explanation (or the relevant passage simply didn't survive to our time) which opened space for centuries of interpretation.

What is the Stoic meaning of catharsis? I will opt for the following interpretation. There is the map of possible activities of the human spirit, and its certain areas are off limits to a Stoic. They represent the specific "commotions of the soul," as the ancients put it, that a follower of Stoicism is committed to avoid. Importantly, these "commotions" are not the same with what we today conceptualize as "emotions." Contrary to the commonly-held view, Stoicism doesn't oblige us to eschew all emotion – that would be neither doable nor desirable. This view is actually another misconception about Stoicism: a Stoic as an ice-blooded, rigid and lifeless figure, devoid of ordinary human passions and thus of humanity itself. This is an erroneous notion indeed. As a matter of fact, a Stoic isn't supposed to avoid emotions as such, but avoid getting irrevocably overcome and carried away by them. Speaking more precisely: a Stoic is obliged to keep clear of these "commotions of soul" which entail a permanent loss of her ability to make autonomous decisions (as Lawrence Becker remarks, this doesn't prohibit temporary renunciation of it). No example is more informative and classic here than Seneca's discussion of the problem of anger in his extensive treatise *On Anger*.

If we express Stoicism in these terms, we can't escape the key question of *how* these undesirable "commotions of soul" are to be eschewed. And here is the thing: this is exactly the point where catharsis can be employed. One way to get rid of these undesirable commotions is to administer certain "vaccination" or "homeopathic therapy" in which a person is subjected to a small, diluted dose of the given sentiment. Having been exposed to it, she is more likely to be immune to this kind of troublesome agitation in the future and less likely to be incapacitated by it. As Henryk Elzenberg states it:

> Art is a way to make one's life force flourish – with no desires and no suffering [...] Art gives vent to our thrills and it facilitates retaining ataraxia in real life. Here is the place where Aristotle's catharsis might fit[411].

Notice, that this approach would be particularly beneficial if another human being was involved. In other words, imagine that we can cure one human being by vaccinating another. Of course, this is impossible in medicine, while it would be ethically doubtful if possible (why expose someone else to an agent we believe is harmful?) How about the cathartic procedure though? This is exactly where the magic of artistic creativity can

The argument

take effect. Unlike in the needle-and-antibody medicine, it allows us to learn not from our own mishap, not from the mishap of the other, but from a staged mishap. Theater is the most obvious example. We don't witness actual sentiments there, but performed sentiments. This, however, doesn't hamper the cathartic potential of theater-going. Furthermore, artistic creativity makes us capable of "staging" the whole situation ourselves. Consider again Goethe and his *The Sorrows of the Young Werther*. The author writes a book about Werther, sick from love, and concludes the narrative arc by killing him. This is like burning in effigy. The author uses the protagonist to commit a proxy suicide which cures the author from his own real-life, ill-fated love. The slate is clean now. The therapy has been administered and is in effect, while no actual humans were harmed in the process. The benefit is there, the collateral damage is zero.

[2] The second viable framework for a possible harmony between Stoicism and the autotherapeutic theme of artistic creativity can be described with one of the techniques of the Stoic training. The gist of it is to constantly keep in mind that in no earthly misery we are alone. In every distress and suffering, in every misfortune and every adversity, we are accompanied by others humans. This awareness provides profound and powerful solace. Furthermore, it disproves an exclamation, so often cried out by people in pain, that the particular blow that has hit them has hit *only them*. In a stronger version (not unheard of though!), the complaint goes that the higher powers of the universe zeroed in on them to persecute them, i.e., that society, fate, nature or God "conspire" against them. In response to this, the Stoics point out that in every human calamity the calamity itself is just a half of calamity. The other half consists in the impression of irrationality and injustice which, apparently, allowed the calamity befall us. The Stoic technique in question ("it happens to others too") helps to squash this impression. It restores our belief in the impartiality of the universe, it reminds us that we are by no means exceptional. Fate neither disfavors nor discriminates against us. Everything that happens to us – happens to many[412].

Seneca puts it this way in the epistle 107. "Have your servants left you? And is that all? Some have robbed their master, others have vilified him, others have betrayed him, others have trampled upon him, some have made an attempt on their master's life with poison [...] These, and all other mischiefs you can imagine, have happened to many."[413] In his treatise on consolation we read:

> It is, therefore, a great consolation to reflect that what has happened to us has happened to everyone before us and will happen to everyone after us. In my opinion, nature has made her cruelest acts affect all men alike, in order that the universality of their lot might console them for its hardship[414].

Marcus Aurelius sums it up briefly: "In everything which happens keep before your eyes those to whom the same things happened."[415]

Where is the link from here to the autotherapeutic theme? There is no denying that suffering can have us cast our gaze down to the dust. Suffering has an overwhelming ability to enclose us in a narrow, radically first-person perspective of pain. On the other hand, artistic creativity and art are able to do just the opposite. They expand our horizon. They remind us that the world is broad and wide, they break open the self-contained loop of self-tormenting thought. As a matter of fact, creativity and art count among the best awareness-raisers and perspective-broadeners ever invented. They are vehicles by which we can do exactly what Marcus Aurelius prompts us to do: "suddenly be raised up above the earth, and [...] look down on human things."[416] "Look down from above on the countless herds of men and their countless solemnities, and the infinitely varied voyagings in storms and calms."[417]

Once our perceptive powers are enhanced, we are able to see other people better, and this includes our co-sufferers. Art and artistic creativity can help us find those with whom we are bound by the chain of shared pain... and not only that. Artistic creativity wields a very specific power that no other pain-reliever does. It's able not only to show pre-existing fellow sufferers, but it can also *create* new ones. Everyone who writes a novel is qualified to populate the pages with whatever characters she wishes – including such who suffer the same way the author does. This is the high point of compatibility between the autotherapeutic theme and Stoicism. Goethe and his Werther again serve as a beautiful example. The author creates a character who not only shares the author's pangs of unfortunate love but takes it one step further by killing himself for this reason. The autotherapeutic theme of artistic creativity is pushed to the limit: an artist brings to life an imaginary figure whom he subsequently sacrifices in order to cure himself.

The possibility of contradiction

There is a simple problem with the "presumption of cooperation" logic I proposed before: there is no *a priori* argument to back it up. I have assumed that this logic is sound and a meaningful discussion followed. Yet, intellectual honesty requires that the other option is discussed as well, i.e., the possibility that Stoicism and the autotherapeutic theme or artistic creativity cannot be pursued together. This possibility is just as open as the possibility of cooperation. Even more than that: a few arguments can be presented to support this position.

[1] The first argument comes from the logical point of view, and it is the opposite of the "assumption of cooperation" approach. It is true that Stoicism and the autotherapeutic theme of artistic creativity share the same goal. They also share the same point of departure: they both spring from the experience of misery, distress, and discontentment. The question is, then, is it possible in Stoicism to travel from point A to point B via two separate routes at the same time?

Let's note in the first place, that these two routes are truly distinct. They are not congruent with each other. After all, among the many precepts of the Stoic teaching, not a single one has anything to do with "living a creative life." Furthermore, as I argued in chapter 3, the Stoics expressed explicit disdain for art and creativity. The divergence between the two walks of life is explicitly expressed e.g. in the introductory book of *Meditations* where Marcus Aurelius expresses his gratitude "to the gods [...] [that] I did not make more proficiency in rhetoric, poetry, and the other studies, in which I should perhaps have been completely engaged, if I had seen that I was making progress in."[418]

That being said, we need to keep in mind that Stoicism promotes coherence. It encourages adherence to a coherent set of principles and organizing one's life along the lines of one framework only. Attempts to kill too many birds with one stone or a habit of swapping distinct mental attitudes are all suspicious from a Stoic point of view. Thus, just as a real-life traveler would have a bit of a problem in running two different itineraries at once (unless she enjoys the gift of bilocation), a Stoic too is skeptical of following two trajectories at once. The Stoic way is to stick to the Stoic way. As Seneca puts it: "A wound is not soon healed, when different salves are tried by way of experiment. A plant thrives not, nor can well take root, if it is moved from place to place."[419]

Seen in this light, it seems that Stoicism and the autotherapeutic theme of artistic creativity cannot be agreed, because they are two distinct treatments for the same ailment. They prompt different medicines, and it's incoherent to administer them both at once. Especially when an essential requirement of one of them is that no incoherent therapy is employed.

[2] The second argument is more elusive but still convincing. The basic idea is that in Stoicism there is no hesitation about the goal of philosophy.

There is some verbal discrepancy and the goal is variously rendered as "happy," "rational," "flourishing" or "virtuous" life. Yet, there is no doubt that arriving at this blessed state of mind is the ultimate end of Stoic toil. Above all, there is no doubt that it should be embraced once accomplished and some Stoics go as far as to assert that to achieve this state of mind once is to achieve it permanently.

In the artistic life, however, the state of affairs can be massively different. An artist may "officially" want to ease her suffering ("heal her soul") through creativity, and she may even sincerely believe that. It is perfectly possible though, that what the creative process actually does is just the opposite. It may well strengthen and reproduce the initial state of discontent. An artist may seem to use creativity to quash her pain and get rid of gloom, but what *de facto* happens is that the creative process sustains and solidifies her misery.

How does it work? A hurting soul fuels creativity, so a truly successful therapy cuts the life-giving root of inspiration. To cure a human is to kill an artist. Thus, it is preferable for an artist to conserve and retain the distress of a human. Biographies of many creative individuals, as described in chapter 3, clearly show that protracting illness by feigning treatment appears to them more fruitful than actual recovery.

Needless to say, this twisted logic is unacceptable from the Stoic point of view. The purpose of Stoicism is to live a good life, and this purpose is defied if someone intentionally eludes it. Moreover, Stoicism is highly demanding when it comes to logical coherence (as remarked before). Hence, the idea of intentionally avoiding getting cured in order to prolong the condition is a contradiction in terms in the eyes of a Stoic.

[3] Finally, the ancient Stoics expressed certain distrust of autotherapy through art. Seneca states that "popular and vulgar acclamations [i.e., displays of culture and literature] are not made or purchased for satisfaction, but with great loss and pains."[420] He argues for example that a speaker shouldn't rely on actual anger to boost her rhetorical skills. Seneca admits that the audience tends to be more impressionable if they see that speaker's performance is fueled by emotion, but despite that, it is in the end still more beneficial to deceive the audience by simulating anger rather than really become angry. "Anger, then, must never become a habit with us, but we may sometimes affect to be angry when we wish to rouse up the dull minds of those whom we address, just as we rouse up horses who are slow at starting with goads and firebrands."[421] And:

"An orator," says our opponent, "sometimes speaks better, when he is angry." Not so, but when he pretends to be angry. For so also actors bring down the house by their playing, not when they are really angry, but when they act the angry man well. And in like manner, in addressing a jury or a popular assembly, or in any other position in which the minds of others have to be influenced at our pleasure, we must ourselves pretend to feel anger, fear, or pity before we can make others feel them. Often the pretense of passion will do what the passion itself could not have done [422].

All this leaves us in an ambiguous situation. There are valid arguments both for and against coherence between the autotherapeutic theme and Stoicism. The possibility of cooperation appears sound, but so does the possibility of contradiction. It is not clear which argument outweighs which and the case appears to be inconclusive. Lack of a clear conclusion, however, shouldn't sadden a philosopher – it's more like an occupational hazard. Let me then say the following. Culturally, the Epicureans are often presented as the major rivals of the Stoics, yet in antiquity, an equally important opposition existed between the Stoics ("the dogmatists") and the Skeptics. Thus, I would like to "make an excursion into the enemy's camp"[423] myself, just as Seneca did, and suspend my judgment in regard to the autotherapeutic theme. I hope that a further study and a more detailed analysis of this scenario will shed more light on it.

13. The didactic theme

> ...the artist attains the power of awakening other souls to a given activity[424].
>
> Ralph Waldo Emerson

We have finally arrived at the last theme to be discussed in this book. The didactic theme frames artistic creativity as a tool to teach, that is, a tool which serves to transmit and propagate knowledge, ideas, and wisdom. The discussion of this theme requires that we confront two questions. First, *what* is being taught? Second, *who* is being taught?

Let's begin with the first one. What can be taught? What kind of knowledge can artistic creativity pass on? One preliminary answer is: every kind. There is no theoretical reason to cross out any type or genre of knowledge. In practice, however, artistic creativity conveys some areas of learning better and some worse. It isn't typically employed to teach advanced mathematical concepts, string theory, rocket science, and brain surgery. Yet, a great deal of wisdom and scholarship have been historically disseminated by various artists. Starting again with the rivals of Stoicism, there is no denying that, among other things, Lucretius wrote his *De Rerum Natura* in order to propagate Epicurean ideas. This is a fine example because Lucretius did what we are hardly able to do today. He not only squeezed concrete physical ideas of his philosophical school into a poetic form but furthermore, it didn't prevent him from making it sophisticated poetry, acclaimed as one of the peaks of Latin verse[425]. Today poetry and concepts from advanced physics don't go together that well.

On the other hand, there is a number of novels by Jules Verne, all of them full of detailed knowledge from various branches of science. From reading *Twenty Thousand Leagues Under the Sea* alone, we can learn about the 19th-century understanding of the principles of undersea voyages, the anti-imperial sentiments in the British Raj, not to mention countless facts about oceanography and marine biology. From *The Mysterious Island*, we can learn lots of survival and engineering tips, ranging from how to produce fire with one's bare hands and how to determine geographic location with neither GPS nor sextant, through the arcana of pottery and brick-making, to smelting ore and producing nitroglycerin. Just consider the following fragment:

> Was [producing soda] difficult? No; for marine plants abounded on the shore, glass-wort, ficoides, and all those fucaceae which form wrack. A large quantity of these plants was collected, first dried, then burnt in holes in the open air. [...] The result was a compact grey mass, [...] known [as] "natural soda."[426]

The didactic content of this passage is incontrovertible.

The same can be said about a great deal of non-fiction literature, including such genres as memoir, diary or essay. Among them, travel literature can serve as a model example. Every travelogue, every book written after or during a journey, every painting painted from life and every photograph taken while on the road, each of them is a good example of the didactic theme of artistic creativity. Each of them attempts to capture some experience and transfer it to those who didn't have the fortune and privilege to experience it themselves. Reports from travels have been an important branch of literature ever since Pausanias' *Description of Greece*. It goes all the way from Marco Polo and Ibn Battuta, through the books yielded by the Romantic fondness of travelling (like Goethe's *Italian Journey* or Chateaubriand's *Travels in Greece*...) to *Carrying the Fire* by Apollo astronaut Michael Collins and the contemporary deluge of travel blogs. A constant and unwavering stream of such literature could be traced back through centuries, and the advance of modern technology doesn't seem to impair it.

Before the advent of photography, which thoroughly transformed the ways of how canvas and brush are used to tell a story, the art of painting was another great example of the didactic theme. It takes just one visit to the Benaki Museum in Athens, Greece, to comprehend first-hand that we would know nothing about what Athens of the Tourkokratia period looked like if not for the effort of the painters who toiled to depict it. And what about modern, nonrepresentational art? It doesn't have to be at odds with the didactic theme either, even though the content of the transmitted knowledge is surely far more abstract and less conceptual. Religious art is another example. It cannot be denied that Rublev's *Trinity* was meant to pass some wisdom to the viewers, although the matter of this wisdom doesn't yield to easy rational explanation.

This list doesn't pretend to be exhaustive, it's rather just a quick outline of the didactic theme. I must also emphasize that I don't assume that any specific work of art has ever been brought to life for didactic purposes only (this, by the way, holds for all the themes studied in this book). By its very definition, the didactic theme is bound to coincide and co-occur at least with the preservation theme as well as with the cognitive theme. As for the former, the key difference is that the preservation theme is aimed at passing some knowledge to the future, while the didactic theme – to other people. As to the latter, the cognitive theme is focused on the very act of acquiring knowledge, while the didactic theme is about transmitting it to others. This connection doesn't present a methodological problem though. In accordance with the general concept of this book, I analyze all themes one-by-one.

It's clear then that the didactic theme can refer to a gamut of understandings and areas of knowledge. Artistic creativity is capable of transmitting a wide variety of practical and theoretical wisdom, yet, among these, one case is certainly of our particular interest. This case is about artistic creativity used to express, teach and advocate... Stoic philosophy. This is the prime example I will refer to in the subsequent analysis since it's the one which is immediately linked to our subject matter. It isn't an oversimplification, however. We need to keep in mind, however, that knowledge in general (being cognizant of facts) is, in the eyes of a Stoic, the preliminary and prerequisite condition of living a good life (as discussed in chapter 9). Thus, if we find out that it's consistent with Stoicism to employ artistic creativity to propagate Stoicism, it will follow that it's consistent with Stoicism to employ artistic creativity to propagate knowledge in general. This holds because valorizing knowledge is an indispensable part of the Stoic doctrine itself.

Let's now turn to the second major question: *who* is being taught? There is one crucial division I must make in this regard. I will first consider the specific but very important case in which, to put it simply, the author herself is her own audience (in Baudrillard's terms, "the sender is identical with the receiver"). The second case is the more traditional view, in which the artist and the audience are separate persons. Certainly, these two cases can interfere with each other, but it doesn't undermine the legitimacy of discussing them separately.

[A] Let's first consider the case in which the artist herself is her own audience. In this case, her didactic pursuit is somehow self-aimed, in other words, she creates in order to teach herself. This can raise eyebrows, and one may justly wonder if it isn't circular reasoning. After all, how can there be any increase of wisdom and growth of knowledge if an X addresses the same X? How can anything new emerge in this loop?

The answer is that in this case "teaching" doesn't refer to the standard concept of transmitting knowledge from one person to another, but to the practice of exercising and improving one's ability to live a Stoic life. It's not about converting to Stoicism but rather about self-affirming in it. It's the practice of perfecting and polishing one's Stoic attitude to life and making it more thoroughgoing and applicable to a wider range of situations. It's the toil of debunking one's doubts about Stoic life and learning how to overcome crises and letdowns. Contrary to what is sometimes held (by those who are overtly attached to the all-or-nothing understanding of virtue) becoming a Stoic is not a singular act of self-transformation and instantaneous conversion. It's no road to Damascus. It's rather a perpetual process of self-evolution, the practice of continuously tailoring one's spirit in the pursuit of the idealized goal. Epictetus says "generally [...] if you would make any thing a habit, do it [...] So it is with respect to the affections of the soul."[427] In a similar vein: "a bull is not made suddenly, nor a brave man."[428] In the words of Diogenes Laertius: "Another tenet of [Stoicism] is the perpetual exercise of virtue, as held by Cleanthes and his followers. For [...] the good man is always exercising his mind."[429] This aspect of Stoic philosophy has been explored in detail by Pierre Hadot in his *The Inner Citadel. The Meditations of Marcus Aurelius*[430] as well as in *Philosophy as a Way of Life: Spiritual Exercises from Socrates to Foucault*[431].

There is a direct link between this processual aspect of adopting Stoicism and the didactic theme. If Stoicism requires constant exercise

The argument

and self-reaffirmation, it follows that it should embrace devices and tools which can contribute to this process. There is no obvious reason to rule out a creative effort as one of these tools. Thus, it is compatible with Stoicism to use artistic creativity to reassure and reconfirm oneself on the Stoic path. An obvious and prominent example of this is Marcus Aurelius' *Meditations*. As Pierre Hadot puts it: "Marcus took the trouble to write down his thoughts, aphorisms, and reflections in a highly refined literary form, since it was precisely the perfection of the formulas which could ensure their psychological efficacy and persuasive force."[432] This is – let me remind – the gist of the didactic theme.

The actual status of Marcus's work is open to many interpretations, none of which is decisive[433], yet there are serious arguments that it was intended for author's personal use only, and not for publication. One simple and convincing argument appeals to Marcus' literary style: his *Meditations* are all written in the second person singular. It doesn't defy logic to assume that Marcus addresses himself[434]. Also, explicitly self-aware self-admonitions about the regularity of spiritual exercise are frequent in *Meditations*. "Often think of,"[435] "frequently consider,"[436] "constantly bring to your recollection"[437] and the like. Moreover, there is a very meaningful passage about the usefulness of keeping carefully prepared, self-addressed notes handy: "to him who is penetrated by true principles even the briefest precept is sufficient."[438] Finally, the "you" of the text has a background which is strikingly similar to Marcus Aurelius' own. "Take care that you are not made into a Caesar, that you are not dyed with this dye; for such things happen."[439] "Let no man any longer hear you finding fault with the court life."[440] "Where a man can live, there he can also live well. But he must live in a palace – well then, he can also live well in a palace."[441]

Within this interpretation, *Meditations* can be seen as a self-addressed handbook to be of aid in moments of adversity or doubt. Furthermore, it seems to be potentially fruitful to study from the viewpoint of the theory of literacy (as advanced by authors like Ong, Havelock, Goody or Olson) how the Stoics employed for their own purposes the practice of producing a written record of one's internal struggle. In particular, the following seem to be promising common points between the theory of literacy and the Stoic habit of spiritual exercise: (i) externalization through writing; (ii) imposing the linear verbal order required by text; (iii) potential rationalization which happens in the process; (iv) the possibility of "back-scanning" (as Goody puts it) allowed by an account in writing.

In sum, the didactic theme in its self-addressed version, when the artist is herself the audience, appears to be in accordance with the logical structure of Stoicism. Artistic creativity, seen through this lens, can greatly help in making ethical progress. There is more textual evidence to prove this, but since it refers to the next case too, I will discuss it in the section which follows.

[B] In this case the artist and the audience are distinct. This is the more traditional view in which we have an artist, who produces a work of art of some kind, and the audience, who perceives it. (In Baudrillard's terms, the "sender" and the "receiver" are distinct). By "audience" I mean an actual or imaginary assembly of viewers, listeners, or readers, of any size. "Audience" in this sense includes a real-time audience at a concert or performance, in which the creative act is simultaneous with the reception of it, but it also includes a case in which a period of time separates the artist's toil and its reception by others. This time span might vary from minutes, as with some types of online artistic activity, to several years, as in the case of voluminous novels that take a long time to write, publish and read. It can surely exceed the artist's lifetime. A work of art can be addressed, voluntarily or involuntarily, implicitly or explicitly, to viewers and audiences of future generations. Finally, an artist can either target her creative effort at a specific, given audience that she is aware of, or, as it happens in most cases, she can address an audience she is unable to predict. All such instances are comprised by the concept of "audience."

All told, we are considering a case in which an artist teaches other people through her creative efforts: she transmits ideas to others, she increases their wisdom, she helps them make progress. What ideas and what progress? As discussed earlier, I organize this analysis around passing Stoic ideas and fostering Stoic progress (and, as remarked, whatever this analysis turns out holds also for the wider sense of transmitting non-stoic knowledge). This can be translated into a situation in which the artist teaches her audience how to be better Stoics than they already are. Or, if the audience is still green and had never been exposed to Stoicism before, it translates into the artist teaching Stoicism from scratch and trying to awaken the Stoic potential present in every human being. This case can be described in terms of artist's care for other humans, or, on the other hand, in terms of her attempt to "convert" them to Stoicism, or even in terms of her being an "apostle" of Stoicism.

An abundance of examples illustrates this case. Passing over the ancient ones, we can find plenty of them in the Neostoicism period. Take a look at a passage from a 1586 poem by Jan Kochanowski, Poland's greatest poet of the Renaissance era:

The argument

> For a mortal it is futile to care,
> About any eternal affair.
> It's enough for him to know he won't avoid that
> What – beyond all times – was commanded for him by God.
>
> He will never get lost,
> Who so aligns his mind,
> That he endures both mishap and happiness
> Withstands the former and isn't carried away by the latter[442]

The Stoic message of these two stanzas is explicit. The same goes for the poem *If* by Rudyard Kipling. Among many pieces of commonplace general advice, it contains clearly Stoic concepts that one's self-esteem should be independent from the judgment of others and – like in Kochanowski – that success and defeat should be treated as indifferents alike[443]. The similar case is the famous *Desiderata* by Max Ehrmann. Besides some new-age-tainted or at least generic concepts, it advances concrete Stoic principles. Comparing with others is to be eschewed, while the readiness of the spirit is to be strengthened through constant exercise and so on[444]. Stoicism and its impact on the way of life is also one of the main themes in the bestselling novel *A Man in Full* by Tom Wolfe[445]. Finally, a clear Stoic stand is present in the poetry of Zbigniew Herbert, one of the eminent European poets of the second half of the 20th century. See, e.g., his short and wisdom-clear works like *Mr. Cogito and the Pearl*[446], *Mr. Cogito on Upright Attitudes*,[447] or a poem which aspires to capture the ontological aspect of Stoic ethics, i.e., *Pebble*[448]. It's also worth to notice in this context that in 1992 Herbert published a poetic epitaph dedicated to Henryk Elzenberg, the philosopher who was the first one to expose the poet to the Stoic doctrines and who I mentioned several times on these pages myself. In it, the praise of the deceased teacher is a praise of the Stoic ideal itself[449].

Having said this, we may now ask our question for the last time. Is using artistic creativity to teach Stoicism to others consistent with Stoicism itself? It appears so. After all, we should expect that Stoicism warrants its own proliferation. The logic behind this can be best manifested by contraposition: a philosophy of life which recommends us not to follow it seems an absurd. The Stoics claim repeatedly that the proof of a philosophy of life is in the life itself (as Epictetus says, "If I were talking to an athlete, I should say, 'Show me your shoulders,' and then he might say, 'Here are my Halteres' [i.e., training equipment]. 'You and your Halteres look to that.' I should reply"[450]). It makes no sense for a philosophy of life to undermine its sole sphere of applicability. The ultimate purpose of Stoicism is to allow humans to live stoically – and it is requisite for this that humans know *how* to do it. Thus, it is a contradiction to argue from a Stoic position against the proliferation of Stoic philosophy. We can conclude that the didactic theme is compatible with Stoicism.

Let's turn to the ancients one last time. Cleanthes explicitly confirms the basic premise of the didactic theme. "Poetic and musical forms are better: that a philosophical treatise may, it is true, well express divine and human matters, yet it lacks the proper words to express divine greatness. For this reason, melodies and rhythms are incomparably better at arriving at the truth about divine matters."[451] Marcus Aurelius asserts that "everybody knows [...] that some good things are said [...] by these writers"[452] [i.e., by the dramatists] and proves this by repeatedly quoting playwrights and other non-philosophical authors, including Euripides[453], Sophocles[454], Aristophanes[455], Menander[456], Homer[457], and Hesiod[458]. In epistle 108 Seneca speaks exhaustively about the role poetry can play in the propagation of philosophy:

> When salutary [i.e., philosophical] precepts are [...] expressed in verse, they descend the readier into the hearts even of the unskillful. For, according to Cleanthes, as our breath gives a more clear and shrill sound when driven through the passage of a trumpet [...] so our understandings are rendered more clear, when confined to the strict laws of a verse. The same things are heard with less attention, and affect us less, when delivered in prose or common discourse, than when decorated with poetical numbers[459].

Epictetus notes an instance of the didactic theme in Homer:

> Do you not suppose that Homer wrote this [referring to *Iliad* XIX.321] that we may learn that those of noblest birth, the strongest and the richest, the most handsome, when they have not the opinions which they ought to have, are not prevented from being most wretched and unfortunate?[460]

Finally, we shouldn't forget that Marcus Aurelius was not the only Stoic author who "took the trouble to write down his thoughts [...] in a highly refined literary form."[461] Given the controversy over how the *Discourses* were written[462] it would be misleading to make any definitive statement with regard to them, yet we can, without much doubt, assert that Seneca painstakingly crafted his philosophical works and went to great lengths to ensure their literary excellence.

There is also one more powerful line of reasoning which supports compatibility between Stoicism and the didactic theme in artistic creativity. As mentioned in the Introduction, one of the most serious challenges that Stoic philosophy faces is the relationship between a Stoic

The argument

and other humans. This relationship is, in brief, anything but clear. It is evident that other humans count as "not in our power" and it follows that a Stoic is obliged to hold them as completely indifferent, neither good nor bad. It follows that a Stoic mustn't shackle her own happiness and good life to other people and that her well-being shall not be diminished by any misfortune that happens to others. Also, she mustn't refer to others in defining her values, goals, and commitments. Other people are on a par with all other objects beyond her control, like rocks, earthquakes, rain, the chemical composition of water and the motion of planets.

This idea conflicts not only with the layman's idea of "moral" understood as "caring for other people," not only with the Christian ideal of loving thy neighbor but also with the specifically Stoic obligation of social and political commitment[463]. How can a Stoic be engaged in social affairs if these affairs are beyond her control and she is to be indifferent to what is beyond her control? How can she be responsible for the community she lives in if she must be responsible only for that which she controls? This question is crucial and, as mentioned, I believe it is one of the most pressing issues that modern Stoicism deals with.

The didactic theme offers a solution to this. One viable way in which a Stoic can express her care, concern, and responsibility for others is by trying to make them Stoic. It is not up to her whether or not such attempt comes to fruition, but the sole decision to attempt – is. Thus, to teach Stoicism to others might be a legitimate way in which a Stoic can do justice to both the requirement of social commitment and the fact that others are not in her power. Goethe once said that "we learn only from those whom we love,"[464] but the reverse of this statement is also true. For us, the Stoics, to love is to teach. To love other humans is to teach them how to be better humans. To love others is to pass the Stoic ideas to them since the Stoic ideas are the most valuable thing that a human can offer a fellow human. Lawrence Becker agrees with this viewpoint, as he concludes his *A New Stoicism* in the following words: "The life of a stoic sage is filled with [...] happiness, as a consequence of her virtue. We imperfect ones [...] cannot wish less for those we love."[465]

Conclusions

This book produces two conclusions. **The first one** is clearly ambiguous: certain understandings of artistic creativity can be agreed with Stoicism, while others cannot. Once we zero in on the specific themes, the result turns out to be around fifty-fifty. About half of the themes is acceptable to Stoicism while the other half is not. The quick recap is as follows.

Artistic creativity is incompatible with Stoicism if it is understood as means of seeking fame (chapter 5), increasing the overall value of the universe (chapter 11), preserving some element of the universe (chapter 7), or expressing the individuality of the artist (chapter 8 – although the incompatibility is less evident here). On the other hand, artistic creativity is a legitimate Stoic endeavor if it is understood as means of seeking profit (chapter 6), comprehending the world (chapter 9), changing it (chapter 10 – this case is not fully unequivocal, though), or as means to teach people (chapter 13). Finally, there is no clear answer as to artistic creativity understood as autotherapy (chapter 12).

This evaluation is detailed yet inconclusive. This, however, as I remarked earlier, shouldn't sadden a philosopher. In philosophy, inconclusiveness is an occupational hazard. One may say that the whole point of the intellectual investigation is to follow the evidence where it leads and to avoid the easy and relative safety of the trenches of superficial conclusiveness. Many philosophical works end up with certain ambiguity, and it is to no detriment of them. It's a sign of philosophical weight if, so to speak, the ambiguity we end up with is more profound, subtler and somehow more revealing than the one we begin with. This is how philosophical writings should be judged, and I can only hope that this book passes the test.

That being said, there is **the second,** much more concrete, conclusion of the book. Over the course of this analysis, I haven't found much evidence that the "ordinary," "mundane," or simply "non-Romantic" understandings of artistic creativity are inconsistent with Stoicism. As I will talk of in a moment, an actual Renoir, i.e., someone who sets new courses for art and opens up new worlds of artistic expression, will have a hard time trying to follow the Stoic principles. But how about mentioned Raymond Dufayel, from Jean-Pierre Jeunet's *Amélie*, who just copies the same Renoir's painting again and again? Or a teenager who plays guitar on a promenade to entertain vacation-goers and earn her college tuition? This book's investigation identifies no obstacle blocking their way to Stoicism. As long as they keep their approach to creativity outside of the Romantic model, they are, in principle, free to live their Stoic lives. This conclusion is valid at least within the scope of the analysis this book offers.

On the other hand, and more importantly, it turns out from this study that the crucial, the most philosophically interesting, as well as the most culturally important understanding of artistic creativity, the "Romantic model of art," as discussed in chapter 2, is at odds with Stoicism. This conclusion follows directly from the breakdown of the partial answers set forth earlier. The themes which are agreeable with Stoicism are not the characteristics of the Romantic view on art (like, e.g., the didactic theme), or even are downright alien to it (e.g., the profit theme, see the seaside guitarist again). In contrast to them, the themes which are associated with the Romantic model of art (preservation, fame of the artist, expression of her individuality) are unacceptable to Stoicism.

In this regard, we get the big answer we sought. Stoicism and the Romantic model of artistic creativity contradict each other. These two models of life, two models of narrating oneself and two models of relationship with the world – they cannot go together. A Romantic poet and a Stoic cannot be rolled into one.

One specific consequence of this is the following. If we agree that a degree of suffering is an inherent part of the Romantic view on creativity (the most explicit manifestation of this is the model of tormented artist or cursed poet described in chapter 3), then the Stoic ethics can't be a shield against this suffering. If the Romantic artist wants protection against her pains (and assuming that the Romantic model even allows for any such protection, for any such "hedgehog skin," to use Nietzsche again) – she needs to seek beyond Stoicism. It's interesting to note that, on some level, this reinforces the tormented artist model. After all, when it comes to the possible ways in which she might want to seek her relief, this analysis closes down one salient way for her.

This was the ramification from the artist's own point of view. If we look at the bigger picture though, we'll apprehend another idea that comes out of this study. Here is what we know. Stoicism and the Romantic model of artistic creativity, the two great manifestations of human spirit, the two great vertices of human capability, cannot be embraced simultaneously.

Conclusions

A person won't be able to achieve both of them at once. In more general terms this means that the human spirit, so to speak, can't fit in itself all at once. In other words, there is more to the human spirit than the narrow logic of any particular expression allows. All its possible expressions and manifestations cannot happen through a single person. Thus, the human spirit, just for the full articulation of its potential, requires wide timespans and many distinct individuals. Some of them may become Stoics, some may become Romantic artists. On some level, there is a tinge of pleasant pluralism in this. If we want to explore all of our human potential, diversity becomes a must. We need to keep the space open for different people to be in their different ways.

On yet another hand however, there is also a bit of sorrow in all this. We have learnt that the entirety of possible human experience will never be accessible to a single individual. Stoic aspirations come at a price of giving up on Romantic creativity and vice versa. We will always have to forgo one pinnacle of spirit to climb another. Sacrifice, thus, becomes an indispensable companion of human life. And one may want to add that this sheds new light on asceticism, i.e., the call for voluntary sacrifice, which hence reemerges as a topic of perennial interest.

* * *

Let's now turn to the impact that these conclusions have on Stoicism itself and particularly on how we interpret and apply it today. Let's look at it this way. It was a common thread in the ancients to underscore the unlimited applicability of Stoic philosophy. "Where a man can live, there he can also live well,"[466] as Marcus Aurelius says. Stoicism was intended to be a philosophy suitable for everyone and viable in all circumstances. But does it hold today? We have concluded that there is at least one way of life (a very important one, to boot) which is at odds with Stoicism. Thus, this books serves as an argument in favor of the following position. It is indeed possible to be a Stoic today, but there is a mandatory reservation that it's not an option open to everybody and at all times.

It's worth of notice that this reservation was not entirely foreign to the ancient Stoics (although, as mentioned, their official position was that Stoicism was perfectly universal). First of all, as discussed in the Introduction, they frequently admitted that due to supremely high standards, an actual full-blown Stoic sage is a rare bird in the woods. Also, it was not unusual for the ancient Stoics to evoke examples of children and implicitly (or not-so-implicitly) suggest that young humans are not capable of reaching the level of agency required for Stoicism. Epictetus says for example that children merely "at one time play as wrestlers, then as gladiators, then blow a trumpet, then act a tragedy, when they have seen and admired such things"[467]. On the other hand, Marcus Aurelius seems to be well aware that a debilitating decline of agency may happen on the other end of the cycle of human life. Here is how he describes the decay of intellect in the old age:

> We ought to consider [...] that if a man should live longer it is quite uncertain whether the understanding will still continue sufficient for the comprehension of things. [...] We must make haste then, not only because we are daily nearer to death, but also because the conception of things and the understanding of them cease first [468].

Today Lawrence Becker seems to agree that there are exceptions to Stoic universality. He states, for example, that it is well plausible that

> there is an identifiable kernel of bodily and psychological health that is a necessary condition of all further development. If this kernel is damaged, so is the capacity to develop agency[469].

Becker suggests brain injury and autism as examples of such damage. The list might possibly go on to include any major condition which significantly impacts the mentioned kernel. Furthermore, Becker clearly entertains the idea that Stoicism may be not suitable for all types of people. He considers "agents whose psychology is radically different from our own"[470] and argues that Stoicism is "largely silent"[471] about them. In this context, certain people openly dismiss the Stoic path. Here is Becker again:

> Acting appropriately, as understood here, is a special kind of optimization project – one that it is logically possible to reject. (And which many people with compulsive, obsessive, or addictive personalities do in fact reject.)[472]

And, let's say, this list can be appended by the Romantic artist. Even though she doesn't have to label herself as "compulsive, obsessive, or addictive personality," she may well reject this "optimization project."

This brings us to the even bigger picture. One of the commonplace ideas of our time is the notion that it's inconceivable to demand sagacity from a human subjected to extreme circumstances. It is impossible to accuse the inmates of Auschwitz, the prisoners of Gulag, or the survivors of the Rwandan genocide, of not handling their horrors stoically. On the other hand, it is equally essential intuition of our time that it was impossible for Winston Smith to demonstrate Stoic sagehood in the rat scene in the Room 101 in George Orwell's *1984*[473].

Modern interpretation of Stoicism needs to take this into account somehow. In this context, I will advance the following idea. Modern

Stoicism needs to concede that there can occur circumstances which make it impossible to retain all three of the following elements: **identity, life, agency**. But let's not be mistaken. In most cases, it's feasible to hold on to the three of them, and the gist of making progress in Stoicism is to learn how not to drop any of them prematurely. Yet, when pushed to the limits, modern Stoics cannot coherently state that it is *always* possible to cling to *all* three. Sometimes it's necessary to forgo one of them to keep the other two (in many cases it will still be up to us which one to let go of, hence the Stoic stance on suicide can be expressed in these terms as the last ditch manifestation of agency). When faced with singularly adverse circumstances, a Stoic must either **(1)** preserve her identity and agency by exiting life, or **(2)** preserve her identity and life by forgoing agency, or **(3)** preserve her life and agency by changing her identity, i.e., altering the story she weaves about herself. The point is that the Stoic's identity is, conceptually, on par with agency and life. This is the key difference between ancient Stoicism and its modern interpretation. In the former, the mere "identity" was not a part of the equation. But it needs to be now. In this vein, identity, agency, and life can be traded for one another.

To illustrate this better, let's turn to the classic, extreme case. Let's imagine a Stoic taken a prisoner of war. She knows that she will be brought to questioning the next day and that she will be tortured unless she betrays someone or something which is dear to her (e.g., a person, an allegiance, or at least a philosophical principle). Let's also assume that holding someone or something "dear" is part of her identity (this seems a fair assumption) and that she can be reasonably certain that if she confesses to whatever the investigators want they will keep their promise and release her. Finally, let's imagine that she managed to somehow smuggle a razor blade into her cell and thus she faces a trilemma. She can either kill herself, or be tortured, or avoid torture through timely confession.

There are three trajectories in this case. **First**, a Stoic can kill herself and thereby preserve her identity as well as her agency (the identity is preserved because she is holding on to her principles till her dying breath, while agency is exercised in the ultimate act of suicide). The martyrological misinterpretation of Stoicism (see chapter 9) holds that doing so is always the duty of a Stoic and I will just underscore again that this is not true. **Second**, she can subject herself to torture and strive to withstand it. Yet (and here is one of the critical differences between modern reading of Stoicism and the orthodox, ancient stance) by doing so she sets herself on a path on which her agency will be lost. True, her life and identity will be preserved (temporarily), but the agency will be lost in torture – sooner or later, but inevitably. This is Orwell's message, which is so dear to our contemporary sensibility. If the external circumstances are applied properly (e.g., by a qualified torturer in a well-equipped torture chamber), then there is no escape from losing agency. Thus, in order to save it, a Stoic has to forgo something else: her identity, or, in other words, the story she weaves about herself. This is the novelty that modern Stoicism must be open to and our **third** possibility that we need to put on the table. This is the third scenario in which a Stoic doesn't kill herself, but immediately provides the investigators the information they want.

This, of course, is blasphemy for the ancient Stoics. In the harsh framework of classical Stoicism, this trajectory isn't even entertained, and there exists only the stark choice between suffering torture or committing suicide. Yet, given our modern understanding that it is counterfactual to expect a human being to endure the heights physical adversity, we must consider this third scenario. If Stoicism is to be understood in terms of constructing *a posteriori* all-things-considered normative propositions for practical reason (Becker), or as cheerful exercise and contemplation of one's agency (as I myself mentioned in the Introduction), then it follows that such a calculated and cold-blooded move in order to avoid devastating pain must be included as a viable option. To zealously write it off would mean committing a grave sin against modern sensibility. It would mean not paying attention to the lesson of *1984* that physical adversity can crush all agency whatsoever[474].

Let's be clear, however. I don't hold that Stoicism praises dishonesty or flip-flopping. The idea is, simply, that if we want a relevant modern version of Stoicism, then we must endow a Stoic with both capacity and right to narrate a new story about herself, i.e., to change her identity if necessary. A modern Stoic must be far more flexible than her ancient counterpart was. It is essential that she is able and apt to shape her own evolution. A Stoic, if she is truly to be an inspiring figure for our time, must be less of a fixed and immutable rock, which antiquity used to praise, and more of a malleable, self-aware and self-conscious person who is capable of defining and re-defining herself.

Let's borrow from Seneca. "Isocrates laid hands upon Ephorus and led him away from the forum, thinking that he would be more usefully employed in compiling chronicles."[475] What has happened there? In order to live a flourishing and fulfilled life, Ephorus had to abandon the activities of the forum and turn to historical research instead. He got his priorities realigned. Yet, we must go much further down this road. First of all, we can't wait for someone else's coercion. We need to rely on our own autonomous decision to set us on a new course. Second, that "new course" doesn't refer merely to our job, industry, or the choice of task we perform. Our latitude is far greater. We, the modern Stoics, are free to meddle at will with the sacred kernel of our mental and spiritual arrangement which our predecessors deemed untouchable.

Specifically, imagine that we define our identity around the values of integrity, trustworthiness, and loyalty. The story we narrate about ourselves is that we follow our idealistic principles, we are loyal to our loved ones, and we never give away the secrets we have been trusted with. Imagine then, that our life takes a sudden turn and we find ourselves facing the torture situation described earlier. How would we react? As already discussed, the ancient understanding of Stoicism compels us either to kill ourselves or to willingly submit to torture. A modern Stoic, however, needs to be free to do whatever she finds reasonable for her, all-things-considered. If she finds that adhering to her principles is not worth the cost of excruciating pain or downright physical annihilation – it is her decision to make, it is her autonomy and her responsibility. She can drop her previous identity and start a new one. This new identity might be, e.g., that she is a commonsensical person, who is not willing to sacrifice herself for mere ideals and who values earthly survival and physical inviolability over loyalty to unmeetable commitments.

In modern Stoicism, this needs to be a licit way of conduct. If Stoicism praises agency unlimited (perfect, "maximized" agency), then no worldly obligation shall tame it. Thus, a coherent, contemporary understanding of Stoic agency must encompass the agency of a higher order. Its domain includes the freedom to pick and choose from the triad of agency, identity, and life. In other words, if one wishes to desist from being a Stoic, one must be free to do it. We arrive at a conclusion that if Stoic agency is to be truly unlimited, then Stoic universality has its limits.

The entire discussion of the limits of Stoicism, all this pondering over Stoics subjected to hellish adversities in torture chambers may seem digressive. Yet, it puts our central problem of Stoicism and artistic creativity in context. The figure of an artist is interesting because of its ambivalence: while some themes of artistic creativity dovetail with Stoicism, others contradict it. In this light, we may say that an artist sits on the very verge of Stoicism's domain of validity and which way she is leaning depends on what view on creativity we assume. This is another reason which makes the issue of Stoicism and artistic creativity so interesting. True, Stoicism has its great merits as a philosophy of life – in most cases of life. Its applicability has its limits, though. And just there, between the two domains of relevance and impossibility, there is the equivocal figure of an artist. She captures the experience of being on the edge. Inquiry into Stoicism and artistic creativity turns out to be a case study for the threshold of applicability of Stoicism.

I will conclude saying that I believe that I "have sufficiently described and illustrated for any fallacies that may be involved in my argument to be patent to anyone, except of course myself at the present moment."[476] I have, to the best of my ability, scrutinized how Stoicism and artistic creativity relate to one another. As I have repeatedly remarked before, it has all been fuelled by a profound conviction that both of them are perennially valuable, both artistic creativity and Stoicism, the two great pinnacles of spirit conceived by humans, for humans, and of humans.

Acknowledgements

There is a long list of individuals who were of help during the process of writing of this book. In alphabetical order, I would like to express my gratitude to the following: to Lawrence C. Becker, a Stoic in flesh and spirit, for his input in my understanding of where modern Stoicism should be headed and invaluable overall support above and beyond; to Janusz Dobieszewski, for his guidance and intellectual patronage; to Michał Dobrzański, for his relentlessly critical insight and for his constant reminder that Stoicism must be down to earth; to Kimberly Harris, for her detailed and careful patience; to Jeffrey Hause for helpful comments; to William Irvine, for his kind help and patience; to Olga Kaczmarek, for permanent inspiration, for thorough and comprehensive critical comments, and for her support when Stoicism failed; to Adam Leszkiewicz, for insightful remarks and for bibliographical and biblical suggestions; to Iwona Lorenc, for her help and guidelines; to Tomasz Mazur, for inspiration and initial setup of my understanding of Stoicism; to Patrick Murray for discussing Stoicism from the Marxist viewpoint; to Massimo Pigliucci, for his friendship and guidance; to Gregory Sadler, for his friendship and insight; to Piotr Schollenberger, for guidelines and advice; to Jeanne Schuller, for inspiring remarks; to Justin Sears, for his commentary and suggestions; to William O. Stephens, for the detailed and exhaustive discussions, meticulous comments and great help. Finally, I would like to express my gratitude to my loving parents, to the University of Warsaw, to Creighton University in Omaha, to Kosciuszko Foundation and to Republic of Poland's National Program for the Developments of Humanities – for the generous support.

Endnotes

[1] Maciej Kropiwnicki and Julian Kutyła, ed., *Žižek. Przewodnik Krytyki Politycznej* (Warszawa: Wydawnictwo Krytyki Politycznej, 2009), 9. In original Polish: "*Podstawą ludzkiej kreatywności jest poszukiwanie nieszczęścia.*"

[2] Friedrich Nietzsche, *The Gay Science*, §306, trans. Walter Kaufmann (New York: Vintage Books, 1974), 245.

[3] Henryk Elzenberg, "Etyka wyrzeczenia. Czym jest i jak bywa uzasadniana," in: Henryk Elzenberg and Michał Woroniecki, ed., *Z filozofii kultury* (Kraków: Znak, 1991), 221.

[4] Henry de Montherlant, *Don Juan*, trans. Adrienne M. Schizzano, in: Oscar Mandel, ed., *The Theatre of Don Juan. A Collection of Plays and Views, 1630-1963* (Lincoln: University of Nebraska Press, 1963), 690. In original French the passage reads: "*Le bonheur écrit à l'encre blanche sur des pages blanches.*"

[5] I'm of course well aware of the problems with defining the proper and ultimate goal of Stoic philosophy. Yet, for brevity, I will throughout this book abbreviate the goal of the Stoic ethics as "living a happy life." For proof that it's in agreement with the ancient Stoics see, e.g., Epictetus, *Discourses*, II.19.24: "Let any of you show me a human soul ready to think as God does, and not to blame either God or man, ready not to be disappointed about anything, not to consider himself damaged by anything, not to be angry, not to be envious, not to be jealous." All quotations from Epictetus used in this book come from: Epictetus, *The Discourses of Epictetus with the Encheiridion and Fragments. Translated with Notes, the Life of Epictetus, and a View of His Philosophy, by George Long*, trans. George Long (London: George Bell and Sons, 1890). I occasionally modernized grammar and spelling and changed it to American English.

[6] Epictetus, *Discourses*, III.23.30.

[7] Michel Foucault, *The Care of the Self* [vol. 3 of *The History of Sexuality*], trans. Robert Hurley (New York: Pantheon Books, 1986), 57.

[8] Marcus Aurelius, *Meditations*, XII.22. All quotations from Marcus Aurelius used in this book come from: Marcus Aurelius, *The Meditations of the Emperor Marcus Aurelius Antoninus. Translated by George Long, M.A. With a Biographical Sketch and a View of the Philosophy of Antoninus by the Translator*, trans. George Long, (New York: A.L. Burt, Publisher, 189?). I occasionally modernized grammar and spelling and changed it to American English.

[9] Epictetus, *Discourses*, III.13.11.

[10] Seneca, *Epistles*, 59.14. All quotations from Seneca used in this book come from: (1) Lucius Anneus Seneca, *The Epistles of Lucius Annus Seneca; With Large Annotations, Wherein, Particularly, the Tenets of the Antient Philosophers Are Contrasted With the Divine Precepts of the Gospel, With Regard to the Moral Duties of Mankind. In Two Volumes. By Thomas Morell, D.D.*, trans. Thomas Morell, vol. I-II (London: W. Woodfall, G.G.J., J. Robinson, 1786); (2) Lucius Anneus Seneca, *Minor Dialogues Together with the Dialogue on Clemency*, trans. Aubrey Stewart (London: G. Bell and Sons, 1889); (3) Lucius Anneus Seneca, *On Benefits*, trans. Aubrey Stewart (London: G. Bell and Sons, Ltd., 1912). I occasionally modernized grammar and spelling and changed it to American English.

[11] Reported in: Davidson, *The Stoic Creed* (Edinburgh: Clark, 1907), v. See also: E. Renan, *Marc Aurèle et la fin du monde antiqua* (Paris, 1882), 157-158.

[12] Davidson, *The Stoic Creed*, 252.

[13] Jacqueline Lagreé, "Constancy and Coherence," in: Steven K. Strange and Jack Zupko, *Stoicism: Traditions and Transformations* (Cambridge: Cambridge University Press, 2004), 168.

[14] Bertrand Russell, *History of Western Philosophy and its Connection with Political and Social Circumstances from the Earliest Times to the Present Day* (London: George Allen & Unwin, 1961), 276.

[15] Meaningful in this respect is the fact that the title of the last section of Peter Gay's biography of Sigmund Freud reads "Death of a Stoic" and that the last sentence of the entire book is: "The old stoic had kept control of his life to the end," Peter Gay, *Freud: A Life for Our Time* (New York: Norton, 1988).

[16] Robert L. Arrington, *Western Ethics. An Historical Introduction* (Malden: Blackwell, 1998), 105. And also, as Long states it, "Not only the words 'stoic' (uncapitalized) and 'stoical' recall [the influence of Stoic philosophy]. In popular language to be 'philosophical' means to show fortitude in the face of adversity recommended by the Stoic writers" (Anthony A. Long, *Hellenistic Philosophy. Stoics, Epicureans, Sceptics* [New York: Charles Scribner's Sons, 1974], 107). And there is still more than that. Some Stoic ideas have become part of folk wisdom and general psychological knowledge. Notice the following passage from Emerson: "the old oracle said, 'All things have two handles. Beware of the wrong one.'" (Ralph Waldo Emerson, "American Scholar," in: Lawrence Buell, ed., *The American Transcendentalists. Essential writings* [New York: Modern Library, 2006], 85). The fact is: it was not an oracle, it was Epictetus: "Every thing has two handles, the one by which it may be borne, the other by which it may not" (Epictetus, *Encheiridion*, §43). All this speaks to the contemporary status of some parts of Stoic ethical teaching. They are an indispensable yet often unacknowledged part of our outlook on life. What happened to Emerson happens on a daily basis on the Internet. For instance, Michael Stevens is an entertainer who created a YouTube channel named "Vsauce" which features "videos relating to various scientific topics, as well as gaming, technology, culture, and other topics of general interest" (en.wikipedia.org/wiki/Vsauce; accessed April 14, 2014). Among other things, he published a video titled "What Is the Greatest Honor?" in which he ponders over what is the greatest honor possible. He starts with mundane examples, like being praised

after completing a marathon, then he discusses various famous accolades like the Oscars, the Nobel Prize and the Medal of Honor, and he concludes with a staggeringly Stoic remark that "a fair argument can be made that simply knowing you did the right thing when presented with a [given] situation [...] is the greatest honor possible" (www.youtube.com/watch?v=P85Fj8m6v84; 9min 02sec – 9min 18sec, accessed April 14, 2014). There are also many images shared as Internet memes which convey specific Stoic ideas and, as of April 2014, the website www.keepcalm-o-matic.co.uk has a variety of items on sale (posters, mugs, keychains, bags, iPhone cases, t-shirts, stickers, magnets, greeting cards, etc.) with the caption "Keep calm and stay Stoic" (sd.keepcalm-o-matic.co.uk/i/keep-calm-and-stay-stoic-2.png ; accessed April 13, 2014).

[17] Arthur Schopenhauer, *The World as Will and Representation* (I.I.16), trans. E.F.J. Payne, (New York: Dover Publications, 1966), vol. 1, 86.

[18] Wilhelm Windelband, *A History of Philosophy*, trans. James H. Tufts, (Westport: Greenwood Press, 1979), 176.

[19] Alasdair MacIntyre, *After Virtue. A Study in Moral Theory* (Notre Dame: University of Notre Dame Press, 2007), 170.

[20] David Hume, *Dialogues Concerning Natural Religion*, in: David Hume, *Essays and Treatises on Several Subjects* (London 1788), 433.

[21] Montesquieu, *The Spirit of the Laws* (XXIV.10), trans. and ed. Anne M. Cohler et al., (Cambridge: Cambridge University Press, 2002), 326-327.

[22] Reported in: F.H.Sandbach, *The Stoics* (London: Bristol Classical Press, 1989), 9.

[23] Emmanuel Levinas, *Otherwise than Being or Beyond Essence*, trans. Alphonso Lingis, (Pittsburgh: Duquesne University Press, 1998), 178.

[24] E.g. Lawrence Becker, *A New Stoicism* (Princeton: Princeton University Press, 1998); Margaret Graver, *Stoicism and Emotion* (Chicago: University of Chicago Press, 2007); Rene Brouwer, *The Stoic Sage: The Early Stoics on Wisdom, Sagehood and Socrates* (Cambridge: Cambridge University Press, 2014); Anthony A. Long, *Epictetus: A Stoic and Socratic Guide to Life* (Oxford: Oxford University Press 2002) and others.

[25] E.g. Margaret Graver and Anthony A. Long (translated), *Letters on Ethics: To Lucilius* (Chicago: University of Chicago Press, 2015); Cynthia King (ed.), *Musonius Rufus: Lectures and Sayings* (CreateSpace, 2011).

[26] E.g. Frank McLynn, *Marcus Aurelius: A Life* (Cambridge: Da Capo Press, 2009); James S. Romm, *Dying Every Day: Seneca at the Court of Nero* (New York: Vintage Books, 2014).

[27] Becker, *A New Stoicism*.

[28] William B. Irvine, *A Guide to The Good Life. The Ancient Art of Stoic Joy* (New York: Oxford University Press, 2009).

[29] Massimo Pigliucci, *How to be a Stoic : Using Ancient Philosophy to Live a Modern Life* (New York: Basic Books, 2017).

[30] Donald Robertson, *Stoicism and the Art of Happiness* (London: Hodder & Stoughton, 2013).

[31] E.g.: William O. Stephens, *Marcus Aurelius: a Guide for the Perplexed* (New York: Continuum, 2011).

[32] Piotr Stankiewicz, *Sztuka życia według stoików* (Warszawa: WAB, 2014).

[33] Becker, *A New Stoicism*, 6.

[34] See: http://modernstoicism.com, accessed February 2, 2017.

[35] Like the Modern Stoicism itself but also, e.g., the New Stoa, founded back in 1996 (see: http://newstoa.com, accessed February 2, 2017).

[36] E.g. there is Massimo Pigliucci's blog "How To Be A Stoic" (see: https://howtobeastoic.wordpress.com, accessed February 2, 2017) and there is the "Stoicism Today" blog hosted by Modern Stoicism and contributed to by many authors (see: http://modernstoicism.com, accessed February 2, 2017).

[37] E.g. there is an online "Stoicism group" on Facebook (see: https://www.facebook.com/groups/Stoicism/, accessed February 2, 2017) and there is a Stoic site authored by yours truly (in Polish): https://www.facebook.com/SztukaZyciaWedlugStoikow/, accessed February 2, 2017).

[38] Seneca, *Epistles*, 113.23.

[39] Long, "Stoicism in the Philosophical Tradition: Spinoza, Lipsius, Butler" in: *The Cambridge Companion to the Stoics*, (Cambridge: Cambridge University Press, 2003), 390.

[40] Seneca, *Epistles*, 113.23. We should also keep in mind that the Stoics' openness to diversification, the malleability of their doctrine and its propensity to evolve fostered vitality of the school and contributed to its lasting influence.

[41] Becker, *A New Stoicism*, 82.

[42] See, ibid., 5.

[43] MacIntyre, *After Virtue*, 169.

[44] See: M. Andrew Holowchak, *The Stoics: A Guide for the Perplexed* (London: Continuum, 2008),72-73.

[45] See also, e.g., R.W.Sharples, *Stoics, Epicureans and Sceptics. An Introduction to Hellenistic Philosophy* (London – New York: Routledge, 1996), 107: "Modern criticism of Stoic ethics has centered on the seeming inhumanity of the Stoic sage."

[46] Denis Diderot, "Essai sur les règnes de Claude et de Néron," in: Denis Diderot, *Oeuvres* (Paris: Brière), vol. 12, 49.

[47] David Hume, "The Skeptic," in: *Essays: Moral, Political and Literary*, ed. Eugene F. Miller (Indianapolis: Liberty Classics, 1985), 168.

[48] Ibid.

[49] Ibid.

[50] Seneca, *Epistles*, 116.7.

Endnotes

[51] Ibid., 116.7.

[52] Seneca, *On Mercy*, II.V.2.

[53] Seneca, *On Firmness*, VII.1.

[54] Ibid.

[55] Ibid.

[56] Seneca, *Epistles*, 42.1.

[57] Epictetus, *Discourses*, II.19.21-24.

[58] William L. Davidson, *The Stoic Creed*, (Edinburgh: Clark, 1907), 188.

[59] Epictetus, *Discourses*, III.24.28.

[60] Ibid., III. 26.4-5.

[61] Epictetus, *Encheiridion*, §3.

[62] Epictetus, *Discourses*, III.24.

[63] Ibid., IV.5.19-22.

[64] Ibid., I.28.14-17. The writings of the ancient Stoics contain many more passages expressing sage's inhumanity towards other people. A broader list of examples can include, first of all, the clear statement that "a wise man is not afflicted at the loss of children or friends" (Seneca, *Epistles*, 74.30). The ancients Stoics make it very clear that death of our loved ones is a neutral thing: "What have you seen ? A man lamenting over the death of a child. Apply the rule. Death is a thing independent of the will" (Epictetus, *Discourses*, III.3.15). "A certain person's son is dead. Answer; the thing is not within the power of the will: it is not an evil" (ibid., III.8.2). The ancient Stoics often evoke venerable examples of fathers who didn't flinch at the loss of their sons (needless to say, mothers and daughters are far less frequent examples). "Lucius Bibulus [...] on the day following that upon which he heard of both his sons deaths, came forth and went through the routine business of his magistracy" (Seneca, *To Marcia on Consolation*, XIV.2). "Greece cannot boast unduly of that father who, being in the act of offering sacrifice when he heard the news of his son's death, merely ordered the flute-player to be silent, and removed the garland from his head, but accomplished all the rest of the ceremony in due form" (ibid., XIII.1). "When he was in the act of [...] dedicating the Capitol the news of his son's death was brought to him. He pretended not to hear it, and pronounced the form of words proper for the high priest on such an occasion, without his prayer being interrupted by a single groan" (ibid., XIII.1-2). "How [...] righteous was he who, on hearing of the death of his son, made a speech worthy of a great man, saying: 'When I begat him, I knew that he would die some day.' [...] And then he added, what showed even more wisdom and courage, 'It was for this that I brought him up' (Seneca, *To Polybius on Consolation*, XI.2-3.). "It is a great thing in all cases to say, I knew that I begot a son who is mortal" (Epictetus, *Discourses*, III.24.105). Furthermore, Epictetus makes it explicit that our friend's misery should not be taken into account: "But you say, I have parted from a certain person, and he is grieved. Why did he consider as his own that which belongs to another? Why, when he looked on you and was rejoiced, did he not also reckon that you are mortal, that it is natural

for you to part from him for a foreign country? Therefore he suffers the consequences of his own folly" (ibid., III.24.4-5). Loving someone is by no account a reason to lose one's cold blood. "'When a good man sees his father or his son being cut down, I suppose he will not weep or faint,' [...] The good man will do his duty without disturbance or fear, and he will perform the duty of a good man, so as to do nothing unworthy of a man. My father will be murdered: then I will defend him: he has been slain, then I will avenge him, not because I am grieved, but because it is my duty" (Seneca, *On Anger*, I.12.1-3). Similarly, sympathizing with someone must not be fully sincere: "When you see a person weeping in sorrow either when a child goes abroad or when he is dead, or when the man has lost his property [...] so far as words then do not be unwilling to show him sympathy, and even if it happens so, to lament with him. But take care that you do not lament internally also" (Epictetus, *Encheiridion*, §16). Finally, based on what Epictetus says, the Stoic sage is not particularly concerned with the earthly fate of his or her significant others: "Take my poor body, take my property, take my reputation, take those who are about me" (Epictetus, *Discourses*, I.29.10). And: "take Socrates and observe that he had a wife and children, but he did not consider them as his own [...] For this reason he was the first to go out as a soldier, when it was necessary" (ibid., IV.1.159-160).

[65] Seneca, *On Firmness*, V.6-7.

[66] Ibid., V.6.

[67] Denis Diderot, "Essai sur les règnes," 47.

[68] Ibid.

[69] Ibid.

[70] Ibid., 48.

[71] Ibid.

[72] Russell, *History of Western Philosophy*, 263.

[73] Ibid.

[74] Ibid.

[75] John Rist, "The Stoic Concept of Detachment," in: John Rist, ed., *The Stoics* (Berkeley: University of California Press, 1978), 265. Another meaningful remark by Rist: "We are [...] only able to 'appropriate' others to ourselves, not treat them as ourselves. [...] The only virtue or moral excellence one can command is one's own. The most the Stoic wise men can feel for one another is mutual respect for virtue achieved," ibid.

[76] Nancy Sherman, *Stoic Warriors. The Ancient Philosophy Behind the Military Mind* (Oxford: Oxford University Press, 2005), 104.

[77] William de Witt Hyde, *The Five Great Philosophies of Life* (New York: Macmillan, 1917), 107. In the subsequent passages of his book William de Witt Hyde unfolds his 1917 gendered understanding of Stoicism. It is heavily outdated but it still provides some insight which is in line with my argument. De Witt Hyde claims that "No woman was ever known to be a consistent and steadfast Stoic. Indeed a Stoic woman is a contradiction in terms" (ibid., 107). In saying so he not only reveals a

great deal about his understanding of femininity and masculinity, but also admits that the Stoic ideal of life is intrinsically incompatible with some part of "being human" (i.e. the feminine part).

[78] Edwyn Bevan, *Stoics and Sceptics* (W.Heffer & Sons, 1959), 66-68. Bevan also states as follows: "I do not think that the Stoic doctrine, forbidding sympathy and pity, forbidding [...] love, was a perversion of their principle: it seems to me the essential consequence of it, [...] – the keystone, as it were, of their system" (ibid.) Two more interesting views on this problem can be found in, respectively, Charles Bigg and Anthony Long. Charles Bigg contrasts the "my soul and God" formula, which he ascribes to the Stoics and to Plotinus, with what he calls the "Christian formula" of "my soul, my brother's soul, and God" (Charles Bigg, *The Church's Task under the Roman Empire*, [Oxford: Clarendon Press, 1905], xiv). While William de Witt Hyde employed his understanding of "masculinity" and "feminity" to argue for an essential fault of Stoicism, Charles Bigg uses the idea of "Christianity" to do so. Christian religion serves as a figure of full-fledged spiritual capability of a human being and incompatibility with it proves a master shortcoming of Stoicism. As for Anthony Long, we there is his description of the harshness of some aspects of the Stoic ethics (in: Anthony A. Long, *Hellenistic Philosophy*, 197-198). He describes an attempt to rescue a child from a fire. He points out that placing virtue in the intention only brings greatly "inhuman" ramifications since the sage is obliged to celebrate the virtue of courage and helpfulness, but is obliged to be indifferent to whether she manages to actually save the child from the flames.

[79] An example of a "highly tautological" interpretation of nature is the understanding that "nature" as "the total sum of things which exist and happen in the universe." If "nature" encompasses everything, then all things that are there and all phenomena that occur conform to it. Incompatibility with nature is a logical impossibility. Needless to say, such an approach is ethically useless, since nothing can be deemed "evil" on the grounds that it is "contrary to nature" (because *nothing* is contrary to nature). In John Stuart Mill's words: "[If] Nature [...] [means] all which is the powers and properties of all things [then] [...] there is no need of a recommendation to act according to nature, since it is what nobody can possibly help doing [...]. [Everything is] conformable to Nature in this sense of the term" (John Stuart Mill, "Nature," in: Louis P. Pojman, *Environmental Ethics: Readings in Theory and Application* [Belmont: Wadsworth/Thomson, 2005], 106-107).

[80] An example of an "ethically empty" interpretation of nature is the understanding that "conformable with nature" signifies "conformable with the scientific laws of the universe, as modern science propounds them." Such an interpretation appeals to common sense, yet it fails as a foundation for practical ethics. If "evil" is that which is contrary to nature, then it turns out that only miracles are evil (miracles taken in the traditional Humean sense of "temporary suspensions of the natural laws"), or, in another view, that levitation, travelling faster than light and even prime numbers greater than 2 are "evil." Either way, it doesn't provide any useful criteria for practical action.

[81] An example of a "redundant" interpretation of nature is the understanding that "conformable with nature" signifies "conformable with reason." In such a case

however, there is no need to use the term "nature" anymore, since all its meaning is represented by "reason" itself. Another example is reading "conformity with nature" as "conformity with facts." The most eminent proposal here is Lawrence Becker's *A New Stoicism*, which is one of the most elaborate and comprehensive attempts to reinstitute Stoic ethics to the contemporary mainstream. Yet, the very term "nature" is again superfluous since it no longer bears any meaning that "facts" don't bear. Becker himself quite openly admits that "nature" serves primarily as a symbol, or, as he says, as a "banner."

[82] Epictetus, *Encheiridion*, §33, 4.

[83] Ibid., §33, 15.

[84] Alexander Pope, "An Essay on Man, In Four Epistles, to H. St. John, Lord Bolingbroke," (epistle 2, lines 101-102), in: Samuel Johnson, ed., *The Works of the English Poets from Chaucer to Cowper* (London: 1810), vol. 12, 221.

[85] John Rist, "The Stoic Concept of Detachment," in: Rist, *The Stoics*, 259.

[86] Dorothea Frede, "Stoic Determinism," in: Brian Inwood, ed., *The Cambridge Companion to the Stoics*, (Cambridge: Cambridge University Press, 2003), 179.

[87] Nietzsche, *The Gay Science*, §306.

[88] In original German the phrase "those whose work is of the spirit" reads "*alle Menschen der geistigen Arbeit.*" Walter Kaufman comments upon his translation that this refers to "artists, scholars, writers." I follow his line of interpretation.

[89] Albert Rothenberg, "Creativity and Psychology," in: Michael Kelly, ed., *Encyclopedia of Aesthetics* (Oxford: Oxford University Press, 1998), vol. 1, 459.

[90] Henryk Elzenberg, *Marek Aureliusz. Z historii i psychologii etyki*, in: Henryk Elzenberg, *Z historii filozofii*, ed., Michał Woroniecki (Kraków: Znak, 1995), 208. In original Polish the relevant passage reads: "*[artyzm] stanowi najwyższe, doskonalsze od innych wcielenie zmysłu życia.*"

[91] Ibid. In original Polish: "*brak u niego najzupełniejszy.*"

[92] Referred in: George Steiner, *Grammars of Creation* (New Haven: Yale University Press, 2001), 355.

[93] Epictetus, *Discourses*, I.4.26.

[94] Richard Rorty, *Contingency, Irony and Solidarity* (New York: Cambridge University Press, 2005), 73.

[95] www.merriam-webster.com/dictionary/presentism ; accessed April 18, 2014.

[96] See. e.g. Seneca, *Epistles*, 113.23.

[97] Long, "Stoicism in the Philosophical Tradition," 366.

[98] Long, *Hellenistic Philosophy*, 233. And also Long : "What was most accessible and influential for the Renaissance and Enlightenment were the treatments of Stoic ethics by Cicero, Seneca, Epictetus and Marcus Aurelius" (Long, "Stoicism in the Philosophical Tradition," 367).

[99] Troels Engberg-Pedersen, *Paul and the Stoics* (Louisville: Westminster John Knox Press, 2000), 46.

Endnotes

[100] Alfred de Vigny, *Stello* (Paris: Flammarion, 1984), 64. In original French: " [...] *du jour où il sut lire il fut Poète*, [...] *dès lors il appartint à la race toujours maudite par les puissants de la terre.*"

[101] "Free artists of themselves" is Harold Bloom's expression denoting the most eminent Shakespearean characters. See: Harold Bloom, *Shakespeare. The Invention of the Human* (New York: Riverhead Books, 1998).

[102] The notion that creativity can be understood as an endeavor of "creating new meanings" requires some commentary. **(1)** One of the basic concerns about utilizing "meaning" to define creativity (besides all the doubts about what "meaning" means) is that such a framework relies too much on the possibility of semantic novelty. We must remember that although a work of art might offer a bracingly fresh significance locally, once the global and diachronic point of view is allowed, it can be argued (and has been argued) that meanings never come *ex nihilo* but are rather constructed and complied from previously existing semantic layers. George Steiner begins his *Grammars of Creation* with a blunt statement that "We have no more beginnings" (Steiner, *Grammars of Creation*, 2) and later argues that meaning consists in the history of words. And then: "The serious writer, the poet above all, is [...] exceptionally attuned to the history of words and to grammatical resources [...] [and she] will hear in the word remote echoes, the soundings in depth [...] the overtones, undertones, connotations [and] family kinships which vibrate around the word" (ibid., 144-147). **(2)** All that being said, Steiner's version of definition of creation as creating new meanings is as follows: "What a poet aims for [...] is that novelty of combinations which will suggest [...] to the reader, a corona, a new-lit sphere or perceptible meanings, of radiant energy, at once understandable and adding to (transcending) what is already at hand" (ibid., 144-147). **(3)** Employing "meaning" to define creativity invites us to call this approach a "hermeneutic" one. Yet, hermeneutics has been primarily occupied with interpreting meanings rather than with their origin. Also, as the very idea of the hermeneutic circle implies, meanings are perceived as rearrangements and recombinations of earlier meanings rather than as coming *ex nihilo*. Finally, historically, hermeneutics was begotten as the study and interpretation of scriptures of allegedly divine provenance, which left little room for inquiry into their origin. **(4)** I will now provide three specific examples to clarify what "creating meanings" can mean in practice. First, poet's devotion to explore previously meaningless usages of words can prompt her to focus on the newest words, i.e. on the most recent additions to the language. Likewise, she might take one more step forward and focus on future words, not yet invented. The Futurist movements of the early 20th century can serve as an example. Second, there have been explicit artistic attempts to draw meanings out of words that have no prior meanings, like in Dadaism. Third, along the same line we can read Heidegger's notion of a work of art bringing the "truth" of the depicted object to the full light of Being. Let me refer to his interpretation of van Gogh's painting. The meanings that are present but concealed in a pair of peasant shoes are brought to plain view by the artist's work: "From the dark opening of the worn insides of the shoes the toilsome tread of the workers stares forth. [...] Van Gogh's painting is the disclosure of what [...] the pair of

peasant shoes *is* in truth. This being emerges into the unconcealment of its Being." (Martin Heidegger, "The Origin of the Work of Art," trans. Albert Hofstadter, in: Martin Heidegger and David Farrell Krell, *Basic Writings: From Being and Time (1927) to The Task of Thinking (1964)* [San Francisco: Harper, 1993], 158-162).

[103] Rothenberg, "Creativity and Psychology."

[104] Keith Negus and Michael Pickering, *Creativity, Communication and Cultural Value* (London: Sage Publications, 2004), vi.

[105] As an illustration to this shift in attributing creativity, we can use this example of a symptomatically biased list from a 1998 encyclopedia entry: "Studies of creativity [...] are found in inquiries about artificial intelligence, hemispherical brain theory, psychoanalysis, literary criticism, experimental and cognitive psychology, and philosophy, among others" (Carl R. Hausman, "Creativity. Conceptual and Historical Overview," in: Michael Kelly, ed., *Encyclopedia of Aesthetics* [Oxford: Oxford University Press, 1998], 453). Another symptomatic fact is that contemporary philosophical dictionaries and encyclopedias are likely to provide more detailed and thoroughgoing entries on "Creationism" than "Creativity."

[106] P. G. W. Glare, ed., *Oxford Latin Dictionary* (Oxford: Oxford University Press, 2012), vol. 1, 501.

[107] Ibid.

[108] Ibid.

[109] Let me add George Steiner's account to this: "In Greek, the denotative and connotative sphere of *poieō* [...] is exceptionally dense. It embraces immediacies of action and complex causality, material fabrication, and poetic license. [...] Latin *creatio* is grounded in biology and in politics: in the engendering of children and the appointment of magistrates," Steiner, *Grammars of Creation*, 21-22.

[110] For the claim that in happened in the 16th century see, e.g.,: Negus et al., *Creativity, Communication and Cultural Value*, 1-2.

[111] Maciej Kazimierz Sarbiewski, *De perfecta poesii*, (I.1), in: Maciej Kazimierz Sarbiewski, *O poezji doskonałej czyli Wergiliusz i Homer. De Perfecta Poesi, sive Vergilius et Homerus*, trans. Marian Plezia (Wrocław: Zakład Ossolińskich, 1954), 3. The quoted passage in original Latin: "*Solus poeta est, qui suo quodam modo instar Dei dicendo seu narrando quidpiam tamquam exsistens facit illud idem penitus, quantum est ex se, ex toto exsistere et quasi de novo creari.*"

[112] Władysław Tatarkiewicz, *A History of Six Ideas*, trans. Christopher Kasparek et al., (Hague: Martinus Nijhoff, 1980), 248.

[113] William Shakespeare, *The Comedy of Errors*, act III, scene II, line 39.

[114] E. M. S. Simpson, ed., *The Sermons of John Donne* (Berkeley: University of California Press, 1959), vol. 4., no. 2, 25. I quote it from: contentdm.lib.byu.edu/cdm/compoundobject/collection/JohnDonne/id/3170/rec/1 ; accessed August 9, 2013.

[115] It is interesting to note at this point that the English language, despite its conceptual precision, lacks a distinction that some other languages are fortunate to

have. For example, in the Polish language we find the term "*stwórca*" which signifies "creator" but solely in the theological sense, an equivalent of the English "creator deity," "the Creator" or "God." On the other hand, there is a term just one letter shorter, "*twórca*," which denotes human actors engaged in creative activities of any sort. It mirrors the English terms "inventor," "originator," "person doing creative work," "artist," or "author of a specific piece of original work" as used in copyright law. The absence of this distinction is meaningful, but it doesn't have a substantial bearing on this investigation.

[116] Gen 1:1, New International Version.

[117] Alexandre Ganoczy, *Der schöpferische Mensch und die Schöpfung Gottes* (Mainz: Matthis-Grünewald-Verlag, 1976), 9. The quoted words are the opening of the book. In original German: "*Wenn heute die philosophische Anthropologie von Schöpfung, die Psychologie von Kreativität und die Umgangssprache vom Schöpfer eines Kunstwerkes sprechen, meinen sie sicherlich damit nichts Theologisches. Der religiöse Sinngehalt dieser Begriffe ist nicht mehr selbstverständlich.*"

[118] Ibid., 10-11. The whole passage in original German: "*Descartes, Kant, Hegel, Marx, Nietzsche, Sartre sowie bestimmten Neomarxisten und Positivisten [...] sind Sprecher des 'homo creator' in seiner Emanzipationsbewegung vom 'deus creator' weg, Nachzeichner des großen Abenteuers, in das die abendländische Menschheit bei ihrem Versuch autonomer Welt- und Selbstgestaltung eintrat.*"

[119] Tatarkiewicz, *A History of Six Ideas*, 249.

[120] Catherine Soussloff, "History of the Concept of the Artist," in: Michael Kelly, ed., *Encyclopedia of Aesthetics* (Oxford: Oxford University Press, 1998), vol. 1, 134. The concept of "art" has a long and convoluted history of its own. For a general outline see, e.g.,: Tatarkiewicz, *A History of Six Ideas*, 11-50.

[121] www.oed.com/view/Entry/11241?redirectedFrom=artistic#eid ; accessed April 10, 2013.

[122] Soussloff, "History of the Concept of the Artist," 130.

[123] www.oed.com/view/Entry/11241?redirectedFrom=artistic#eid ; accessed April 10, 2013.

[124] As K. Negus and M. Pickering put it: "Creativity is a social process, entailing a dynamic of according value and receiving recognition, [...] it is never realized as creative act until it is achieved within some social encounter," Negus et al., *Creativity, Communication and Cultural Value*, 23.

[125] It seems justified to claim that intersubjective dynamics and extra-subjective references present significant challenges, or at least questions, to Stoicism. This, however, is beyond the scope of this book.

[126] This view can be found in Gadamer's *The Relevance of the Beautiful* (see: Hans-Georg Gadamer, *The Relevance of the Beautiful and Other Essays*, trans. Nicholas Walker, [Cambridge: Cambridge University Press, 1986]). Gadamer argues there that the defining point of "new" (non-classical) art is the acknowledgement (which happened sometime in the 19th century) that the universal and common code

exists no more. In his view, the Christian religion used to be the essential provider of this code.

[127] The passages which follow are based mostly on: Isaiah Berlin, *The Roots of Romanticism*, ed. Henry Hardy, (Princeton: Princeton University Press, 1999), and Isaiah Berlin, "The Apotheosis of the Romantic Will," in: Isaiah Berlin, *The Crooked Timber of Humanity. Chapters in the History of Ideas*, ed. Henry Hardy (London: John Murray Publishers, 1990).

[128] See, e.g., Berlin, *The Roots of Romanticism*, 1-2, 5, 20.

[129] See, e.g., ibid. 141, or Berlin, "The Apotheosis of the Romantic Will," 226.

[130] See, e.g., Berlin, *The Roots of Romanticism*, 103, 105-106.

[131] See, e.g., Berlin, "The Apotheosis of the Romantic Will," 231.

[132] See, e.g., Berlin, *The Roots of Romanticism*, 139.

[133] See, e.g., Berlin, "The Apotheosis of the Romantic Will," 232, or Berlin, *The Roots of Romanticism*, 98-99, 140.

[134] See, e.g., Berlin, "The Apotheosis of the Romantic Will," 231, or Berlin, *The Roots of Romanticism*, 119.

[135] See, e.g., Berlin, "The Apotheosis of the Romantic Will," 227.

[136] See, e.g., ibid. 228.

[137] See, e.g., Berlin, *The Roots of Romanticism*, 133.

[138] Reported by Diogenes Laertius: "But for Chrysippus, there had been no Porch" (Diogenes Laertius, *Lives of Eminent Philosophers*, VII.183, in: Diogenes Laertius, *Lives of Eminent Philosophers*, vols. 1-2, translated by Robert Drew Hicks [London: Heinemann, 1942]).

[139] See, e.g., Berlin, *The Roots of Romanticism*, 141, 146-147.

[140] Ludwig Wittgenstein, *Tractatus Logico-Philosophicus*, §7.

[141] Jean Baudrillard, "The Precession of Simulacra," in: Jean Baudrillard, *Simulacra and Simulation*, trans. Sheila Faria Glaser (Ann Arbor: The University of Michigan Press, 1994), 41.

[142] Boris Groys, *The Total Art of Stalinism. Avant-garde, Aesthetic Dictatorship, and Beyond*, trans. Charles Rougle (Princeton: Princeton University Press, 1992).

[143] Piotr Kozak, introduction to Boris Groys, *Stalin jako totalne dzieło sztuki*, trans. Piotr Kozak (Warszawa: Sic, 2010), 9. (It is a Polish edition of Groys' book). In original Polish: "*największego awangardowego artystę, a nawet najwybitniejsze dzieło awangardowej sztuki.*" I'm grateful to Adam Leszkiewicz for indicating this passage to me.

[144] Interestingly, Joseph Stalin did write poetry in his youth. This, however, is beside the point.

[145] Kropiwnicki [ed.], *Žižek. Przewodnik Krytyki Politycznej*, 9. In original Polish: „*Szczęście to reakcyjne pojęcie dla głupich ludzi. Podstawą ludzkiej kreatywności jest poszukiwanie nieszczęścia*". There are a few more passages in Žižek which convey a

very similar idea: "'Happiness' relies on the subject's inability or unreadiness fully to confront the consequences of its desire [...] In our daily lives, we (pretend to) desire things which we do not really desire, so that, ultimately, the worst thing that can happen is for us to get what we 'officially' desire." (Slavoj Žižek, *Welcome to the Desert of the Real*, [London: Verso, 2002], 59-60). "Happiness is for me a very conformist category [...] When you are in a creative endeavor, that wonderful fever, 'My God, I am on to something,' happiness doesn't enter it. You are ready to suffer [...] This is how we function: we don't really want what we think we desire" (source: the video "Why Be Happy When You Could Be Interesting?", www.youtube.com/watch?v=U88jj6PSD7w; accessed September 27, 2014). Presumably, a Stoic defense against these attacks comes along the line that Žižek's understanding of "happiness" is too close to "having one's desires satisfied" and thus it is nonstoic.

[146] Marcus Aurelius, *Meditations*, VI.46.

[147] Ibid., VII.3.

[148] Ibid., V.28.

[149] Epictetus, *Encheiridion*, §33.10.

[150] Epictetus, *Discourses*, I.4.26.

[151] Ibid., I.28.12.

[152] Ibid., I.28.32-33.

[153] Seneca, *Epistles*, 49.5.

[154] Seneca, *On Benefits*, I.III.10.

[155] Ibid., I.IV.5.

[156] Ibid., I.IV.6.

[157] Marcus Aurelius, *Meditations*, I.17.

[158] Seneca, *Epistles*, 88.3.

[159] Ibid., 88.7.

[160] Ibid., 88.9-10.

[161] Władysław Tatarkiewicz, *History of Aesthetics*, ed. J. Harrell, trans. Adam and Ann Czerniawski (The Hague: Mouton, 1970), vol. 1, 200. The Chrysippus's words were transmitted by Chalcidius in *Ad Timaeum* 167. This equals to *Stoicorum Veterum Fragmenta* III.229. English translation by J.C.B. Lowe. In original Latin (by Chalcidius): "Pictores quoque et fictores, nonne rapiunt animos ad suavitatem ab industria?"

[162] Seneca, *Epistles*, 108.35.

[163] Ibid., 115.11-12.

[164] Ibid., 123.9.

[165] Musonius Rufus, *Lectures and Sayings*, 77. Passage transmitted by Stobaeus (3.1.209).

[166] Seneca, *Epistles*, 115.8-9.

¹⁶⁷ Ibid., 115.1-2.

¹⁶⁸ Plato, *Ion*, 534a. Trans. Paul Woodruff. In: John. M. Cooper and D. S. Hutchinson, ed., *Plato. Complete Works* (Indianapolis: Hackett, 1997), 941.

¹⁶⁹ Plato, *Ion*, 534b. Trans. Paul Woodruff. Ibid., 942.

¹⁷⁰ Seneca, *On Tranquility of Mind*, XVII.10. Seneca seems to refer to Plato's *Phaedrus* 245a (where we read: "If anyone comes to the gates of poetry and expects to become an adequate poet by acquiring expert knowledge of the subject without Muses' madness, he will fail," translated by Alexander Nehamas and Paul Woodruff, in: John. M. Cooper and D. S. Hutchinson, ed., *Plato. Complete Works*, 523) and to Aristotle's *Problemata*, XXX.1, 953a (where we read: "Why is it that all those who have become eminent in philosophy or politics or poetry or the arts are clearly of an atrabilious temperament, and some of them to such an extent as to be affected by diseases caused by black bile [...] ?," W. D. Ross, ed., *The Works of Aristotle*, trans. E.S. Forster [Oxford: Clarendon Press, 1927], vol. 7, page unspecified).

¹⁷¹ Johann Wolfgang von Goethe, *Conversations with Eckermann (1823-1832)*, trans. John Oxenford (San Francisco: North Point Press, 1984), 203 (entry dated March 11, 1828).

¹⁷² Hausman, "Creativity. Conceptual and Historical Overview," 454.

¹⁷³ Theodor W. Adorno, *Philosophy of Modern Music*, trans. Anne G. Mitchell and Wesley V. Blomster, (New York: The Seabury Press, 1973), 22.

¹⁷⁴ Berlin, "The Apotheosis of the Romantic Will," 228-229.

¹⁷⁵ Michel Foucault, *The Care of the Self* [vol. 3 of *The History of Sexuality*], trans. Robert Hurley (New York: Pantheon Books, 1986), 46.

¹⁷⁶ Ibid., 47.

¹⁷⁷ Ibid.

¹⁷⁸ Ibid., 46.

¹⁷⁹ D.E.Hahm, *The Origins of Stoic Cosmology* (Columbus: Ohio State University Press, 1977), 3.

¹⁸⁰ Trans. Constance Garnett. Source: en.wikisource.org/wiki/Anna_Karenina/Part_One/Chapter_1 ; accessed September 8, 2014.

¹⁸¹ See: Sergei Esenin, *Selected Poetry*, trans. Peter Tempest (Moscow: Progress Publishers, 1982), 235.

¹⁸² Søren Kierkegaard, *Either/or* [abridged edition], trans. George L. Stengren, ed. Steven L. Rossfrom (London: Harper, 1986), 13.

¹⁸³ See: Paul Verlaine, *The Cursed Poets*, trans. Chase Madar (Copenhagen – Los Angeles: Green Integer, 2003). This book, first published in original French in 1884, is devoted to six French poets: Tristan Corbière, Arthur Rimbaud, Stéphane Mallarmé, Marceline Desbordes-Valmore, Auguste Villiers de l'Isle-Adam and Paul Verlaine himself. The very phrase "cursed poet" ("*poète maudit*" in French) can be traced back at least to the novel *Stello* by Alfred de Vigny, first published in 1832.

Therein we read: "*Je veux dire qu'il avait raison de se plaindre de savoir lire, parce que du jour où il sut lire il fut Poète, et dès lors il appartint à la race toujours maudite par les puissants de la terre*" (Vigny, *Stello*, 64) which can be rendered in English as: "I mean that he was right to complain about knowing how to read because from the day when he learnt to read he became a poet and thus he belonged to the race forever cursed by the powerful of the earth."

[184] Albert Rothenberg, *Creativity and Madness. New Findings and Old Stereotypes* (Baltimore: The Johns Hopkins University Press, 1994).

[185] Kenneth Schuyler Lynn, *Hemingway* (New York: Simon and Schuster, 1987), 527. The remark was made by Buck Lanham during his trip to visit Hemingway in Cuba in 1949.

[186] Jeffrey Meyers, *Hemingway, a Biography* (New York: Harper & Row, 1985), 352.

[187] Jeffrey A. Kottler, *Divine Madness. Ten Stories of Creative Struggle* (San Francisco: Jossey-Bass, 2006), 94.

[188] Myra Friedman, *Buried Alive: The Biography of Janis Joplin*, (New York: William Morrow & Company, 1973), 219.

[189] Ibid., 218.

[190] Stephen B. Oates, *William Faulkner, the Man and the Artist: A Biography* (New York: Harper & Row, 1987), 256.

[191] Ibid., 257.

[192] Gerald Clarke, *Capote: A Biography* (New York: Simon and Schuster, 1988), 498.

[193] Bob Thomas, *Joan Crawford, a Biography* (New York: Simon and Schuster, 1978), 95-96.

[194] Arnold M. Ludwig, *The Price of Greatness. Resolving the Creativity and Madness Controversy* (New York – London: Guilford, 1995), 144.

[195] Elwira Watała and Wiktor Woroszylski, *Życie Sergiusza Jesienina* (Warszawa: PIW, 1982), 297. In original Polish: "*Usiłował* [...] *wyskoczyć przez okno na klatce schodowej. Isadora* [...] *kazała zmoczyć mu głowę zimną wodą. Kiedy to nie pomogło, związano Jesienina* [...] *sznurem do suszenia bielizny. Stawiał opór* [...] *krzyczał, że poskarży się na nich Trockiemu, wołał: Ukrzyżujcie mnie!*"

[196] This is not to prohibit a more quantitative approach, though. Quite the contrary, it might yield some interesting results. For instance, Arnold M. Ludwig goes to great lengths to provide a detailed scientific account of the problem. See: Arnold M. Ludwig, *The Price of Greatness*.

[197] John Dryden, *Absalom and Achitophel*, lines 163-164,

[198] Berlin, "The Apotheosis of the Romantic Will," 228-229.

[199] Pierre Hadot, *Philosophy as a Way of Life: Spiritual Exercises from Socrates to Foucault*, translated by Michael Case, (Oxford: Blackwell, 1995), 191.

[200] www.oed.com/view/Entry/122712?rskey=eirXNk&result=1&isAdvanced=false#eid; accessed April 30, 2014.

[201] www.oed.com/view/Entry/200321?result=1&rskey=mxF2Rk&;

accessed December 5, 2016.

[202] Ibid.

[203] Ibid.

[204] Seneca, *Epistles*, 65. 5-6.

[205] The reason why I leave out the theme of "creating in order to satisfy the desire to create" is that the Stoic view on "satisfying our desires" is much more complicated than the commonly-held and simplified view may hold. This approach would provide no specific key to our problem in question. It would just be too broad.

[206] "Rallying everything that remains, and not to sanctify nor propound" comes from Harold Bloom, who in turn draws it from the first oration that Satan delivers to the fallen angels in Milton's *Paradise Lost*. The due passage in Bloom's *Anxiety of Influence* is: Harold Bloom, *The Anxiety of Influence. A Theory of Poetry* (Oxford: Oxford University Press) 1973, 21-22. The due passage from Milton is:

> Better to reign in Hell, then serve in Heav'n.
> But wherefore let we then our faithful friends
> Th'associates and copartners of our loss
> Lye thus astonisht on th'oblivious Pool,
> And call them not to share with us their part
> In this unhappy Mansion, or once more
> With rallied Arms to try what may be yet
> Regained in Heav'n, or what more lost in Hell?
>
> (John Milton, *Paradise Lost*, I.262-270)

[207] Seneca, *Epistles*, 2.3.

[208] Soussloff, "History of the Concept of the Artist," 134.

[209] Epictetus, *Encheiridion*, §1, 1-2.

[210] Seneca, *Epistles*, 102.9.

[211] Ibid., 52.9.

[212] Ibid., 52.11.

[213] Epictetus, *Discourses*, I.21.4.

[214] Henryk Elzenberg, *Marek Aureliusz. Z historii i psychologii etyki*, in: Henryk Elzenberg, *Z historii filozofii*, ed., Michał Woroniecki (Kraków: Znak, 1995), 97-213.

[215] With thanks to William O. Stephens for help in clarifying this passage.

[216] Marcus Aurelius, *Meditations*, IV.20.

[217] Ibid., V.33.

[218] Ibid., IV.3.

[219] Ibid., IV.19.

[220] Hyde, *The Five Great Philosophies of Life*, 103-104.

[221] Irvine, *A Guide to The Good Life*.

[222] Ibid., 45. Irvine further explores the concept of "withdrawing from the social hierarchy game" in his subsequent book, i.e. William B. Irvine, *A Slap in the Face. Why Insults Hurt And Why They Shouldn't* (New York: Oxford University Press, 2013).

[223] Foucault, *The Care of the Self*, 59-60.

[224] Ibid., 59.

[225] Ibid., 60.

[226] Seneca, *Epistles*, 20.13.

[227] Ibid., 17.5.

[228] Ibid., 17.6-7.

[229] Epictetus, *Encheiridion*, §41.

[230] Ibid., §33.7.

[231] Marcus Aurelius, *Meditations*, I.5.

[232] Seneca, *Epistles*, 2.5.

[233] Ibid., 2.6. "Cheerful poverty is an excellent thing" is the exact line from Epicurus that Seneca admits to have stolen from the "enemy's camp." The locus in Epicurus is: Usener, *Fragmenta*, 475.

[234] Seneca, *Epistles*, 60.4. The phrase "belly-mongers" (*ventri oboedientes*) comes from, as Seneca acknowledges, Sallust, *Catiline*, I.1.

[235] Seneca, *Epistles*, 25.4-5.

[236] Ibid., 110.18.

[237] Cicero, *On Moral Ends*, III.43. Trans. Raphael Woolf. In: Cicero, *On Moral Ends*, ed. Julia Annas (Cambridge: Cambridge University Press, 2001), 79.

[238] For an excellent (and far more thorough than I provide) account of the doctrinal difference between the Stoics and Aristotle see: Becker, *A New Stoicism*, 140-141 (the subchapter "Good times").

[239] Diogenes Laertius, *Lives of Eminent Philosophers*, VII.27. Diogenes Laertius also quotes a passage from Poseidippus's *Men Transported*: "So that for ten whole days / More temperate than Zeno's self he seemed," (ibid.).

[240] Epictetus, *Encheiridion*, §33.4.

[241] Peter J. Vernezze, *Don't Worry, Be Stoic: Ancient Wisdom for Troubled Times* (Lanham: University Press of America, 2005).

[242] Sharon Lebell, *The Art of Living. The Classical Manual on Virtue, Happiness, and Effectiveness* (San Francisco: Harper, 1995).

[243] William B. Irvine, *A Guide to The Good Life*.

[244] Becker, *A New Stoicism*.

[245] Henryk Elzenberg, *Kłopot z istnieniem* (Toruń: UMK, 2002), 386. Entry dated January 29, 1951.

[246] See: Becker, *A New Stoicism*, 39.

[247] We need to remember that a great part of what we know about Stoicism is not first-hand reports, but an outcome of a long course of tradition of fragments and quotes. It might be reasonably suspected that ancient and mediaeval authors and scholars who contributed to this process were inclined to transmit the most typical and most defining Stoic passages. (Lawrence Becker points out in a similar line of thought: "Both Stoic and anti-Stoics alike have developed an unwholesome fascination with a picture of the Stoic sage drawn for extreme circumstances. We persist, in high art and low journalism, in telling and retelling stories of good people who resolutely endure horrors [...] [Such] fascination with them can be seriously misleading" [Lawrence C. Becker, "Stoic Emotion," in: Steven K. Strange and Jack Zupko, *Stoicism: Traditions and Transformations* {Cambridge: Cambridge University Press, 2004} 250-251]).

[248] This metaphor was coined by professor Marian Przełęcki.

[249] Marcus Aurelius, *Meditations*, V.16.

[250] As remarked, the "all-things-considered" phrase and concept are borrowed from Lawrence C. Becker. For a detailed account of this framework, see: Becker, *A New Stoicism*.

[251] Epictetus, *Discourses*, III.20.12-13.

[252] Ibid., II.5.1-4.

[253] Ibid., II.5.6-7.

[254] Ibid., II.5.21-23.

[255] Seneca, *Epistles*, 82. 10-12.

[256] Marcus Aurelius, *Meditations*, VII.68.

[257] John Rist, *Stoic Philosophy* (Cambridge: Cambridge University Press, 1969), 8.

[258] Schopenhauer provides a good example of reluctance to the ascetic reading of Stoicism. "[The Stoics] were of opinion that *actual* dispensing with everything that can be discarded is not required, but that it is sufficient for us constantly to regard possession and enjoyment as *dispensable*, and as held in hand of chance." Schopenhauer, *The World as Will and Representation*, vol. 2, 155 (chapter XVI).

[259] Seneca, *On the Happy Life*, XXV.2.

[260] Epictetus, *Discourses*, IV.11.33-34.

[261] Marcus Aurelius, *Meditations*, I.6.

[262] It's a passage from a letter sent by Marcus Cornelius Fronto to Marcus Aurelius, dated year 162. C.R.Haines, ed., *The Correspondence of Marcus Cornelius Fronto with Marcus Aurelius Antoninus, Lucius Verus, Antoninus Pius, and Various Friends*, trans. C.R.Haines (Cambridge: Harvard University Press, The Loeb Classical Library, 1963), vol. 2, 11.

[263] Becker, *A New Stoicism*, 140.

[264] Paul Auster, *Hand to Mouth. A Chronicle of Early Failure* (New York: Henry Holt and Company, 1998), 3-4.

[265] Salvador Dalí, *Diary of a Genius*, trans. Richard Howard (New York: Prentice Hall Press, 1986), 21.

[266] Ibid., 82.

[267] See: Harold Bloom, *Shakespeare. The Invention of the Human*.

[268] I have also argued against the ascetic misinterpretation in: Piotr Stankiewicz, "Stoics Are Not Ascetics," in: Patrick Ussher [ed.], *Stoicism Today. Selected writings*, vol. II (Stoicism Today, 2016), 253-255. Available also online: https://blogs.exeter.ac.uk/stoicismtoday/2015/10/03/stoic-avoidance-of-asceticism-by-piotr-stankiewicz/ (accessed January 23, 2017).

[269] Marcus Aurelius, *Meditations*, XII.27. See also: Stephens, *Marcus Aurelius*, 101-107.

[270] Marcus Aurelius, *Meditations*, VII.6.

[271] Ibid., VII.19.

[272] Seneca, *Epistles*, 21.5. Due passage in *Aeneid* is IX.445-447.

[273] See: Ricardo Salles, *The Stoics on Determinism and Compatibilism* (Aldershot, Hants, England: Ashgate Pub, 2005), 19-29.

[274] Ibid., 19-20 (see also: *Stoicorum Veterum Fragmenta* II.625). Translation from Greek by Long and Sedly, modified by Salles.

[275] Seneca, *On Anger*, II. XXXI.4.

[276] Seneca, *Epistles*, 107.5. See also: ibid., 107.1-2.

[277] Seneca, *To Polybius on Consolation*, I.4.

[278] Marcus Aurelius, *Meditations*, III.3. See also: Seneca, *To Polybius on Consolation*, XIV.2-3.

[279] Marcus Aurelius, *Meditations*, VII.1.

[280] Ibid., IX.14.

[281] Ibid., IV.44.

[282] Ibid., VI.37.

[283] Ibid., VII.49.

[284] This line plays on the following remark by Henryk Elzenberg: "The goal of a serious and great writer is to tell a generation about the eternal things [...] The goal of a less serious writer is to tell the eternity about a generation" (Elzenberg, *Kłopot z istnieniem*, 91 [entry dated February 22, 1914]). In original Polish: "*Celem pisarza serio, tego 'wielkiego', jest powiedzieć pokoleniu o rzeczach wiecznych [...] Celem tego mniej serio jest powiadomić wieczność o pokoleniu.*"

[285] Marcus Aurelius, *Meditations*, X.27.

[286] Diogenes Laertius, *Lives of Eminent Philosophers*, VII.123.

[287] Marcus Aurelius, *Meditations*, XII.13.

[288] Seneca, *To Marcia on Consolation*, IX.5.

[289] Seneca, *On Anger*, II.XXXI.4.

[290] Seneca, *Epistles*, 91.4.
[291] Seneca, *On Anger*, III. XXXVII.3-4.
[292] Seneca, *Epistles*, 91.3.
[293] John Ashbery, "Pourquoi Écrivez-vous," *Libération*, March 1985, 47. Reported in: Timothy Clark, *The Theory of Inspiration. Composition as a crisis of subjectivity in Romantic and post-Romantic writing* (Manchester: Manchester University Press, 1997), 19.
[294] Reported in: Clark, *The Theory of Inspiration*, 18.
[295] Reported in: Elzenberg, *Kłopot z istnieniem*, 17 (entry dated October 13, 1907). In original French: "*Je ne pense jamais, mes idées pensent pour moi.*"
[296] Viktor E. Frankl, *The Unconscious God. Psychotherapy and Theology* (London: Hodder and Stoughton, 1977), 29.
[297] Stephen Davies, "Artistic expression," in: *Routledge Encyclopedia of Philosophy*, Edward Craig. ed., (London – New York: Routledge, 1998), vol. 1, 495.
[298] Rorty, *Contingency, Irony and Solidarity*, 3.
[299] With thanks to William Stephens for discussing this with me.
[300] Epictetus, *Discourses*, IV.5.23-26.
[301] Seneca, *On Firmness*, IV.1-2
[302] Seneca, *On Anger*, III. XXV.3.
[303] Epictetus, *Discourses*, I.25.29.
[304] Marcus Aurelius, *Meditations*, IV.49.
[305] Ibid., XII.22.
[306] Epictetus, *Discourses*, III. 24. 24-26.
[307] Seneca, *On Anger*, III.VI.1.
[308] Seneca, *Epistles*, 59. 16.
[309] Seneca, *On Benefits*, VII.I.7.
[310] Seneca, *Epistles*, 72.4-5.
[311] Marcus Aurelius, *Meditations*, XII.3.
[312] Pierre Hadot, *The Inner Citadel. The Meditations of Marcus Aurelius*, trans. Michael Chaes (Cambridge, London: Harvard University Press, 1998), 119-120. Passage from Empedocles equals to fragments 27-28 in: Hermann Diels and Walther Kranz, *Die Fragmente der Vorsokratiker, griechisch und deutsch* (Berlin: Weidman, 1951).
[313] Rorty, *Contingency, Irony and Solidarity*, 23 ff.
[314] See: Philip Larkin, *Collected Poems*, ed. Anthony Thwaite (New York: Farrar, Strauss and Giroux), 2003, 177.
[315] Rorty, *Contingency, Irony and Solidarity*, 23.
[316] Ibid.

[317] Ibid.

[318] Obviously, Rorty is not the only one thinker to uphold the concept of art as a rendition of author's idiosyncrasies. "The theoretical proposition that the work of art is a product of an original mind that imposes its unique imprint on it has been widely accepted in Western culture since the Greeks" (Soussloff, "History of the Concept of the Artist," 130).

[319] Rorty, *Contingency, Irony and Solidarity*, 189-198. A brief summation of this idea is as follows: "In my utopia, human solidarity [...] is to be achieved [...] by imaginative ability to see strange people as fellow sufferers," ibid., xvi.

[320] Ibid., 192.

[321] Such an interpretation can rely, e.g., on the "System of Transcendental Ideas" section of *Critique of Pure Reason* (A333-A338). E.g.: "Properly speaking, an objective deduction of these transcendental ideas, such as we were able to supply for the categories, is impossible. For precisely because they are only ideas, they have in fact no reference to any object that could be given congruently with them." Immanuel Kant, *Critique of Pure Reason*, (A335-A336), trans. Werner S. Pluhar (Indianapolis: Hackett Publishing Company, 1996), 377-378.

[322] Marcus Aurelius, *Mediations*, V.10.

[323] Consider, e.g., this passage from Epictetus: "For it is a great thing in all cases to say, 'I knew that I begot a son who is mortal.' For so you also will say, 'I knew that I am mortal'" (*Discourses* III.24.104-105). Application of the argument from mortality somehow makes the persons it is applied to equal to one another. To say "you are mortal" is not only akin to saying "I am mortal" but suggests that both "you" and "I" are merely manifestations of the same principle of mortality .

[324] Diogenes Laertius, *Lives of Eminent Philosophers*, VII. 142-143.

[325] Epictetus, *Discourses*, I.14.6-7.

[326] Ibid., I.13.3-4.

[327] Seneca, *On Benefits*, III.28.1-2.

[328] Marcus Aurelius, *Mediations*, VIII.7.

[329] Ibid., VII.9.

[330] Epictetus, *Discourses*, I.12.12-14.

[331] E.Zeller, *The Stoics, Epicureans and Sceptics*, trans. Oswald J. Reichel (London, New York: Longmans, Green, 1892), 403.

[332] Galatians 3:28 (New International Version).

[333] See: Willard Van Orman Quine, *On What There Is* (Washington: Catholic University of America, Philosophy Education Society, 1948).

[334] Epictetus, *Discourses*, III.15.10.

[335] Seneca, *On Tranquility of Mind*, VII.2.

[336] Marcus Aurelius, *Meditations*, V.3.

[337] Becker, *A New Stoicism*, 108.

[338] "Zeno rejected the results of the 'second voyage' and, no less than Epicurus, he took a clear materialistic position. He denied not only the transcendent existence of the Ideas, but he refused to attribute to them even the ontological meaning which Aristotle [...] maintained." Giovanni Reale, *A History of Ancient Philosophy*, trans. John R. Catan (Albany: State University of New York Press, 1985), vol. 3, 10.

[339] Two comments here. First, there was no single and definite stance among the ancient Stoics as to what exactly becomes of humans after our biological death. The common notion is quite clear, though. Whatever happens to us after the last breath, it has no great importance from a Stoic perspective. Second, the quoted formula about earthly life and afterlife is drawn from William B. Irvine. See: Irvine, *A Guide to The Good Life*, 22.

[340] "Following the facts" is Becker's phrasing. See: Becker, *A New Stoicism*.

[341] Phrase proposed by Michał Dobrzański.

[342] For the brief discussion of the problems with "following nature," see section "Challenges Facing Stoicism" in the Introduction.

[343] See: Becker, *A New Stoicism*.

[344] http://www.vatican.va/edocs/ENG0216/__P1.HTM ; accessed June 10, 2013.

[345] Becker, *A New Stoicism*, 9.

[346] Ibid., 42. See also: ibid., 44.

[347] "First-order endeavor" in Becker's terms.

[348] A lovely passage from Epictetus illustrating the martyrological misinterpretation is this. "In this way an athlete also acted who was in danger of dying unless his private parts were amputated. His brother came to the athlete, who was a philosopher, and said, 'Come, brother, what are you going to do? Shall we amputate this member and return to the gymnasium?' But the athlete persisted in his resolution and died." (Epictetus, *Discourses*, I.2.25).

[349] Epictetus, *Discourses*, II.15.4-13.

[350] William Shakespeare, *As You Like It*, act 2, scene 7, lines 139-140.

[351] Friedrich Nietzsche, *Twilight of the Idols or How to Philosophize with a Hammer*, §3 (in: "Morality as Anti-Nature" section), in: Friedrich Nietzsche, *Twilight of the Idols and The Anti-Christ*, trans. R.J.Hollingdale (Harmondsworth: Penguin, 1974), 44.

[352] Obviously, this statement is a certain approximation. If we examine it closer, it becomes manifest that there are some roles which humans choose by themselves. In Shakespeare's *Twelfth Night* Malvolio says that "Some are born great, some achieve greatness, and some have greatness thrust upon'em" (William Shakespeare, *Twelfth Night*, act II, scene V) and the same holds in our case. Some roles are innate (like "being someone's brother"), some might be chosen by us (like "being a wrestler" or "being a philosopher") and some are forced on us (like "being a disabled person"). This distinction is not foreign to the Stoics, since they acknowledged that we do have a degree of latitude in the selection of roles. "You must decide whether your disposition is better suited for vigorous action or for

tranquil speculation and contemplation, and you must adopt whichever the bent of your genius inclines you for" (Seneca, *On Tranquility of Mind*, VII.2). This, however, doesn't affect the train of argument because the Stoics define the quality of "being in one's power" as "being *completely* in one's power." If this formula holds, it turns out that the selection of the roles we play in life is still not in our power. (With thanks to William O. Stephens for a meaningful discussion of this issue).

[353] As argued for in the previous chapter, it is rewarding for modern Stoicism to avoid exposing the idea that it is some superhuman higher power which assigns roles for us to play. The gain from this omission is twofold: first, we circumvent risky metaphysical entanglements, second, we avoid the dangerous moment of taking responsibility away from human beings.

[354] Epictetus, *Encheiridion*, §17.

[355] Epictetus, *Discourses*, III.24.96-99.

[356] See: C.M. Bowra, ed. and trans., *A Second Book of Russian Verse* (Westport: Greenwood Press, 1971), 131-132.

[357] See: ibid., 125.

[358] William Shakespeare, *Romeo and Juliet*, act I, scene II, lines 39-45.

[359] www.krytykapolityczna.pl/English/Applied-Social-Arts/menu-id-113.html; accessed August 22, 2013.

[360] Ibid.

[361] Andrei Voznesensky, "Prophecies of a Greedy Observer," *The New York Times*, November 27, 1988. (It is a review of V. S. Pritchett, *Chekhov. A Spirit Set Free* [New York: Random House], 1988.)

[362] www.oed.com/view/Entry/39569?redirectedFrom=conservative#eid; accessed June 26, 2013.

[363] Ivan Goncharov, *Oblomov*, trans. Natalie Duddington (London, New York: Dent, Dutton, 1953), 4-5.

[364] See section "Challenges Facing Stoicism" in the Introduction.

[365] Marcus Aurelius, *Meditations*, X.27.

[366] Ben Kimpel, *Stoic Moral Philosophies: Their Counsel for Today* (New York: Philosophical Library, 1985), 130.

[367] William Shakespeare, *As You Like It*, act 2, scene 7, lines 139-140.

[368] The phrase "adopted, adapted or abandoned" was suggested to me by William O. Stephens.

[369] With thanks to William O. Stephens for helpfully commenting on this paragraph.

[370] See my Stoic handbook for details on this.

[371] Of necessity, this discussion is a very brief one and leaves many important issues aside. For more on the topic of roles in the Stoic ethics see: Brian Johnson, *The Role Ethics of Epictetus: Stoicism in Ordinary Life* (Lanham: Lexington Books, 2014).

[372] See: Stankiewicz, *Sztuka życia według stoików*.

[373] Epictetus, *Discourses*, I.25.8-9.

[374] Seneca, *On Tranquility of Mind*, IV.2-4.

[375] Becker, *A New Stoicism*, 20.

[376] Ibid., 21. See also: ibid., 110. For further discussion see: ibid., 5-6, 19, 44, 131-132, 145-146 and 156-157.

[377] Epictetus, *Encheiridion*, §43.

[378] An example of the "failing Epicurean state argument" can be found in Epictetus, *Discourses*, III.7.19-20. "Are you thinking of a city of Epicureans? [In it one person would say] 'I do not marry.' [Another would say] 'Nor I, for a man ought not to marry; nor ought we to beget children, nor engage in public matters.' What then will happen? From where will the citizens come? Who will bring them up? Who will be governor of the youth, who [will] preside over gymnastic exercises?" A few lines further Epictetus explicitly states that Epicurean ideas are "subversive of a state." For more on this see: Geert Roskam, *Live Unnoticed (Lathe Biosas) : on the Vicissitudes of an Epicurean Doctrine* (Leiden: Brill, 2007).

[379] Such instances do happen, but they are beyond the scope of this chapter and this book.

[380] Diogenes Laertius, *Lives of Eminent Philosophers*, VII. 142-143.

[381] Epictetus, *Discourses*, I.14.6-7.

[382] Marcus Aurelius, *Mediations*, VII.9.

[383] Ibid., VIII.7.

[384] Seneca, *To Marcia On Consolation*, XVIII.2-4.

[385] Epictetus, *Discourses*, I.13.3-4.

[386] Seneca, *On Benefits*, III.28.1-2.

[387] Ibid., III.28.1-2.

[388] Seneca, *On Providence*, II.1.

[389] Seneca, *On Firmness*, IV.2.

[390] Seneca, *Epistles*, 91. 5-6.

[391] Marcus Aurelius, *Meditations*, IV.50.

[392] Ibid., VI.36.

[393] Ibid., X.17.

[394] Ibid., II.17.

[395] Seneca, *Epistles*, 107. 7-8.

[396] Marcus Aurelius, *Meditations*, XI.27.

[397] Seneca, *On Firmness*, VIII.2.

[398] Ibid., XVIII.4.

[399] Seneca, *To Helvia On Consolation*, VIII.6

Endnotes

400 Plato, *Meno*, 78a. Trans. G.M.A. Grube. In: John. M. Cooper and D. S. Hutchinson, ed., *Plato. Complete Works* (Indianapolis: Hackett, 1997), 877.

401 Friedrich Nietzsche, *The Birth of Tragedy Out of the Spirit of Music*, §7, trans. Ian Johnston, records.viu.ca/~johnstoi/Nietzsche/tragedy_all.htm; accessed June 1, 2014.

402 Abraham H. Maslow, "A Theory of Human Motivation," in: Cary L. Cooper and Lawrence A. Pervin, ed., *Personality: Critical Concepts in Psychology*, (London: Routledge, 1998), 177.

403 Meyers, *Hemingway*, 545.

404 www.arttherapy.org/upload/whatisarttherapy.pdf; accessed June 1, 2014.

405 Foucault, *The Care of the Self*, 55.

406 Ibid., 57.

407 Donald M. Borchet, ed., *Encyclopedia of Philosophy* (Detroit: Macmillan, 2006), vol. 5, 44.

408 Ross, ed., *The Works of Aristotle*, vol. 10.

409 Ibid.

410 Ibid., vol. 11.

411 Elzenberg, *Kłopot z istnieniem*, 20-21. Entry dated December 6, 1907.

412 Notice, that the method of consolation based on "everything that happens to us, happens to many" is in a sense the exact opposite of Rorty's view in which suffering is always specifically and inevitably ours.

413 Seneca, *Epistles*, 107.5.

414 Seneca, *To Polybius on Consolation*, I.4.

415 Marcus Aurelius, *Meditations*, VII.58.

416 Ibid., XII.24.

417 Ibid., IX.30.

418 Ibid., I.17.

419 Seneca, *Epistles*, 2.3.

420 Ibid., 59.15.

421 Seneca, *On Anger*, II. 14.1.

422 Ibid., II. 17.1.

423 Seneca, *Epistles*, 2.5.

424 Ralph Waldo Emerson, "History," in: Jean Ferguson Carr, Alfred Riggs Ferguson and Joseph Slater, ed., *The Collected Works of Ralph Waldo Emerson* (Cambridge, London: Belknap Press of Harvard University Press, 1979), vol. 2, 10.

425 See, e.g., book I, lines 507-524 in: Titus Lucretius Carus and William Ellery Leonard, trans., *Lucretius: Of the Nature of Things: A Metrical Translation*, (London: Dent, 1921).

[426] Jules Verne, *The Mysterious Island*, trans. unspecified, in: Charles F. Horne, ed., *Works of Jules Verne* (New York, London: Vincent Parke and Company, 1911), vol. 6, 21-22.

[427] Epictetus, *Discourses*, II.18.4-5. See also: William O. Stephens, "The Roman Stoics on Habit," in: T. Sparrow and A. Hutchinson, ed., *A History of Habit: From Aristotle to Bourdieu* (Lanham: Lexington Books, 2013), 37-65.

[428] Epictetus, *Discourses*, I.2.32.

[429] Diogenes Laertius, *Lives of Eminent Philosophers*, VII.128.

[430] Hadot, *The Inner Citadel*.

[431] Hadot, *Philosophy As a Way of Life*.

[432] Hadot, *The Inner Citadel*, 34.

[433] For more on this see, e.g.: Hadot, *The Inner Citadel*, or R.B. Rutherford, *The Meditations of Marcus Aurelius: A Study* (Oxford: Clarendon Press, 1989), or P. A. Brunt, "Marcus Aurelius in His Meditations," in: "The Journal of Roman Studies," 64 (1974), 1-20; or Elzenberg, *Marek Aureliusz*.

[434] As William O. Stephens insists in his book, this is the reason why the title *Meditations* is misleading. Stephens advocates the use of *Memoranda* instead: Stephens, *Marcus Aurelius*, 2-3.

[435] Marcus Aurelius, *Meditations*, V.23.

[436] Ibid., VI.38.

[437] Ibid., XII.27.

[438] Ibid., X.34.

[439] Ibid., VI.30.

[440] Ibid., VIII.9.

[441] Ibid., V.16.

[442] http://staropolska.pl/renesans/jan_kochanowski/piesni/piesni_10.html ; accessed August 22, 2018. It's a passage from *Canto IX* from the first book of cantos by Jan Kochanowski (in original Polish: *Pieśń IX, Księgi Pierwsze*). 1586 is the poem's publication date, two years after author's death. The exact composition date of the poem is not known. The original Polish lines are as follows:

> "*Prózno ma mieć na pieczy*
> *Śmiertelny wieczne rzeczy;*
> *Dosyć na tym, kiedy wie, że go to nie minie,*
> *Co z przejźrzenia Pańskiego od wieku mu płynie.*
>
> *A nigdy nie zabłądzi,*
> *Kto tak umysł narządzi,*
> *Jakoby umiał szczęście i nieszczęście znosić,*
> *Temu mężnie wytrzymać, w owym sie nie wznosić.*"

[443] See: Rudyard Kipling, "If," in: Rudyard Kipling, *Rudyard Kipling's Verse* (New York : Doubleday, Doran and Co., 1944), 578.

[444] See: Max Ehrmann, "Desiderata," in: Max Ehrmann, *The Desiderata of Happiness* (New York: Crown Publishers, 1992), 10.

[445] See: Tom Wolfe, *A Man in Full: A Novel* (New York: Farrar, Straus and Giroux, 1998). See also: William O. Stephens, "Real Men Are Stoics: An Interpretation of Tom Wolfe's *A Man in Full*," in: "Stoic Voice Journal," vol. 1, no. 3 (April 2000).

[446] See: Zbigniew Herbert, *The Collected Poems, 1956-1998*, translated by Alissa Valles, Czeslaw Milosz and Peter Dale Scott (London: Atlantic Books, 2009), 276.

[447] See: ibid., 330-332.

[448] See: ibid., 197.

[449] See: ibid., 467.

[450] Epictetus, *Discourses*, I.4.13-14.

[451] Tatarkiewicz, *History of Aesthetics*, vol. 1, 199. The quoted words of Cleanthes were reported by Philodemus (*De musica*, 28, 1). English translation by J.E. King.

[452] Marcus Aurelius, *Meditations*, XI.6.

[453] Ibid., VII.38, VII.40, VII.50, VII.51 and X.21.

[454] Ibid., XI.6.

[455] Ibid., VII.42.

[456] Ibid., V.12.

[457] Ibid., V.31, X.34 and XI.31.

[458] Ibid., V.33 and XI.32.

[459] Seneca, *Epistles*, 108.9-10. Fragment quoted from Cleanthes equals to: von Arnim, frag. 487.

[460] Epictetus, *Discourses*, IV.10.36.

[461] Hadot, *The Inner Citadel*, 34.

[462] See Robert F. Dobbin's introduction in: Epictetus, *Discourses*, trans. Robert. F. Dobbin (Oxford: Oxford University Press, 1998). Dobbin declares that he "side[s] with Stellwag" in "suspect[ing] that E[pictetus] committed his thoughts to writing, in the form of diatribes, in a like effort to reach an audience beyond his immediate time and place. Arrian's foreword played its part in putting this slight deception across," ibid., xxi-xxii.

[463] The writings of the ancient Stoics provide numerous formulas for the obligation of social and political commitment. E.g.: "the men among whom you have received your portion, love them, but do it truly" (Marcus Aurelius, *Meditations*, VI.39). "As you are a component part of a social system, so let every act of yours be a component part of social life" (ibid., IX.23). "[The Stoics] argue that a friend is worth having for his own sake and that it is a good thing to have many friends" (Diogenes Laertius, *Lives of Eminent Philosophers*, VII.124.). "The wise man will love" (ibid., VII.129). Zeller comments upon this that "[the Stoics] hold that the further man

carries the work of moral improvement in himself, the stronger he will feel drawn to society" (Zeller, *The Stoics, Epicureans and Sceptics*, 311).

[464] Goethe, *Conversations with Eckermann*, 93 (entry dated May 12, 1825).

[465] Becker, *A New Stoicism*, 149.

[466] Marcus Aurelius, *Meditations*, V.16.

[467] Epictetus, *Discourses*, III.15.5.

[468] Marcus Aurelius, *Meditations*, III.1.

[469] Becker, *A New Stoicism*, 143.

[470] Ibid., 118.

[471] Ibid., 118.

[472] Ibid., 120.

[473] Room 101 is a chamber of horrors in George Orwell's *1984* where every prisoner faces the worst fear of their life. Winston Smith confronts an alternative: he will either betray Julia, his lover, or his face will be ripped apart by hungry rats, the deepest of his nightmares. He betrays, in order to avoid the rats. Doing so marks the final disintegration of his personality and agency, as well as his ultimate surrender to the totalitarian Big Brother.

[474] Lawrence Becker's viewpoint appears to be the same. See: e.g. Becker, *A New Stoicism*, 143.

[475] Seneca, *On Tranquility of Mind*, VII.2.

[476] P. Leon, "Suggestions from Aesthetics for the Metaphysic of Quality (III)," in: *Mind*, New Series, vol. 33, no. 130 (1924), 147.

Bibliography

Books and articles

Adorno, Theodor W. *Philosophy of Modern Music.* Translated by Anne G. Mitchell and Wesley V. Blomster. New York: The Seabury Press, 1973.

Arnim, Ioannes ab, ed. *Stoicorum Veterum Fragmenta,* vols. 1-4. Lipsiae: Teubner, 1905.

Arrington, Robert L. *Western Ethics. An Historical Introduction.* Malden: Blackwell, 1998.

Auster, Paul. *Hand to Mouth. A Chronicle of Early Failure.* New York: Henry Holt and Company, 1998.

Baudrillard, Jean. "The Precession of Simulacra." In Jean Baudrillard, *Simulacra and Simulation.* Translated by Sheila Faria Glaser. Ann Arbor: The University of Michigan Press, 1994.

Becker, Lawrence C. *A New Stoicism.* Princeton: Princeton University Press, 1998.

Becker, Lawrence C. "Stoic Emotion." In *Stoicism: Traditions and Transformations,* edited by Steven K. Strange and Jack Zupko, 250-276. Cambridge: Cambridge University Press, 2004.

Berlin, Isaiah. "The Apotheosis of the Romantic Will." In Isaiah Berlin, *The Crooked Timber of Humanity. Chapters in the History of Ideas.* Edited by Henry Hardy. London: John Murray Publishers, 1990.

Berlin, Isaiah. *The Roots of Romanticism.* Edited by Henry Hardy. Princeton: Princeton University Press, 1999.

Bevan, Edwyn. *Stoics and Sceptics.* W. Heffer & Sons, 1959.

Bigg, Charles. *The Church's Task under the Roman Empire.* Oxford: Clarendon Press, 1905.

Bloom, Harold. *The Anxiety of Influence. A Theory of Poetry.* Oxford: Oxford University Press, 1973.

Bloom, Harold. *Shakespeare. The Invention of the Human.* New York: Riverhead Books, 1998.

Borchet, Donald M., ed. *Encyclopedia of Philosophy,* vol. 5. Detroit: Macmillan, 2006.

Bowra, C.M., ed. and trans. *A Second Book of Russian Verse.* Westport: Greenwood Press, 1971.

Brouwer, René. *The Stoic Sage: The Early Stoics on Wisdom, Sagehood and Socrates.* Cambridge: Cambridge University Press, 2014.

Brunt, P. A. "Marcus Aurelius in His Meditations." *The Journal of Roman Studies* 64 (1974): 1-20.

Cicero, *On Moral Ends*. Translated by Raphael Woolf, edited by Julia Annas. Cambridge: Cambridge University Press, 2001.

Clark, Timothy. *The Theory of Inspiration. Composition as a crisis of subjectivity in Romantic and post-Romantic writing*. Manchester: Manchester University Press, 1997.

Clarke, Gerald. *Capote: A Biography*. New York: Simon and Schuster, 1988.

Dalí, Salvador. *Diary of a Genius*. Translated by Richard Howard. New York: Prentice Hall Press, 1986.

Davidson, William L. *The Stoic Creed*. Edinburgh: Clark, 1907.

Davies, Stephen. "Artistic expression." In *Routledge Encyclopedia of Philosophy*, vol. 1. Edited by Edward Craig. London – New York: Routledge, 1998.

Diderot, Denis. "Essai sur les règnes de Claude et de Néron." In *Oeuvres*, vol. 12, 1-148. Paris: Brière.

Diels, Hermann, and Walther Kranz. *Die Fragmente der Vorsokratiker, griechisch und deutsch*. Berlin: Weidman, 1951.

Diogenes Laertius, *Lives of Eminent Philosophers*, vols. 1-2. Translated by Robert Drew Hicks. London: Heinemann, 1942.

Dobbin, Robert F. Introduction to *Discourses*, by Epictetus, translated by Robert.F.Dobbin, i-xiv. Oxford: Oxford University Press, 1998.

Dryden, John. *Absalom and Achitophel*.

Ehrmann, Max. *The Desiderata of Happiness*. New York: Crown Publishers, 1992.

Elzenberg, Henryk. "Etyka wyrzeczenia. Czym jest i jak bywa uzasadniana." In Henryk Elzenberg, *Z filozofii kultury*, edited by Michał Woroniecki, 203-224. Kraków: Znak, 1991.

Elzenberg, Henryk. *Kłopot z istnieniem*. Toruń: UMK, 2002.

Elzenberg, Henryk. "Marek Aureliusz. Z historii i psychologii etyki." In Henryk Elzenberg, *Z historii filozofii*, edited by Michał Woroniecki, 97-213. Kraków: Znak, 1995.

Emerson, Ralph Waldo. "American Scholar," in: *The American Transcendentalists. Essential writings*, edited by Lawrence Buell, 89-99. New York: Modern Library, 2006.

Emerson, Ralph Waldo. "History." In *The Collected Works of Ralph Waldo Emerson*, vol. 2, edited by Jean Ferguson Carr, Alfred Riggs Ferguson and Joseph Slater. Cambridge – London: Belknap Press of Harvard University Press, 1979.

Engberg-Pedersen, Troels. *Paul and the Stoics*. Louisville: Westminster John Knox Press, 2000.

Epictetus, *The Discourses of Epictetus with the Encheiridion and Fragments. Translated with Notes, the Life of Epictetus, and a View of His Philosophy, by George Long*, trans. George Long. London: George Bell and Sons, 1890.

Esenin, Sergei. *Selected Poetry.* Translated by Peter Tempest. Moscow: Progress Publishers, 1982.
Foucault, Michel. *The Care of the Self* [vol. 3 of *The History of Sexuality*]. Translated by Robert Hurley. New York: Pantheon Books, 1986.
Frankl, Viktor E. *The Unconscious God. Psychotherapy and Theology.* London: Hodder and Stoughton, 1977.
Frede, Dorothea. "Stoic Determinism." In *The Cambridge Companion to the Stoics*, edited by Brian Inwood, 179-205. Cambridge: Cambridge University Press, 2003.
Friedman, Myra. *Buried Alive: The Biography of Janis Joplin.* New York: William Morrow & Company, 1973.
Gadamer, Hans-Georg. *The Relevance of the Beautiful and Other Essays.* Translated by Nicholas Walker. Cambridge: Cambridge University Press, 1986.
Ganoczy, Alexandre. *Der schöpferische Mensch und die Schöpfung Gottes.* Mainz: Matthis-Grünewald-Verlag, 1976.
Gay, Peter. *Freud: A Life for Our Time.* New York: Norton, 1988.
Glare, P.G.W., ed. *Oxford Latin Dictionary.* Oxford: Oxford University Press, 2012.
Goethe, Johann Wolfgang von. *Conversations with Eckermann (1823-1832).* Translated by John Oxenford. San Francisco: North Point Press, 1984.
Goncharov, Ivan. *Oblomov.* Translated by Natalie Duddington. London – New York: Dent, Dutton, 1953.
Graver, Margaret. *Stoicism and Emotion.* Chicago: University of Chicago Press, 2007.
Groys, Boris. *Stalin jako totalne dzieło sztuki.* Translated by Piotr Kozak. Warszawa: Sic, 2010.
Groys, Boris. *The Total Art of Stalinism. Avant-garde, Aesthetic Dictatorship, and Beyond.* Translated by Charles Rougle. Princeton: Princeton University Press, 1992.
Hadot, Pierre. *The Inner Citadel. The Meditations of Marcus Aurelius.* Translated by Michael Chaes. Cambridge – London: Harvard University Press, 1998.
Hadot, Pierre. *Philosophy As a Way of Life: Spiritual Exercises from Socrates to Foucault.* Translated by Michael Chase. Oxford: Blackwell, 1995.
Hahm, David E. *The Origins of Stoic Cosmology.* Columbus: Ohio State University Press, 1977.
Haines, C.R. ed., *The Correspondence of Marcus Cornelius Fronto with Marcus Aurelius Antoninus, Lucius Verus, Antoninus Pius, and Various Friends*, vol. 2. Translated by C.R.Haines. Cambridge: Harvard University Press, The Loeb Classical Library, 1963.
Heidegger, Martin. "The Origin of the Work of Art." Translated by Albert Hofstadter. In Martin Heidegger and David Farrell Krell, ed., *Basic Writings: From Being and Time (1927) to The Task of Thinking (1964)*, 139-212. San Francisco: Harper, 1993.

Herbert, Zbigniew. *The Collected Poems, 1956-1998*. Translated by Alissa Valles, Czeslaw Milosz and Peter Dale Scott. London: Atlantic Books, 2009.

Holowchak, M. Andrew. *The Stoics: A Guide for the Perplexed*. London: Continuum, 2008.

Hume, David. "Dialogues Concerning Natural Religion." In David Hume, *Essays and Treatises on Several Subjects*. London: 1788.

Hume, David. "The Skeptic." In David Hume, *Essays: Moral, Political and Literary*, edited by Eugene F. Miller. Indianapolis: Liberty Classics, 1985.

Hyde, William de Witt. *The Five Great Philosophies of Life*. New York: Macmillan, 1917.

Irvine, William B. *A Guide to The Good Life. The Ancient Art of Stoic Joy*. New York: Oxford University Press, 2009.

Irvine, William B. *A Slap in the Face. Why Insults Hurt And Why They Shouldn't*. New York: Oxford University Press, 2013.

Johnson, Brian. *The Role Ethics of Epictetus: Stoicism in Ordinary Life*. Lanham: Lexington Books, 2014.

Kant, Immanuel. *Critique of Pure Reason*. Translated by Werner S. Pluhar. Indianapolis: Hackett Publishing Company, 1996.

Kelly, Michael, ed. *Encyclopedia of Aesthetics*, vol. 1. Oxford: Oxford University Press, 1998.

Kierkegaard, Søren. *Either/or* [abridged edition]. Translated by George L. Stengren, edited by Steven L. Rossfrom. London: Harper, 1986.

Kimpel, Ben. *Stoic Moral Philosophies: Their Counsel for Today*. New York: Philosophical Library, 1985.

Kipling, Rudyard. *Rudyard Kipling's Verse*. New York: Doubleday, Doran, 1944.

Kottler, Jeffrey A. *Divine Madness. Ten Stories of Creative Struggle*. San Francisco: Jossey-Bass, 2006.

Kropiwnicki Maciej, and Julian Kutyła, ed. *Žižek. Przewodnik Krytyki Politycznej*. Warszawa: Wydawnictwo Krytyki Politycznej, 2009.

Lagreé, Jacqueline. "Constancy and Coherence," in: in *Stoicism: Traditions and Transformations*, edited by Steven K. Strange and Jack Zupko, 148-176. Cambridge: Cambridge University Press, 2004.

Larkin, Philip. *Collected Poems*. Edited by Anthony Thwaite. New York: Farrar, Strauss and Giroux, 2003.

Lebell, Sharon. *The Art of Living. The Classical Manual on Virtue, Happiness, and Effectiveness*. San Francisco: Harper, 1995.

Leon, P. "Suggestions from Aesthetics for the Metaphysic of Quality (III)." *Mind*, New Series, vol. 33, no. 130 (1924) : 146-165.

Letters on Ethics: To Lucilius, translated by Margaret Graver and Anthony A. Long. Chicago: University of Chicago Press, 2015.

Levinas, Emmanuel. *Otherwise than Being or Beyond Essence*. Translated by Alphonso Lingis. Pittsburgh: Duquesne University Press, 1998.

Long, Anthony A. *Epictetus: A Stoic and Socratic Guide to Life*. Oxford: Oxford University Press, 2002.

Long, Anthony A. *Hellenistic Philosophy. Stoics, Epicureans, Sceptics.* New York: Charles Scribner's Sons, 1974.

Long, Anthony A. "Stoicism in the Philosophical Tradition: Spinoza, Lipsius, Butler." In *The Cambridge Companion to the Stoics*, edited by Brian Inwood, 365-392. Cambridge: Cambridge University Press, 2003.

Lucretius, Titus Carus, and William Ellery Leonard, trans. *Lucretius: Of the Nature of Things: A Metrical Translation.* London: Dent, 1921.

Ludwig, Arnold M. *The Price of Greatness. Resolving the Creativity and Madness Controversy.* New York – London: Guilford, 1995.

Lynn, Kenneth Schuyler. *Hemingway.* New York: Simon and Schuster, 1987.

MacIntyre, Alasdair. *After Virtue. A Study in Moral Theory.* Notre Dame: University of Notre Dame Press, 2007.

Marcus Aurelius, *The Meditations of the Emperor Marcus Aurelius Antoninus. Translated by George Long, M.A. With a Biographical Sketch and a View of the Philosophy of Antoninus by the Translatori*, trans. by George Long. New York: A.L. Burt, Publisher, 189?.

Maslow, Abraham H. "A Theory of Human Motivation." In *Personality: Critical Concepts in Psychology*, edited by Cary L. Cooper and Lawrence A. Pervin. London: Routledge, 1998.

McLynn, Frank. *Marcus Aurelius: A Life.* Cambridge: Da Capo Press, 2009.

Meyers, Jeffrey. *Hemingway, a Biography.* New York: Harper & Row, 1985.

Mill, John Stuart. "Nature." In *Environmental Ethics: Readings in Theory and Application*, edited by Louis P. Pojman, 122-128. Belmont: Wadsworth-Thomson, 2005.

Montesquieu. *The Spirit of the Laws.* Translated and edited by Anne M. Cohler, Basia C. Miller and Harold Stone. Cambridge: Cambridge University Press, 2002.

Montherlant, Henry de. *Don Juan.* Translated by Adrienne M. Schizzano. In *The Theatre of Don Juan. A Collection of Plays and Views, 1630-1963*, edited by Oscar Mandel, 675-694. Lincoln: University of Nebraska Press, 1963.

Musonius Rufus, *Musonius Rufus: Lectures and Sayings.* Translated by Cynthia King, edited by William B. Irvine. CreateSpace: 2011.

Negus, Keith, and Michael Pickering. *Creativity, Communication and Cultural Value.* London: Sage Publications, 2004.

Nietzsche, Friedrich. *The Gay Science.* Translated by Walter Kaufmann. New York: Vintage Books, 1974.

Nietzsche, Friedrich. *Twilight of the Idols and The Anti-Christ.* Translated by R.J.Hollingdale. Harmondsworth: Penguin, 1974.

Oates, Stephen B. *William Faulkner, the Man and the Artist: A Biography.* New York: Harper & Row, 1987.

Pigliucci, Massimo. *How to be a Stoic: Using Ancient Philosophy to Live a Modern Life.* New York: Basic Books, 2017.

Plato, *Ion.* Translated by Paul Woodruff. In *Plato. Complete Works*, edited by John. M. Cooper and D. S. Hutchinson, 937-949. Indianapolis: Hackett, 1997.

Plato, *Meno*. Translated by G.M.A. Grube. In *Plato. Complete Works*, edited by John M. Cooper and D. S. Hutchinson, 870-897. Indianapolis: Hackett, 1997.

Plato, *Phaedrus*. Translated by Alexander Nehamas and Paul Woodruff. In *Plato. Complete Works*, edited by John. M. Cooper and D. S. Hutchinson, 506-556 Indianapolis: Hackett, 1997.

Pope, Alexander. "An Essay on Man, In Four Epistles, to H. St. John, Lord Bolingbroke." In *The Works of the English Poets from Chaucer to Cowper*, edited by Samuel Johnson, vol. 12. London: 1810.

Pritchett, V. S. *Chekhov. A Spirit Set Free*. New York: Random House, 1988.

Quine, Willard Van Orman. *On What There Is*. Washington: Catholic University of America, Philosophy Education Society, 1948.

Reale, Giovanni. *A History of Ancient Philosophy*, vol. 3. Translated by John R. Catan. Albany: State University of New York Press, 1985.

Renan, Ernest. *Marc Aurèle et la fin du monde antiqua*. Paris: 1882.

Rist, John. "The Stoic Concept of Detachment." In *The Stoics*, edited by John Rist, 259-272. Berkeley: University of California Press, 1978.

Rist, John. *Stoic Philosophy*. Cambridge: Cambridge University Press, 1969.

Robertson, Donald. *Stoicism and the Art of Happiness*. London: Hodder & Stoughton, 2013.

Romm, James S. *Dying Every Day: Seneca at the Court of Nero*. New York: Vintage Books, 2014.

Rorty, Richard. *Contingency, Irony and Solidarity*. Cambridge – New York: Cambridge University Press, 2005.

Roskam, Geert. *Live Unnoticed (Lathe Biosas): on the Vicissitudes of an Epicurean Doctrine*. Leiden: Brill, 2007.

Ross, W. D. ed. *The Works of Aristotle*, vols. 7, 10, 11. Translated by E .S. Forster, Ingram Bywater and Benjamin Jowett. Oxford: Clarendon Press, 1927-1966.

Rothenberg, Albert. *Creativity and Madness. New Findings and Old Stereotypes*. Baltimore: The Johns Hopkins University Press, 1994.

Russell, Bertrand. *History of Western Philosophy and its Connection with Political and Social Circumstances from the Earliest Times to the Present Day*. London: George Allen & Unwin, 1961.

Rutherford, R.B. *The Meditations of Marcus Aurelius: A Study*. Oxford: Clarendon Press, 1989.

Salles, Ricardo. *The Stoics on Determinism and Compatibilism*. Aldershot: Ashgate Pub, 2005.

Sandbach, F.H. *The Stoics*. London: Bristol Classical Press, 1989.

Sarbiewski, Maciej Kazimierz. *O poezji doskonałej czyli Wergiliusz i Homer. De Perfecta Poesi, sive Vergilius et Homerus*. Translated by Marian Plezia. Wrocław: Zakład Ossolińskich, 1954.

Schopenhauer, Arthur. *The World as Will and Representation*, vol. 1 and 2. Translated by E.F.J. Payne. New York: Dover Publications, 1966.

Seneca, Lucius Anneus. *On Benefits*, trans. Aubrey Stewart. London: G. Bell and Sons, Ltd., 1912.

Seneca, Lucius Anneus. *The Epistles of Lucius Annus Seneca; With Large Annotations, Wherein, Particularly, the Tenets of the Antient Philosophers Are Contrasted With the Divine Precepts of the Gospel, With Regard to the Moral Duties of Mankind. In Two Volumes. By Thomas Morell, D.D.*, trans. Thomas Morell, vol. I-II. London: W. Woodfall, G.G.J., J. Robinson, 1786.

Seneca, Lucius Anneus. *Minor Dialogues Together with the Dialogue on Clemency*, trans. Aubrey Stewart. London: G. Bell and Sons, 1889.

Shakespeare, William. *As You Like It.*

Shakespeare, William. *The Comedy of Errors.*

Shakespeare, William. *Romeo and Juliet.*

Shakespeare, William. *Twelfth Night.*

Sharples, R.W. *Stoics, Epicureans and Sceptics. An Introduction to Hellenistic Philosophy.* London – New York: Routledge, 1996.

Sherman, Nancy. *Stoic Warriors. The Ancient Philosophy Behind the Military Mind.* Oxford: Oxford University Press, 2005.

Simpson, E. M. S., ed. *The Sermons of John Donne*, vol. 4. Berkeley: University of California Press, 1959.

Stankiewicz, Piotr. "Stoics Are Not Ascetics," in: Patrick Ussher [ed.], *Stoicism Today. Selected writings*, vol. II (Stoicism Today, 2016), 253-255.

Stankiewicz, Piotr. *Sztuka życia według stoików.* Warszawa: WAB, 2014.

Steiner, George. *Grammars of Creation.* New Haven: Yale University Press, 2001.

Stephens, William O. *Marcus Aurelius. A Guide for the Perplexed.* New York: Continuum, 2012.

Stephens, William O. "Real Men Are Stoics: An Interpretation of Tom Wolfe's *A Man in Full*," "Stoic Voice Journal," vol. 1, no. 3 (April 2000).

Stephens, William O. "The Roman Stoics on Habit," in: *A History of Habit: From Aristotle to Bourdieu*, edited by T. Sparrow and A. Hutchinson, 37-66. Lanham: Lexington Books, 2013.

Tatarkiewicz, Władysław. *History of Aesthetics.* Edited by J. Harrell, translated by Adam and Ann Czerniawski. Hague: Mouton, 1970.

Tatarkiewicz, Władysław. *A History of Six Ideas.* Translated by Christopher Kasparek et al. Hague: Martinus Nijhoff, 1980.

Thomas, Bob. *Joan Crawford, a Biography.* New York: Simon and Schuster, 1978.

Verlaine, Paul. *The Cursed Poets.* Translated by Chase Madar. Copenhagen – Los Angeles: Green Integer, 2003.

Verne, Jules. *The Mysterious Island.* Translator unspecified. In *Works of Jules Verne*, vol. 6., edited by Charles F. Horne. New York – London: Vincent Park and Company, 1911.

Vernezze, Peter J. *Don't Worry, Be Stoic: Ancient Wisdom for Troubled Times.* Lanham: University Press of America, 2005.

Vigny, Alfred de. *Stello.* Paris: Flammarion, 1984.

Voznesensky, Andrei. "Prophecies of a Greedy Observer." *The New York Times*, November 27, 1988.

Watała, Elwira, and Wiktor Woroszylski. *Życie Sergiusza Jesienina*. Warszawa: PIW, 1982.
Windelband, Wilhelm. *A History of Philosophy*. Translated by James H. Tufts. Westport: Greenwood Press, 1979.
Wolfe, Tom. *A Man in Full: A Novel*. New York: Farrar, Straus and Giroux, 1998
Zeller, E. *The Stoics, Epicureans and Sceptics*. Translated by Oswald J. Reichel. London – New York: Longmans, Green, 1892.
Žižek, Slavoj. *Welcome to the Desert of the Real*. London: Verso, 2002.

Online sources

American Art Therapy Association; accessed June 1, 2014. www.arttherapy.org/upload/whatisarttherapy.pdf
Bible Gateway; accessed September 16, 2014. www.biblegateway.com/
Facebook, "Stoicism group," accessed February 2, 2017 https://www.facebook.com/groups/Stoicism/
Facebook, "Sztuka życia według stoików" fanpage, accessed February 2, 2017. https://www.facebook.com/SztukaZyciaWedlugStoikow/
Harold B. Lee Library Digital Collections; accessed August 9, 2013. contentdm.lib.byu.edu/cdm/compoundobject/collection/JohnDonne/id/3170/rec/1
Holy See, official website; accessed June 10, 2013. www.vatican.va/edocs/ENG0216/__P1.HTM
Keepcalm-o-matic; accessed April 14, 2014. sd. keepcalm-o-matic.co.uk/i/keep-calm-and-stay-stoic-2.png
Kochanowski, Jan, poems; accessed August 22, 2018. http://staropolska.pl/renesans/jan_kochanowski/piesni/piesni_10.html
"Krytyka Polityczna"; accessed August 22, 2013. www.krytykapolityczna.pl/English/Applied-Social-Arts/menu-id-113.html
Merriam-Webster dictionary; accessed April 18, 2014. www.merriam-webster.com/dictionary/presentism
Milton, John. *Paradise Lost*; accessed September 17, 2014. www.poets.org/poetsorg/poem/paradise-lost-book-i-lines-221-270
Modern Stoicism website, accessed February 2, 2017 http://modernstoicism.com
New Stoa website, accessed February 2, 2017. http://newstoa.com
Nietzsche, Friedrich. *The Birth of Tragedy Out of the Spirit of Music*. Translated by Ian Johnston; accessed June 1, 2014. records.viu.ca/~johnstoi/Nietzsche/tragedy_all.htm
Oxford English Dictionary; accessed April 10, 2013, June 26, 2013, April 30, 2014 and December 5, 2016. www.oed.com/view/Entry/11241?redirectedFrom=artistic#eid www.oed.com/view/Entry/122712?rskey=eirXNk&result=1&isAdvanced=false#eid

Bibliography

www.oed.com/view/Entry/200321?result=1&rskey=mxF2Rk&
www.oed.com/view/Entry/39569?redirectedFrom=conservative#eid

Pigliucci, Massimo. "How To Be A Stoic" blog, accessed February 2, 2017. https://howtobeastoic.wordpress.com

Stankiewicz, Piotr. "Stoic Avoidance of Asceticism," in: Stoicism Today blog, accessed January 23, 2017. https://blogs.exeter.ac.uk/stoicismtoday/2015/10/03/stoic-avoidance-of-asceticism-by-piotr-stankiewicz/

Tolstoy, Leo. *Anna Karenina*. Translated by Constance Garnett. Accessed September 8, 2014. en.wikisource.org/wiki/Anna_Karenina/Part_One/Chapter_1

Wikipedia; accessed April 14, 2014. en.wikipedia.org/wiki/Vsauce

Wittgenstein, Ludwig. *Tractatus Logico-Philosophicus*; accessed September 17, 2014. en.wikipedia.org/wiki/Tractatus_Logico-Philosophicus

Youtube. Video "Why Be Happy When You Could Be Interesting?"; accessed September 27, 2014 www.youtube.com/watch?v=U88jj6PSD7w

Youtube. Video "What Is the Greatest Honor?"; accessed April 14, 2014 www.youtube.com/watch?v=P85Fj8m6v84

Index

A

Adorno, 14, 130, 145
Anne Frank, 44
Aristotle, 14, 24, 35, 91, 92, 130, 138, 141, 142, 150, 151
artist, ix, 1, 2, 4, 5, 9, 10, 14, 15, 16, 17, 19, 20, 22, 24, 26, 29, 30, 38, 40, 41, 42, 47, 50, 51, 52, 55, 64, 65, 72, 74, 84, 85, 88, 89, 94, 96, 97, 100, 101, 102, 107, 108, 110, 113, 125, 127
ascetic misinterpretation, xviii, 30, 31, 33, 34, 35, 36, 37, 38, 39, 40, 68, 75, 81, 83, 135
autotherapeutic, 23, 89, 90, 91, 93, 94, 95, 97
axiological, 23, 38, 84, 85, 87, 88, 89
Axiom of Futility, 67, 68

B

Balzac, 64
Baudrillard, 9, 100, 102, 128, 145
Becker, xi, xii, xx, 33, 34, 39, 63, 66, 67, 81, 92, 105, 110, 112, 115, 119, 120, 124, 133, 134, 137, 138, 140, 144, 145
Berlin, xviii, 7, 8, 10, 15, 128, 130, 131, 136, 145, 146

C

Capote, 19, 131, 146
Christian, 60, 105, 123, 128

Chrysippus, xii, 8, 12, 39, 43, 58, 128, 129
Cicero, 11, 33, 124, 133, 146
Cleanthes, xii, 100, 104, 143
clinamen, 45
cognitive, 23, 62, 63, 64, 65, 66, 67, 68, 69, 70, 99, 126
conservatism, 75, 82
conservative misinterpretation, xviii, 37, 68, 75, 76, 77, 78, 80, 81, 82, 83
creativity, 4, ix, x, xvii, xviii, xix, xx, 1, 2, 4, 5, 6, 8, 9, 10, 11, 13, 14, 15, 16, 17, 18, 19, 21, 22, 23, 24, 25, 26, 27, 28, 29, 30, 40, 41, 42, 43, 44, 49, 50, 52, 55, 62, 63, 66, 67, 68, 69, 70, 72, 73, 74, 75, 83, 84, 87, 88, 89, 90, 91, 92, 93, 94, 95, 96, 97, 98, 99, 102, 103, 104, 107, 108, 109, 113, 114, 125, 126
Croce, 52

D

Darwin, xii
death, xiv, 25, 38, 39, 40, 42, 46, 55, 61, 69, 110, 121, 138, 142
Descartes, xii, 4, 127
desire, xiv, 2, 12, 25, 27, 28, 29, 68, 129, 132
Dickinson, 51
didactic, 23, 65, 97, 98, 99, 100, 101, 104, 105, 108
Diogenes Laertius, 33, 48, 58, 85, 100, 128, 133, 135, 137, 140, 142, 143, 146
diversity, 36, 48, 60, 61, 81, 109
Donne, 3, 126, 151

E

egalitarianism, x, 60, 61
Elzenberg, xvii, 28, 33, 92, 103, 117, 124, 132, 133, 135, 136, 141, 142, 146
Emerson, 118, 141, 146
Epictetus, x, xiv, xvi, xvii, xx, 11, 27, 28, 32, 33, 38, 39, 43, 53, 54, 58, 59, 62, 69, 71, 80, 82, 85, 100, 103, 104, 109, 117, 118, 119, 121, 124, 129, 132, 133, 134, 136, 137, 138, 139, 140, 142, 143, 144, 146, 148
epistemology, 63
eternal return, 44, 45, 49, 77
expressive, 23, 50, 52, 61, 62

F

fame, 23, 24, 26, 27, 28, 29, 30, 38, 40, 43, 107, 108
Faulkner, 18, 131, 149
Foucault, x, 15, 31, 90, 100, 117, 130, 131, 133, 141, 147

G

God, 3, 4, 9, 16, 27, 58, 70, 93, 103, 117, 123, 127, 129, 136, 147
Goethe, 14, 63, 90, 93, 94, 98, 105, 130, 144, 147
Groys, 10, 128, 147

H

Hadot, 21, 55, 100, 101, 131, 136, 142, 147
happiness, ix, x, xviii, 1, 17, 32, 34, 38, 54, 103, 105, 129
Hemingway, 18, 90, 131, 141, 149
Horvath, 46, 47
Houellebecq, 63, 64
Hume, xi, xii, xiii, 119, 120, 148

I

inhumanity, xiv, 120, 121

K

Kant, xii, 4, 57, 66, 127, 137, 148
knowledge, 12, 59, 62, 63, 64, 65, 66, 67, 68, 70, 97, 98, 99, 100, 102, 118, 130

L

Lampedusa, 64
Larkin, 55, 56, 136, 148
Lennon, 72
Logos, 57, 58, 59, 60, 81, 88
Long, xii, xx, 118, 119, 120, 123, 124, 135, 148, 149
love, xv, 13, 42, 61, 65, 90, 93, 105, 123, 143
Lucretius, 98, 141, 149

M

MacIntyre, xi, xii, 119, 120, 149
Marcus Aurelius, x, xvii, xx, 11, 12, 15, 21, 28, 32, 39, 43, 46, 47, 48, 50, 54, 55, 58, 62, 85, 87, 94, 95, 100, 101, 104, 109, 110, 117, 119, 120, 124, 129, 132, 133, 134, 135, 136, 137, 139, 140, 141, 142, 143, 144, 146, 147, 149, 150, 151
martyrological misinterpretation, 67, 68, 69, 111, 138
Marx, xii, 4, 127
materialists, 16, 66
Mayakovsky, 72
Merleau-Ponty, 52
methodology, xix, 10, 21, 22, 24, 25, 61
Mill, 17, 123, 149

N

naturalism, 64, 82

nature, xiii, xv, xvi, 3, 9, 19, 58, 62, 66, 67, 70, 71, 77, 78, 82, 86, 87, 93, 94, 123, 138
Nietzsche, 4, xvii, 4, 34, 89, 108, 117, 124, 127, 138, 141, 149, 152

O

ontology, 58
Orwell, 57, 64, 65, 110, 112, 144

P

Panaetius, xx, 39
Plato, 1, 14, 24, 45, 55, 66, 89, 130, 141, 149, 150
pleasure, 9, 12, 25, 31, 91, 97
poet, ix, 1, 3, 4, 5, 14, 18, 20, 40, 56, 71, 89, 102, 103, 108, 125, 130
Posidonius, xx, 58
preferred indifferents, 33
preservation, 23, 42, 43, 44, 45, 46, 47, 49, 50, 62, 65, 99, 108
profit, 23, 24, 30, 31, 40, 107, 108

R

reason, xi, xii, xiv, xv, xvii, xx, 11, 16, 23, 30, 33, 34, 38, 52, 68, 69, 70, 71, 94, 97, 101, 104, 112, 113, 122, 123, 132, 142
revolutionary, 23, 70, 72, 74, 75, 76, 78, 83, 84, 85
Romantic, 6, 8, 9, 10, 13, 14, 16, 17, 20, 40, 41, 52, 98, 107, 108, 109, 110, 128, 130, 131, 136, 145, 146
Romanticism, 7, 8, 57, 128, 145
Rorty, xviii, 52, 55, 56, 57, 124, 136, 137, 141, 150
Russell, x, xv, 118, 150

S

sameness, 61
science, 59, 63, 67, 68, 70, 73, 97, 98, 123

second voyage, 66, 138
self, xiii, xiv, xv, 3, 7, 15, 16, 18, 19, 22, 50, 51, 52, 53, 55, 56, 57, 59, 60, 61, 62, 82, 89, 90, 91, 94, 100, 101, 103, 133
Seneca, x, xii, xiii, xv, xx, 12, 14, 20, 21, 24, 25, 28, 32, 39, 43, 44, 46, 48, 53, 54, 58, 62, 80, 86, 87, 92, 93, 95, 96, 97, 104, 112, 118, 119, 120, 121, 122, 124, 129, 130, 132, 133, 134, 135, 136, 137, 139, 140, 141, 143, 144, 150
Shakespeare, xvii, 3, 5, 41, 56, 65, 73, 125, 126, 135, 138, 139, 145, 151
Socrates, 14, 43, 45, 46, 56, 89, 100, 119, 122, 131, 145, 147
spontaneity, 14
Steiner, xvii, 124, 125, 151
Stephens, xi, 115, 120, 132, 135, 136, 139, 142, 143, 151
Stoic, 4, ix, x, xi, xii, xiii, xiv, xv, xvi, xvii, xviii, xix, xx, xxi, 1, 6, 9, 13, 14, 16, 17, 18, 19, 20, 21, 25, 26, 27, 29, 30, 31, 32, 33, 34, 35, 36, 37, 38, 39, 40, 44, 45, 47, 48, 49, 53, 54, 55, 57, 58, 59, 60, 62, 65, 66, 67, 68, 69, 70, 71, 74, 75, 76, 77, 78, 80, 81, 82, 83, 85, 87, 88, 89, 90, 91, 92, 93, 95, 96, 99, 100, 101, 102, 103, 104, 105, 107, 108, 109, 110, 111, 112, 113, 115, 117, 118, 119, 120, 121, 122, 123, 124, 129, 130, 132, 133, 134, 138, 139, 143, 145, 146, 147, 148, 150, 151, 153
Stoicism, 4, ix, x, xi, xii, xiii, xiv, xv, xvi, xvii, xviii, xix, xx, xxi, 1, 6, 10, 11, 15, 16, 17, 20, 21, 23, 25, 27, 29, 30, 31, 33, 34, 35, 36, 37, 38, 39, 40, 41, 44, 48, 49, 53, 59, 61, 62, 63, 65, 66, 67, 68, 70, 74, 75, 76, 79, 81, 82, 83, 87, 88, 89, 90, 91, 92, 93, 94, 95, 96, 97, 99, 100, 102, 103, 104, 105, 107, 108, 109, 110, 111, 112, 113, 114, 115, 118, 119, 120, 122, 123, 124,

127, 133, 134, 135, 137, 138, 139, 140, 144, 145, 147, 148, 149, 150, 151, 152, 153
Sturm und Drang, 53
subject, xii, xviii, xix, 2, 4, 6, 16, 21, 23, 25, 30, 48, 50, 63, 69, 74, 84, 91, 99, 111, 129, 130
suffering, ix, xvi, 17, 20, 39, 56, 57, 62, 78, 89, 92, 93, 94, 96, 108, 112, 141

T

Tolstoy, 16, 44, 64, 153
transcendence, 16, 36, 66

U

unhappiness, 4, 11, 17
universalism, 60
unpreferred indifferents, 33

V

Vigny, 18, 125, 130, 151
virtue, xi, xii, xv, xvi, 5, 12, 16, 39, 42, 68, 73, 76, 100, 105, 122, 123
Vysotsky, 17, 89

W

Wittgenstein, 9, 25, 128, 153

Y

Yesenin, 17, 18

Z

Zeno, xi, 15, 33, 58, 133, 138
Žižek, 4, 117, 128, 148, 152
Żmijewski, 73
Zola, 64

www.ingramcontent.com/pod-product-compliance
Lightning Source LLC
Chambersburg PA
CBHW052047300426
44117CB00012B/2018